COINS

CATALOGUE NO. 1.

MYSORE.

COINS

CATALOGUE NO.1.

MYSORE.

WITH ELEVEN PLATES.

EDGAR THURSTON.

GYAN

Published by

Gyan Publishing House
5, Ansari Road
Daryaganj, New Delhi-110002
Phone: 011-47034999, 9811692060
E-mail: books@gyanbooks.com

Distribution Network
gyanbooks.com
India, USA, Canada, UK, Australia, France

ISBN : 978-81-212-9560-4 (PB)
First Published, 1888

2nd Impression 2023

Printed at: Gyan Press, Delhi.

COINS . CATALOGUE No . 1 MYSORE .
Author: EDGAR THURSTON,

2.

1.

3.

GOVERNMENT CENTRAL MUSEUM,
MADRAS.

COINS.

CATALOGUE No. 1.

MYSORE.

With Eleven Plates.

BY

EDGAR THURSTON,
SUPERINTENDENT, MADRAS GOVERNMENT CENTRAL MUSEUM.

1888.

PREFACE.

In issuing the present catalogue, I have to gratefully acknowledge the assistance which I received, in writing the Introduction, from Mr. Lewis Rice's "Mysore Gazetteer" and Colonel H. P. Hawkes' "Coins of Mysore," of which the latter, published in 1856, is now very scarce. From both these sources I have, in many cases, copied extracts *verbatim.*

To Captain R. H. Campbell Tufnell, I am indebted for the pains and trouble which he took in correcting and revising the proof sheets, and for comparing the inscriptions in the text with those on the coins.

The frontispiece represents in the centre the obverse of the medal struck in commemoration of the taking of Seringapatam in 1799, and above and below, the silver medals struck "for services in Mysore" in 1791-2.

EDGAR THURSTON,
Superintendent.

Government Central Museum,
Madras,
6th January 1888.

CONTENTS.

ABBREVIATIONS.

Nág.	=	Nágarí.	Au.	=	Gold.
Kan.	=	Kanarese.	Ar.	=	Silver.
Eng.	=	English.	Ae.	=	Engish.

INTRODUCTION.

THE present province of Mysore long formed part of the empire of Vijáyanagar, and the origin of the Mysore Rajas is traced[1] to the heroes of a chivalrous exploit. Vijaya and Krishna, two young Kshatriyas of Yádava descent, who, according to tradition, had left Dváraka in Gujarat with the view of establishing themselves in the south, on arriving at Haḍi-nád or Hada-nád, a few miles south-east of the present city of Mysore, learned that the chief of the place had wandered away in a state of mental derangement, and that the neighbouring chief of Kárugahalli, who was of inferior caste, taking advantage of the defenceless condition of the family, had demanded the only daughter of the house in marriage. To this a consent had been given under compulsion, and arrangements unwillingly made for the ceremony. The two brothers espoused the cause of the distressed maiden, and, having secreted themselves with some followers, fell upon the chief and his retinue while seated at a banquet, and slew them. Marching at once on Kárugahalli, they surprised it and returned in triumph to Hadanád. The girl became the willing bride of Vijaya, who took the title of Oḍeyar or Woḍeyar[2] ("lord"), and assumed the government of—Hadanád and Kárugahalli, adopting at the same time the religion of the Jangamas or Lingavantas.

The immediate descendants of Vijaya are thus given by Mr. Bowring:

	A.D.
Vijaya	1399–1422
Hire Beṭṭada Cháma Raja	1423–1457
Timma Raja	1458–1477
Cháma Raja, Ár-beral[3]	1478–1512
Beṭṭada Cháma Raja	1513–1551

Beṭṭada Cháma Raja divided his dominions during his lifetime among his three sons. To Appana Timma Raja he gave Hemanhalli, to Krishna Raja he gave Kembala, and to Chama Raja, surnamed Ból or Bald, he gave Mysore, then called Puragere. A fort was either built

[1] Rice, Mysore Gazetteer, 1877, vol. I, pp. 239-40.
[2] Uḍaiyâr, *vulgo* Woḍeyar or Woḍeiyar.
[3] Six-fingered.

or restored in the year 1524, to which the name of Mahish-úru[4] (buffalo town) was probably given, though Rice says (op. cit., p. 241) that "reasons have been given for supposing that it may have been known by that designation before the Christian era. The vulgar name of the place when Cháma Raja received it as his portion was Puragere, conjectured to be the same as Pirikere, wherein the Kongu king Avinita acquired the recognition of royal rights in the fifth century. It is undoubted that for the last three centuries the name Mysore (Mahishúr) has been the common name of the fort and town erected or repaired by Hire Cháma Raja."

Beṭṭada Cháma Raja was succeeded by his son Appana Timma Raja, who ruled from 1552–1570, and, no male heir surviving to him or his brother Krishna Raja, the succession was continued in the junior or Mysore branch represented by Hire Cháma Raja Ból, who was succeeded in 1576 by Bettaḍa Woḍeyar. The latter only reigned for a very short time, and in the following year his brother Raja Woḍeyar came to the throne, and, casting off even the semblance of subjection to Vijáynagar, acquired the city of Seringapatam and its dependencies from his former master, Vencataputty Rayeel, who resided with scarcely a shadow of authority at Chendragerry.

About this time also the numerous chieftains in the south of India, who had hitherto yielded a nominal obedience to Vijáyanagur, profiting by the dismemberment of the empire consequent on the battle of Talikota in 1565, began to assume the name and importance of Polygars,[5] the chief among whom were the Polygars of Chittledroog, Raidroog, Harponhully, &c.

Raja Woḍeyar was followed successively by Cháma Raja, and Immaḍi Raja who was shortly after his accession poisoned by the daḷavâyi, and Kanṭhirava Narasa Raja placed on the throne. The year after his accession Kanṭhirava successfully defended Seringapatam against the Bijapur forces under Ran-dulha Khan, and subsequently carried his conquests over a wide area. He improved and enlarged the fortifications of Seringapatam, and was the first Raja of Mysore who established a mint, in which was struck the "Agala" or broad Kanṭhiráya haṇa (Kanteroy fanam), a gold coin, which was, together with the "Gidd" or thick Kanṭhiráya hana (a re-coinage by Dewan Purnaiya), for a long time the established currency of Mysore.

The Kanteroy fanam bears on the obverse a representation of the Narasinga avatár, and on the reverse the symbols of the sun and

---

[4] So called with reference to Mahish ásura, the buffalo-headed monster, who was destroyed by Chámundi, the tutelary goddess of Mysore.

[5] The coins issued by the Polygars are reserved for a future catalogue.

moon (?) bounded by cross lines [Pl. I, 1-2]. It appears to be assumed by Wilks[6] that a "Cantyrai hoon" (Canteroy pagoda) was also struck by Kanṭhirava, but Hawkes states[7] that "the Canteroy pagoda is only a *nominal* coin equivalent to ten fanams or Rs. 2-14-8. There is, however, a coin of this name current in the Ceded districts, and valued at about three rupees." Further, Rice says,[8] "even after the coins struck by him (Kanṭhirava) had become obsolete, the accounts continued to be kept in Kanthiraya varaha and hana—the Canteroy pagodas and fanams of the English treaties with Mysore and of the official accounts down to the time of the British assumption. Kanthi Raya coined fanams only (*Kanthiráya hana*), but ten of these were taken to be equal to a varaha or pagoda, which had, however, no actual existence, but was a nominal coin used in accounts only. The Mysore Rajas did not coin varaha or pagodas. These were coined by the Ikkeri rulers of Bednur."

Kanṭhirava died without issue, and was followed successively by Kempa[9] Deva Raja, Chikka Deva Raja, Kanṭhirava Raja Múk-arasu[10] and Doḍḍa Krishna Raja, on whose death in 1731 the direct descent ended. Cháma Raja, a member of the Hemanhalli family, was next elected, but being deposed by the dalaváyi Deva Raja and the minister Nanja Raja, was succeeded by Chikka or Immaḍi Krishna Raja, and Cháma Raja who died childless in 1775. Another Chama Raja, son of Devaraj Arasu of Arkotar, was then selected at random by Haidar Ali Khan, who had usurped the government and was really the ruler.

Haidar died at the age of eighty in camp at Chittore after a virtual reign of nearly thirty years, and was succeeded by his son Tippoo Sultan, who, after a reign of sixteen years, was found among the slain at the storming of Seringapatam on the 4th of May 1799.

The coins struck by Haidar were characterised by their general rudeness, and by the retention of the Hindu figures on the coins of the conquered states; whilst, on the other hand, Tippoo's coinage is remarkable both for the greater number and variety of his gold, silver, and copper pieces, and for the superior neatness of the inscriptions. Haidar's well-known laxity in religious matters rendered him careless on this point, and we accordingly see him, on reducing the neighbouring states to subjection, retaining the current coins of the district with their representations of heathen gods and goddesses, merely substituting his

---

[6] History of Mysore, vol. I, p. 32, ed. II, 1869.

[7] Coinage of Mysore, 1856, p. 3.

[8] Op. cit., vol. I, app., p. 8.

[9] Kempa Deva Raja took the title of "Dodda" (Great) as opposed to "Chikka" (Small).

[10] The dumb king. He was born deaf and dumb.

own initial for the inscription on the reverse. This was done perhaps as much with a view of conciliating his newly-conquered subjects as with that of saving time and expense. An illustration of this is seen in the gold coin called the *Bahâduri* or *Ikkéri pagoda*, the original of which was struck at Bednur by the Polygars of Ikkéri, and bore on the obverse the figures of Síva and Párvati (*Uma and Mahesvara*), and on the reverse the word *Śri*, an appellation of Lakshmi, the Hindu goddess of prosperity, in Nágarí. On the conquest of Ikkéri in 1763, Haidar established a mint at Bednur, and, erasing the word *Śri* on the current coins, substituted his own initial on a granulated surface, still retaining the original obverse. This constitutes the *old Baháduri* or *Ikkéri pagoda* [11] (Pl. I, 3–5), and was the first coin struck by Haidar in his own name. In process of time, the dies wearing out, new dies were manufactured of precisely the same device, but with an inferior degree of skill. Coins struck with these dies are called the *new Baháduri* or *Ikkéri pagodas*. The late Raja of Mysore, on his restoration to the throne, effaced Haidar's initial, and substituted for it his own name (*vide* Krishna Ráj Pagoda, pp. 14 and 24) (Pl. I, 19).

The *Baháduri* or *Ikkéri fanam* (Pl. I, 7) is of precisely the same design as the *new Ikkéri pagoda*.

Haidar conquered Calicut in A.D. 1773, but it was again reduced by General Meadows with the Bombay army after the defeat of the Mysore army under Sirdar Khan in 1782. The small gold coin known as the *Calicut fanam* [12] (Pl. I, 16, 17) bears on the obverse Haidar's initial surrounded by a line and row of dots, and on the reverse the word كليكوت (Kalikút) surmounted by the date.

The coins of Tippoo are much more numerous than those of Haidar, whose initial he retained on his gold and silver coins struck a long time subsequent to his father's death. "This," says Marsden, [13] "is by some attributed to a sentiment of filial duty and respect, but we may rather conclude that he adopted the term (signifying in Arabic a lion, and by misapplication a tiger) as an emblematical designation equivalent to a family name. There appears also an obvious allusion to the attribute of Haidar, or Asad Allah (lion of God) bestowed upon the Khalif Ali, from whom the Sultan affected to trace his maternal descent, and whom he considered as his patron and model."

---

[11] "*The Bangalore pagoda* was struck by Haidar at Bangalore. It resembles the Bahâduri pagoda, but is distinguished by the name of Pedda-talei Bangaloori, or 'big-headed' Bangalore pagoda. None of these coins bear any date." Hawkes, op. cit., p. 5.

[12] Hawkes describes (op. cit.) a Calicut fanam bearing the date 1166. The fanams in the Madras Museum collection bear the dates 1198, 1199, and 1215, respectively, and are known as *Sultán Calicut fanams*.

[13] Numismat. Orient., 1825. Pt. II, p. 699.

With respect to Tippoo's peculiar method of dating his coins, Marsden says,[14] "It will be found to have varied at different periods of his reign. From the year after his accession in the year 1197 of the *Hejrah* until 1200 inclusive, he appears to have employed the usual Muhammadan era; but on his coinage of the following year, instead of 1201, we observe the date 1215, being a difference of fourteen years. To discover the principle of this new reckoning seemed difficult, until it was observed that on some copper coins of the year 1221 the date is accompanied by the word مولودی signifying from "the birth," and upon one of 1222 by the still more express words مولودی محمد from "the birth of Muhammad," which do not leave a doubt of the era being intended to date from the time of that event as recorded (although not without contradiction) by historians."

One of the first gold pieces struck by Tippoo was the *Ahmedi* or *Sultáni gold mohur* (Pl. I, 8). *The Sidáki* or *half mohur* is about half its value. Tippoo is also said to have coined *double mohurs* called *Emaumis*.

Under the general name of *Sultáni pagodas* are included a number of gold coins struck by Tippoo, bearing a general resemblance, but differing slightly as regards the mint towns. Thus the pagodas in the Madras Museum collection which were struck in 1198, 1199 and 1200 bear on the obverse Haidar's initial with the word نگر (Nuggur)[15] and the year of the reign (Pl. I, 9, 10). In 1216 two types of pagodas were issued, one bearing on the obverse Haidar's initial with the word دهاروار (*Dharwar*) and the year of the reign (Pl. I, 11) and the other the same with the substitution of the words فاروقی نگر (*Fárúkhi Nuggur*) for دهاروار (Pl. I, 12).

The pagodas of the year 1221 bear on the obverse Haidar's initial with the words فاروقی پٹن (*Fárúkhi Puttun*)[16] and the year of the reign (Pl. I, 13). The two latter types of coin are known as the *Fárúkhi* or *Fárókhi pagodas*.

Tippoo's *Sultáni fanams* are of two kinds, the *aval* or first, and *duyam*[17] or second, the words *aval* and *duyam* pointing to the difference in their sizes. The latter is sometimes called the *Gidd fanam*. They bear on the obverse Haidar's initial and on the reverse the inscription, ضرب پٹن (*struck at Puttun*) and the date (Pl. I, 14).

---

[14] Op. cit., p. 700.

[15] "The name of *Nuggur* or *Nagar* was given to Bedenore by Haidar when he annexed that province to the usurped sovereignty of Mysore, and it is by Mussulmans called Nugger, or Haidar Nugger; but the Canarese call it by its old name Bednore, or rather Bednoor." Moor, Narrative of Little's Detachment, 1794, p. 477.

[16] *Puttun* = Seringapatam.

[17] *Awul* and *dooyem*. Hawkes, op. cit., p. 6.

The *Nuggur Salay fanam* was minted by Tippoo at Bednur and bears on the obverse Haidar's initial and on the reverse the inscription ضرب نگر (struck at Nuggur) with the date (Pl. I, 15).

The *Dhotie fanam* (Pl. I, 18) bears Haidar's initial on the obverse, and the word فرخی (*Furhi*) [18] with the date on the reverse. It is said to have derived its name from the fanciful resemblance of Haidar's initial to the hook used in gathering fruit. But the same would apply equally to numerous other coins bearing a similar mark.

The *Syed Salee fanam* bears Haidar's initial on the obverse and the inscription ضرب خالق آباد (*struck at Khálakhábád*) with the date on the reverse. The name Khálakhábád was given by Tippoo to the town of Chandagál near Seringapatam.

The following list of gold coins issued by Haidar, Tippoo and Krishṇa Rája Woḍeyar is extracted from Rice's Table of Mysore Gold Coins [19] :

Name.	By whom coined.	Where coined.	Earliest date.
			A.D.
Baháduri hun	Haidar Ali ..	Bednur	1763
Do.	Do. ..	Bangalore ..	..
Sultáni hun	Tippu Sultan ..	Seringapatam, &c.	1783
Kuki Sultáni hun ..	Do. ..	Do. ..	..
Fárokhi hun	Do. ..	Do. ..	..
Krishna Raja Varaha ..	Krishna Raja ..	Mysore ..	1811
Kalikat haṇa	Haidar Ali ..	Calicut	1773
Addakalikat haṇa ..	Do. ..	Do.	..
Sultáni Kalikat haṇa ..	Tippu Sultan ..	Do.	1778
Sultáni hana (*aval*) ..	Do. ..	Seringapatam ..	..
Do. (duyam) ..	Do. ..	Do. ..	..
Nagar Sale haṇa ..	Do. ..	Bednur	1786
Dhoti haṇa do. ..	Do. ..	....	..
Sayad Sale do. ..	Do. ..	Chandgal ..	..
Badshahi do. ..	Haidar Ali (?) ..	....	..
Chick Ballapur haṇa ..	Do. (?) ..	....	..
Ahmadi or Sultani Ashrufi	Tippu Sultan ..	Seringapatam ..	1783
Imámi (double mohur) ..	Do. ..	....	..
Sidáki (half mohur) ..	Do. ..	....	..

[18] Marsden says (op. cit., p. 717), "the word فرخی *ferkhi* or *ferrokhi* might seem to be intended for the name of the coin, but others of the same minute description, bearing the date of 1218, do not contain this word, and on some of the copper money we shall find it to stand apparently for the name of a place, otherwise called New Calicut," which was, according to Wilks, a fort near Calicut named *Ferrockhee*. Dr. Bidie (J. As. Soc., Beng., vol. LI., pl. I, 1883) inclines to the belief that "the term was originally adopted as a pious token of respect for one of Muhammad's successors, and subsequently in some cases did double duty by expressing this and also the place of mintage."

[19] Op. cit., app., p. 2.

The silver coins struck by Tippoo were—

1. The Haidari, Nokára, or double Sultání rupee (Pl. II, 1–3).
2. The Imámí or single rupee (Pl. II, 4).
3. The Ábidí or half rupee (Pl. II, 5).
4. The Bákhrí or quarter rupee (Pl. III, 2, 3).
5. The Jazri [20] or two-anna piece (Pl. III, 4).
6. The Kázmí or one-anna piece (Pl. III, 5).
7. The Kizri or half-anna piece.

The following is a table of Tippoo's silver coins as given by Rice [21]:

Name of coin.	Mint.	Earliest date of coin.
		A.D.
Nokára (double rupee)	Seringapatam ..	1784
Sultáni rupáyi	Do. ..	,,
Do. Âdha rupáyi ($\frac{1}{2}$ r.)	Do. ..	,,
Bákri ,, ,, ($\frac{1}{4}$ r.)	Do. ..	1789
Jasri ,, ,, ($\frac{1}{8}$ r.)	Do. ..	..
Kajmi ,, ,, ($\frac{1}{16}$ r.)	Do. ..	1794
Kizri ,, ,, ($\frac{1}{32}$ r.)	Do. ..	..

Copper coins struck prior to the Muhammadan usurpation seem to have generally borne an elephant on the obverse, with crossed lines on the reverse (Pl. IV, 20). To this was subsequently added the symbol of the moon placed above the elephant, and later still that of the sun was also inserted (Pl. IV, 21, 22).

Haidar probably made simple recoinages of these, but Tippoo's currency was much more extensive and consisted of :

1. A half paisah, bearing the figure of a lion or tiger on one side, and a battle-axe on the other. Marsden says [22] that this coin seems to have been the pattern piece of a coin that did not afterwards become a part of the currency. The specimen (Pl. X, 8) in the Madras Museum collection, which was obtained at Bangalore, differs in some trifling points from those figured by Marsden [23] and Moor.[24]

2. The *Mashrabi, Mushtari, Double Paisah* or *Dub*, which has on the obverse an elephant carrying a flag, and an inscription on the reverse. The coin struck in the year 1219 (Pl. VI, 1) has the word عثمانی (*Usmáni*) on the reverse *inter alia*. On coins bearing the dates 1222, 1224 and 1225, the word مشربی (*Mashrabi*) or مشتری (*Mushtari*) (Pl. VI, 3) appears on the reverse, and coins dated 1222 are inscribed with the word مولودی

[20] *Jáfari.* Marsden, op. cit., p. 720.

[21] Op. cit., app., pp. 6, 7.

[22] Op. cit., p. 725.

[23] Op. cit., Pl. XLVI, Fig. MXLIX.

[24] Op. cit., Pl. I, Fig. 13.

(*Múlúdi*) on the obverse (Pl. VI, 3). The flag on the coins of 1224 bears the numeral ۱ (*alif*) (Pl. VII, 2) and on the coins of 1225 the numeral ب (*be*) (Pl. VII, 5).

3. The *Zahra, Zohra, Single Paisah* or *Dub.*

4. The *Bahrám, Half Paisah* or *Dub.*

5. The *Akhter, Quarter Paisah* or *Dub.*

The single, half and quarter Paisahs of 1224 bear the numeral ۱ over the elephant on the obverse in lieu of the date, those of 1225 and some of 1222 the numeral ب and those of 1226 the numeral ت (*te*).

The object of these numerals is not apparent, but it is suggested by Marsden [25] that they may have reference to the system of depreciation which the coinage in some parts of India is liable to after the lapse of the current year.

The fact is mentioned by Buchanan [26] that the value of his different coins was frequently changed by Tippoo in a very arbitrary manner. When he was about to pay his troops, the nominal value of each coin was raised very high, and kept at that standard for about ten days; during which time the soldiers were allowed to pay off their debts at the high valuation. After this the standard was reduced to the proper value.

Two coins, which are not in the Madras Museum collection, are mentioned by Marsden [27] viz., a minute coin intended for a *half Akhter* or eighth part of a peisah, bearing on the obverse an elephant with the letter ت and on the reverse the denomination of the money, being a word that may be read قطب (katib), but is by no means distinct; and another coin of octagonal form, having on one side the word نواب (nawáb) with some additional characters not legible, and on the other تحرنکر (Trichinopoly?) as the name of the place, with the date 1207.

As bearing indirectly on the subject of Tippoo's coinage, the fact is worthy of mention that Tippoo imitated the mark of the East India Company on its coins, and placed it on his muskets and cannon, substituting the letters of his father's name ح ی د ر for the usual V.E.I.C. (Pl. X, 11).

On the death of Tippoo in 1799, the British Government restored the Hindu Raj and placed on the throne Krishna Raja Woḍeyar, son of the last Cháma Raja, during whose minority Purnaiya acted as regent.

The Baháduri pagoda was changed by Kṛishṇa Rája, the figures of Síva and Párvati being retained, but the Nágari inscription "*Srí Kṛishṇa Rája*" substituted for Haidar's initial (Pl. I, 19).

---

[25] Op. cit., p. 723.

[26] Journey to Mysore, vol. I, p. 129.

[27] Op. cit., p. 726.

His silver coinage consisted of :

1. A rupee, half and quarter rupee, bearing an inscription in Hindustani on the obverse and reverse, which were originally coined by Purnaiya, but afterwards recoined by Kṛishṇa Rája (Pl. III, 6–9).

2. A quarter rupee bearing on the obverse the figure of Chámundi, and on the reverse the date and inscription کشن راج و دیر ضرب مہی سور (Kishen Ráj Woḍeyar : struck at Mahisur) (Pl. III, 10, 11).

3. The Aḍḍa or half fanam (Pl. III, 12).

4. The Hága or quarter fanam (Pl. III, 13).

The two latter coins bear on the obverse the figure of Chámundi, and on the reverse the Kanarese inscription *Mayiḷi hanna.* They are also known as the large and small *Mayili* [28] or *Cali* fanams.

On the accession of Kṛishṇa Rája, a small copper cash was struck bearing on the obverse an elephant with the symbols of the sun and moon, and on the reverse the Nágarí inscription *Śrí Kṛishṇa Rája* (Pl. IX, 3).

The next coinage bore the same obverse with the addition of the word *Śrí ;* while the reverse bore the inscription "*V.*" "*X.*" or "XX Cash" (Eng.) "*Mayili kásu* 5," "10" or "20" (Kan.) (Pl. IX, 5–7).

A later coinage had the English characters of the reverse below the Kanarese; and still later the word *Chá* (in Kanarese for Chámundi) was added above the inscription on the reverse, and in a subsequent issue the entire word *Chámundi* (Kan.) was inserted above the elephant on the obverse, and the word *Kṛishṇa* (Kan.) added to the inscription on the reverse (Pl. IX, 8).

The next step was the substitution of the lion of Chámundi for the elephant, and the modification of the inscription on the reverse, which now stood as follows on the 25 cash pieces : in the centre *Kṛishṇa* (Kan.) surrounded by the inscription "*XXV Cash*" (Eng.), "*Zerb Mahisur*" (Hind.), "*Mayili kasu 25*" (Kan.) (Pl. X, 1). The smaller coins had merely the word "*Kṛishṇa*" (Kan.), "*Zerb Mahisur*" (Hind.), together with the numeral *5* or *10* in later issues.

The following list of coins, issued by Kṛishṇa Rája Woḍeyar, is given by Rice.[29]

---

[28] Rice says (op. cit., app., p. 7) "The meaning of the word *Mayili* is not very clear. It may be connected with an old Kannada word *Muyyi,* signifying *token, exchange ;* unless it refers in any way to Mayiliapur (St. Thomé) at Madras."

[29] Op. cit., app., pp. 2–7.

Name of coin.	Mint.	Earliest date.	Obverse.	Reverse.
Krishna Raj Varaha ..	Mysore.	1811	Uma and Mahesvara.	Sri Krishna Raja.
Rája rupáyi	Seringapatam.	1800	..	
Do. ardha rupáyi (½ r.)	Do. ..	..	..	
Do. pávali ,, (¼ r.)	Mysore..	1828	Figure of Chámundi surrounded by dots.	*Kishen Raj Wodeyar, San., 1244. Julûs Zarb Mahisúr*; surrounded by dots.
Do. Aḍḍa (½ fanam) ..	Do. ..	..	Figure of Chámundi.	*Mayili hanna.*
Do. Hága (¼ ,,)..	Do. ..	..	Do. ..	Do.
Kásu or Áne kásu ..	Do. ..	After 1811	Elephant with sun and moon.	*Sri Krishna Raja.*
Mayili kásu	Do. ..	Later than above.	Do. with *Sri* above.	*V.X.* or *XX Cash* (Eng.), *Mayili kásu 5, 10, or 20* (Kan.)
Do.	Do. ..	Do.	Do. ..	*Chá Mayili kásu 5* (Kan.) *V Cash* (Eng.).
Do.	Do. ..	Do.	Do. with *Sri Chámundi* above.	*Krishna* (Kan.) *Mayili kásu ipattu* (Kan.) *XX Cash* (Eng.).
Do.	Do. ..	Do.	Lion of Chámundi, *Sri*, sun and moon above.	*Krishna* (Kan.) *XXV Cash* (Eng.) *Zarb Mahisur* (Hind.) *Mayili 25 kásu* (Kan.)
Do.	Do. ..	Do.	Do. ..	*Krishna* (Kan.) *Zarb Mahisur* (Hind).
Do.	Do. ..	Do.	Do. with date 1843 below.	Do. do.

The copper mint was removed from Mysore to Bangalore in 1833 and abolished in 1843. Since 1863 the native copper coins, though still current among the people, have ceased to be issued from the public treasuries, and are thus being gradually withdrawn from circulation. Many specimens, however, of the copper coins of Tippoo and Kṛishṇa Rája Woḍeyar can still be obtained in the bazaars at Bangalore, Mysore, Seringapatam, &c.

Rice says,[30] "The following coins now (1877) in circulation are those of British India, together with a few native copper coins which, however, are being withdrawn and sold, and broken up as old copper:

Copper	Kásu	.. Pie or cash.
Do.	Duggáni	.. ½ duddu, 2 pies.
Do.	Múr kásu	.. ¼ anna.
Do.	Duddu	.. ⅛ do.
Do.	Ardháne	.. ½ do.
Do.	Áne ..	.. anna.
Silver	Doddáne	.. 2 annas.
Do.	Pávali	.. ¼ rupee.
Do.	Ardha rupai.	½ do.
Do.	Rupai	.. rupee.

Government Central Museum,
Madras,
6th January 1888.

EDGAR THURSTON,
Superintendent.

[30] Op. cit., app., p. 8.

TABLE

OF

THE MYSORE RAJAHS.[31]

Name.	Date of reign.
Vijaya	1399–1422
Hire Bettada Cháma Raja	1423–1457
Timma Raja	1458–1477
Cháma Raja, Ár-beral	1478–1512
Beṭṭada Cháma Raja	1513–1551
Appana Timma Raja	1552–1570
Hire Cháma Raja, Ból	1571–1575
Bettaḍa Wodeyar	1576–1577
Raja Woḍeyar	1578–1617
Cháma Raja	1617–1636
Immaḍi Raja	1637–1638
Kanṭhirava Narasa Raja	1638–1658
Doḍḍa Deva Raja	1659–1672
Chikka Deva Raja	1672–1704
Kanṭhirava Raja, Múk-arasu	1704–1714
Doḍḍa Krishna Raja	1714–1731
Cháma Raja	1731– ..
Chikka or Immaḍi Krishna Raja	1734–1766
Cháma Raja	1766–1775
Cháma Raja	1775–1796
Muhammadan Usurpation, 1761–1799.	
Kṛishṇa Rája Woḍeyar	1799–1868
Cháma Rájendra Woḍeyar	1868– ..

[31] Rice, Op. cit., vol. I, p. 240.

TABLE

OF

THE WODEIYAR DYNASTY OF MAISUR.[32]

Name.	Date of reign.
Ráj Wodeiyar	1578–1617
Cháma Rája IV	1617–1637
Immaḍí Rája	1637–1638
Kaṇṭhíráva Narasa Rája	1638–1659
Kempa Déva Rája	1659–1672
Chikka Déva	1672–1704
Kaṇṭhíráva Rája II	1704–1714
Doḍḍa Kṛishṇa Rája	1714–1731
Cháma Rája V	1731–1733

COMPARATIVE TABLE OF THE DATES ON THE COINS OF TIPPOO SULTAN, AND THE YEARS OF THE CHRISTIAN ERA.

Muhammadan.	Christian.	Muhammadan.	Christian.
1198	1783-84	1220	1791-92
1199	1784-85	1221	1792-93
1200	1785-86	1222	1793-94
1215	1786-87	1223	1794-95
1216	1787-88	1224	1795-96
1217	1788-89	1225	1796-97
1218	1789-90	1226	1797-98
1219	1790-91		

[32] Elliot, Numismat. Orient., 1885, p. 104.

GOLD: PRIOR TO MUHAMMADAN USURPATION.

No.	Mint: Date.	Obverse.	Reverse.
		KAṆṬHÍRÁVA NARASA RÁJA.	
		KANTEROY FANAM.	
1	Seringapatam.	Figure of the Narasinga Avatár.	Symbols of sun and moon (?) [Pl. I, 1.]
1.1	Seringapatam.	Same as 1.	Same as 1. [Pl. I, 2.]
2	Seringapatam.	Same.	Same.
2.1	Seringapatam.	Same.	Same.
		FANAM OF HAIDAR.	
2.2	1179.	Haidar's initial: surrounded by a ring of dots.	سنہ ۱۱۸۹ : surrounded by a ring of dots.

GOLD: MUHAMMADAN USURPATION.

No.	Mint: Date.	Obverse.	Reverse.
		BAHÁDURI OR IKKÉRI PAGODA.	
3	Bednur.	The figures of Síva and Párvati (Uma and Mahesvara).	Haidar's initial on a granulated surface. [Pl. I, 3.]
4	Bednur.	Same as 3.	Same as 3. [Pl. I, 4.]
5	Bednur.	Same.	Same. [Pl. I, 5.]
		BAHÁDURI OR IKKÉRI FANAM.	
6	Bednur.	The figures of Síva and Párvati (Uma and Mahesvara).	Haidar's initial on a granulated surface. [Pl. I, 7.]
7	Bednur.	Same as 6.	Same as 6.

GOLD: Muhammadan usurpation—*continued.*

No.	Mint: Date.	Obverse.	Reverse.
		Ahmedi or Sultání Mohur.	
8	Seringapatam, 1219.	دین احمد درجهان روشن است زفتح حیدر ح احمدی ضرب پتن سال زبرجد سنه ۹۱۲۱ "The religion of Muhammad is made illustrious in the world by the victory of Haidar. H.[1] *Ahmedi.* Struck at *Puttun*[2] in the year of the cycle *Zabarjad:*[3] year (of the new era) 1219:" encircled by a ring of dots. (Marsden).	هو السلطان الوحید العادل تاریخ جلوس سال سخ سیوم بهاری سنه ۹ جلوسی "He is the only just Sultan. Third (day of the month) *Bahárí*:[4] year of the cycle *Sakh*:[5] year of the reign 9:" encircled by a ring of dots. (Marsden). [Pl. I, 8.]
		Sidáki[6] or Half Gold Mohur.	
8.1	....	محمد دین احمد در جهان روشن ح حیدر صدیقی ضرب پتن سال سراب سنه ۷۱۲۱ Same as 8, but bearing the name *Sidíki* and the year 1217 of the cycle *Siráb* (see footnote, page 25).	Same as 8, but bearing year of the reign 7.

[1] Haidar's initial.

[2] "The word پتن [*Puttun* or vulgarly *Patan*] signifies the city per excellentiam and is meant to denote Seringapatam, the capital of the Mysore dominion." Marsden, op. cit. p. 710.

"Seringapatam" (says Buchanan, op. cit., vol. I, p. 62) is commonly called *Patana* or *Patan*, *i.e.*, the city; but the name used in our maps is a corruption from *Srí Rangapatna*, the city of *Srí Ranga*, from its containing a temple dedicated to Vishnu under that name.

[3] زبرجد Zabarjad = a Topaz. The names of the years of the cycle mentioned by Marsden as occurring on Tippoo's mohurs or half mohurs are:—سراب *siráb*, هتا *shitá*, زبرجد *zabarjad*, and سخ *sakh*. *See* supplement.

[4] "The third day of Baháríor second month of the calendar is the day of Tippu's accession, on which he declared himself Sultan. It corresponds to the 4th of May 1783 A.D., at which period Tippu was flushed with the victory recently obtained over a British army on the Malabar coast." Marsden, op. cit., p. 710.

[5] سخ Sakh, lit. beads, *i.e.*, of glass, is here made to signify 37.

[6] This coin is referred to as the *Siddekie*, *Sedduckee*, *Seddaky*, and *Sedaky* Pagodas in the accounts of the Madras Mint in the early part of the present century.

GOLD : MUHAMMADAN USURPATION—*continued.*

No.	Mint : Date.	Obverse.	Reverse.
		SULTÁNÍ PAGODA.	
9	Bednur, 1198.	ح نگر ٢ "H.[1] *Nuggur*. (Year of the reign) 2" on a granulated surface, surrounded by lined circles and ring of dots.	هو السلطان العادل سنه ١١٩٨ هجری "He is the just Sultan. Year hejirah 1198:" surrounded by lined circle and ring of dots. [Pl. I, 9.]
10	Bednur, 1199.	Same as 9; but year 3.	Same as 9; but year 1199.
11	Bednur, 1200.	Same;[2] but year 4.	Same; but year 1200. [Pl. I, 10.]
12	Dharwar, 1216.	ح دهاروار ٦ "H. *Dharwar*.[3] (Year of the reign) 6" on granulated surface: surrounded by lined circle and ring of dots.	محمد هوالسلطان العادل سنه ١٢١٦ "Muhammad. He is the just Sultan. Year 1216:" surrounded by lined circle and ring of dots. [Pl. I, 11.]
		FÁRÚKHÍ PAGODA.	
13	Bednur, 1216.	فاروقی نگر ح سنه ٦ "*Fárúkhí*[4] *Nuggur*. H. Year 6:" surrounded by lined circle and ring of dots.	محمد هوالسلطان الوحيدالعادل سنه ٦١٢١ "Muhammad. He is the only just Sultan. Year 1216:" surrounded by lined circle and ring of dots. [Pl. I, 12.]
14	Bednur, 1216.	Same as 13.	Same as 13.

[1] Haidar's initial.

[2] A copper coin of the same type was struck, of which the only specimen seen by me is in the cabinet of Captain Tufnell. *Auct.*

[3] A Fárúkhí pagoda was struck by Tippoo in which the word خورشيد سواد (*Khorshid-suád*) is supposed to stand for Dharwar.

[4] "Farûkhî is the appellation given in Tîpû's nomenclature to the small gold coin that has already been noticed as equivalent to the *varaha*, hûn, or pagoda of the preceding Government..... It is the quarter part of the *Ahmedi*."

"With respect to the name of Muhammad which appears at the top of the inscriptions it is evident that it cannot be placed in the construction assigned to it in describing the Sultání rupee of 1215, and I am led to think that, notwithstanding the disjunction of the words it should be understood to follow the word year, and to designate the new era." Marsden, op. cit., p. 716.

GOLD: Muhammadan usurpation—*continued.*

No.	Mint: Date.	Obverse.	Reverse.
		Fárúkhí Pagoda—*continued.*	
15	Seringapatam, 1221.	فاروقی پٹن ح سنہ ۱۱ "*Fárúkhí Puttun.*[1] H. Year 11:" surrounded by lined circle and ring of dots.	Same as 13, but date 1221. [Pl. I, 13.]
16	Seringapatam, 1221.	Same as 15.	Same as 15.
16.1	Dharwar, 1217	فاروقی خورشید سواد سنہ ۷ "*Fárúkhí Khorshíd-suád.*[2] Year 7:" surrounded by lined circle and ring of dots.	Same: but date 1217. [Pl. I, 6.]
		Sultání Fanam (Thin).	
17	Seringapatam, 1217.	Haidar's initial surrounded by lined circle and ring of dots.	ضرب پٹن ۷۱۲۱ "Struck at *Puttun*, 1217:" surrounded by lined circle and ring of dots. [Pl. I, 14.]
18	Seringapatam, 1219.	Same as 17.	Same as 17: but date 1219.
		Sultání Fanam (Thick).	
19	Seringapatam.	Same as 17.	Same as 17: but date illegible.
20	Seringapatam.	Same.	Same.

[1] Haidar's initial is combined in this coin, with the word *Puttun*.

[2] "The new name which Tippu has given, we understand, to Darwar, but we do not recognise in it any analogy to existing circumstances, or any direction in the application than what seems to have arisen from whim and caprice; خورشید "the sun," prefixed to سواد which means blackness, darkness, riches, population, &c., may be supposed to have a variety of meanings: suwad means also the circumference: and possibly the inscription may be translated "Stricken on the sun's circumference," alluding to the circular figure of the die. We are not clear whether سواد does not also signify light or splendour; therefore we may give the word divers meanings, but should not, perhaps, among them hit upon that which was intended." Moor, op. cit., app. p. 478.

GOLD: Muhammadan usurpation—*continued.*

No.	Mint: Date.	Obverse.	Reverse.
			[1] Nuggur Fanam.
21	Bednur, 1199.	Same.	ضرب نگر ۱۱۹۹ "Struck at *Nuggur*, 1199:" surrounded by lined circle and ring of dots. [Pl. I, 15.]
22	Bednur, 1220.	Same.	Same as 21: but date 1220. Reading from l to r.
			Calicut Fanam.
23	Calicut, 1215.	Same.	كليكوت سنه ۵۱۲۱ "*Kalikút.*[2] Year 1215" (reading from r to l): surrounded by lined circle. [Pl. I, 16.]
24	Calicut, 1215.	Same.	كليكوت سنه ۱۲۱۵ Same as 23: but date reading from l to r. [Pl. I, 17.]
			Dhotie Fanam.
25	New Calicut? 1216.	Same.	فرخی ۶۱۲۱ "*Furrokhi.* 1216:" surrounded by lined circle and ring of dots. [Pl. I, 18.]
26	New Calicut? 1217.	Same.	Same as 25: but date 1217.

[1] The "Nuggur Salay" fanam of Hawkes.
[2] *Kullekoot.* Moor, op. cit., p. 478.

GOLD: Kṛishṇa Rája Woḍeyar.

No.	Mint: Date.	Obverse.	Reverse.
		GOLD: Kṛishṇa Rája Woḍeyar.	
		Kṛishṇa Ráj Pagoda.[1]	
27	**Mysore.**	The figures of Síva and Párvati holding trisúla and deer: emblems of sun and moon above.	"*Śrí Kṛishṇa Rája*" (Nág). [Pl. I, 19.]
28	**Mysore.**	Same as 27.	Same as 27.
29	**Mysore.**	Same as 27.	Same as 27.

[1] Also called Kurtur Ikkéri pagoda. "The name Kurtur was given to the reigning Raja of Mysore to distinguish him from the head of another branch of the family called also Raja, but having in addition the title of Dalawai." Buchanan, op. cit., vol. I, p. 46.

SILVER: MUHAMMADAN USURPATION.

No.	Mint: Date.	Obverse.	Reverse.
		NOKÁRA OR DOUBLE SULTÁNÍ RUPEE.	
1	Seringapatam, 1200.	دین احمد محمددرجهان روشن است زفتح حیدر ضرب پتن سال دلوسنه ۱۲۰۰ هجری "The religion of Muhammad is made illustrious in the world by the victory of Haidar. H. Struck at *Puttun* in the year of the cycle *dalú*;[1] year hejirah 1200:" surrounded by lined circle and ring of dots.	هوالسلطان الوحید العادل سیوم بهاری سال دلو سنه ۴ جلوس "He is the only just Sultan. Third (day of the month) *Bahárí*;[2] year of the cycle *dalú*; year of the reign 4:" surrounded by lined circle and ring of dots. [Pl. II, 1.]
2	Seringapatam, 1216.	دین احمد محمد درجهان روشن زفتح حیدر است ح حیدری ضرب پتن سال سارا سنه ۶۱۲۱ "The religion of Muhammad is made illustrious in the world by the victory of Haidar. H. *Haidarí*.[3] Struck at *Puttun* in the year of the cycle *Sárá*:[4] year (of the new era) 1216:" surrounded by lined circle and ring of dots.	هوالسطان الوحید العادل تاریخ جلوس سال سخ سیوم بهاری سنه ۶ جلوسی "He is the only just Sultan. Epoch of the accession in the year *Sakh*: third (day of the month) *Bahárí*: year of the reign 6:" surrounded by lined circle and ring of dots. [Pl. II, 2.]
3	Seringapatam, 1217.	دین احمد محمد درجهان روشن زفتح حیدر است ح حیدری ضرب پتن سال سراب سنه ۷۱۲۱ Same as No. 2: but year of the cycle *Siráb*:[5] year (of the now era) 1217.	هو السلطان الوحید العال تاریخ جلوس سال سخ سیوم بهاری سنه ۷ جلوسی Same as No. 2: but year of the reign 7. [Pl. II, 3.]

[1] The name of the cycle is here دلو *dalú*, a water-bucket or the sign of the Zodiac Aquarius, the letters of which produce the number 40. The names of the years of the cycle on Tippoo's's silver coins are:—
ازل *ázal*, جلو *jalú*, دلو *dalú*, ها *shá*, سارا *sárá*, and سراب *siráb*. See supplement.

[2] V. ant. p. 20, foot-note.

[3] The word حیدری Haidarí is one of the names which was given to this coin.

[4] "The word سارا *Sárá* means odoriferous, and is produced by adding together س 30, ا 1, ا 10, and again ا 1, which make up the number 42." Marsden, op. cit., p. 703.

[5] The word سراب *Siráb* means "the undulating refraction of the sun's rays striking on a sandy plain" (mirage).

SILVER : Muhammadan usurpation—*continued.*

No.	Mint : Date.	Obverse.	Reverse.
		Imámí or Sultání Rupee.	
4	Seringapatam, 1216.	دین احمد محمد درجہان روشن زفتح حیدر است ح امامی ضرب پٹن سال سارا سنہ ۱۲۱۶ "The religion of Muhammad is made illustrious in the world by the victory of Haidar. H. *Imámí*. Struck at *Puttun* in the year of the cycle *Sárá* : year (of the new era) 1216 :" surrounded by lined circle and ring of dots.	ھوالسلطان الوحیدالعادل تاریخ جلوس سال سخ سیوم بہاری سنہ ٦ جلوسی "He is the only just Sultan. Epoch of the accession in the year *Sakh*. Third (day of the month) *Bahárí* Year of the reign 6 :" surrounded by lined circle and ring of dots. [Pl. II, 4.]
4.1	Seringapatam, 1216.	Same as 4.	Same as 4.
4.2	Seringapatam, 1216.	The same legends on the obverse and reverse as those of No. 4.1 ; but the coin is much thicker, and has a plain rim on the face instead of a lined circle and ring of dots.	
		Ábidí or Half Sultání Rupee.	
5	Seringapatam.	دین احمد محمد درجہان روشن زفتح حیدر است ح عابدی ضرب پٹن سال راسخ سنہ ... "The religion of Muhammad is made illustrious in the world by the victory of Haidar. H. *Ábidí*. Struck at *Puttun* in the year of the cycle ......: year (of the new era ....):" surrounded by lined circle and ring of dots.	Same as No. 4 : but year of the reign 2. [Pl. III, 1.]
6	Seringapatam, 1216.	Same as No. 5 : but year 1216.	Same : but year of the reign 6. [Pl. II, 5.]

SILVER: MUHAMMADAN USURPATION—*continued.*

No.	Mint: Date.	Obverse.	Reverse.
		BÁKHRÍ OR QUARTER RUPEE.	
7	Seringapatam, 1217.	محمد هو السلطان الوحيد العادل سنه ۷۱۲۱ "Muhammad. He is the only just Sultan. Year 1217:" surrounded by lined circle and ring of dots.	باقری سنه ۷ ح پٹن "*Bákhri.*[1] Year 7. H. *Puttun*:" surrounded by lined circle and ring of dots. [Pl. III, 2.]
8	Seringapatam, 1218.	Same as No. 7.	Same as No. 7. [Pl. III, 3.]
		JAZRI OR TWO ANNAS.	
9	Seringapatam, 1221.	سنه ۱۲۲۱ محمد ضرب پٹن "Year of Muhammad, 1221. Struck at *Puttun*:"[2] surrounded by lined circle and ring of dots.	جعفری سنه ۱۱ جلوس "*Jazri.* Year of the reign 11:" surrounded by lined circle and ring of dots. [Pl. III, 4.]
		KÁZMÍ OR ONE ANNA.	
10	Seringapatam, 1221.	سنه ۱۲۲۱ محمد ضرب پٹن "Year of Muhammad, 1221. Struck at *Puttun*:" surrounded by lined circle and ring of dots.	کاظمی سنه ۱۱ جلوس "*Kázmí.* Year of the reign 11:" surrounded by lined circle and ring of dots. [Pl. III, 5.]
10.1	Seringapatam, 1221.	Same as No. 10.	Same as No. 10.

[1] "Mahomed Báker was the 4th khalif from Ali, father of Imam Jaeffer: and to him Tippoo may, perhaps, desire to show some reverence; but his reverence seems always ambiguous: for باقر *baker* means also abundance of riches, excelling in science, *&c.*" Moor, op. cit., p. 476.

[2] Haidar's initial joined to the word *Puttun*.

SILVER: KṚISHṆA RÁJA WOḌEYAR.

No.	Mint: Date.	Obverse.	Reverse.
		ONE RUPEE.	
11	Mysore.	سکہ زد بر هفت کشور سایہ [1] فضل الہ حامی دین محمد شاه عالم بادشاه "Defender of the Muhammadan faith, Reflection of Divine excellence, the Emperor Sháh Álam struck this coin to be current throughout the seven climates." [2] (Marsden.)	ضرب مہی سور سنہ ۷۴ جلوس میمنت مانوس "Struck at Mysore in the 47th year of the auspicious reign." [Pl. III, 6.]
12	Mysore.	Same as 11.	Same as 11: but year 48. [Pl. III, 7.]
		HALF RUPEE.	
13	Mysore.	Same.	Same. [Pl. III, 8.]
13.1	Mysore.	Same.	Same.
		QUARTER RUPEE.	
14	Mysore.	Same.	Same: but year 45. [Pl. III, 9.]
14.1	....	Same.	Same.
15	Mysore, 1244.	Figure of Chámundi: [3] encircled by ring of dots.	کشن راج ودیر سنہ ۴۴۲۱ جلوس ضرب مہی سور "*Kishen Ráj Woḍeyar*: Year of the reign 1244. Struck at Mysore:" encircled by ring of dots. [Pl. III, 10.]
16	Mysore, 1244.	Same as 15.	Same as 15. [Pl. III, 11.]
		AḌḌA OR HALF CANTEROY FANAM.	
17	Mysore.	Same.	"*Mayili hanna*" [4] (Kan). [Pl. III, 12.]
17.1	Mysore.	Same.	Same.

[1] Only a portion of the inscription occurs on each coin.

[2] "When Timur, establishing his throne in India, overcame the kings of Cashmeer, Bengal, Decan, Gudjraat, Lahore, Poorub, and Paishoor, he united the kingdoms, and called himself conqueror and sovereign of the seven climates or countries; which title has been retained by his successors." Moor, op. cit., app., p. 472.

[3] Bala Krishṇa. Elliot, Numismat. orient., 1885, p. 106.

[4] V. ant., Foot-note, p. 15.

SILVER: Kṛishṇa Rája Woḍeyar—*continued.*

No.	Mint: Date.	Obverse.	Reverse.
		Hága or Quarter Canteroy Fanam.	
18	Mysore.	Same.	Same. [Pl. III, 13.]
18.1	Mysore.	Same.	Same.

COPPER: Chequered reverse.[1]

No.	Mint: Date.	Obverse.	Reverse.
1	....	Gryphon l.	Cross lines.
2	....	Gryphon r.	Single lines at right angles, with a cross in each interspace. [Pl. IV. 1.]
3	....	Gryphon l.	Cross lines with symbols.
4	....	Lion r.	Double cross lines with symbols. [Pl. IV, 4.]
5	....	Prancing horse, l: encircled by a ring of dots.	Same. [Pl. IV, 2.]
6	....	Fish, l: encircled by a ring of dots.	Single cross lines. [Pl. IV, 11.]
7	....	Same.	Same.
8	....	Bull, l, with moon above: encircled by a ring of dots.	Double cross lines with symbols. [Pl. IV, 6.]
9	....	Bull, r, with sun and moon above: encircled by a ring of dots.	Same. [Pl. IV, 3.]
10	....	Boar, r; encircled by a ring of dots.	Same.
11	....	Deer, r, with sun and moon above: encircled by a ring of dots.	Same. [Pl. IV, 7.]
12	....	Same.	Same.

[1] Many of the following coins with chequered reverse do not probably belong specially to Mysore, though those which bear Kanarese numerals on the obverse have been attributed to a Cháma Raja. They are introduced here for convenience, as they are very common in the Mysore bazaars.

COPPER : CHEQUERED REVERSE—*continued.*

No.	Mint : Date.	Obverse.	Reverse.
13	....	Peacock, r.	Same. [Pl. IV, 8.]
14	....	Peacock, r : encircled by a ring of dots.	Same. [Pl. IV, 9.]
15	....	Same.	Same.
16	....	Bird, r : encircled by a ring of dots.	Same. [Pl. IV, 12.]
17	....	Figure of Ganesa.	Same.
18	....	Same.	Double stamped with cross lines and symbols.
19	....	Same.	Double stamped with (1) cross lines, (2) elephant with trunk elevated. [Pl. IV, 10.]
20	....	Figure of Ganesa.	Double cross lines with symbols.
21	....	Figure of Lakshmi : encircled by a ring of dots.	Same. [Pl. IV, 14.]
22	....	Figure of Hanumán : encircled by a ring of dots.	Single cross lines with symbols. [Pl. IV, 16.]
23	....	Dagger : encircled by a ring of dots.	Double cross lines with symbols. [Pl. IV, 13.]
24	....	Flower : encircled by a ring of dots.	Same.
		COINS WITH KANARESE NUMERALS.	
25	....	Numeral ೧ (1): encircled by a ring of dots.	Same. [Pl. IV, 17.]
26	....	Numeral ೨ (2): encircled by a ring of dots.	Same.
27	....	Numeral ೩ (3): encircled by a ring of dots.	Same.
28	....	Numeral ೪ (4): encircled by a ring of dots.	Same.

COPPER: Chequered reverse—*continued.*

No.	Mint : Date.	Obverse.	Reverse.
		Coins with Kanarese numerals—*cont.*	
29	....	Same.	Same.
30	....	Numeral ೬ (6): encircled by a ring of dots.	Same.
31	....	Numeral ೯ (9): encircled by a ring of dots.	Same.
32	....	Numeral ೧೦ (10): encircled by a ring of dots.	Same.
33	....	Numeral ೧೧ (11): encircled by a ring of dots.	Same. [Pl. IV, 16.]
34	....	Numeral ೧೨ (12): encircled by a ring of dots.	Same.
35	....	Numeral ೧೫ (15): encircled by a ring of dots.	Same.
36	....	Numeral ೧೭ (17): encircled by a ring of dots.	Same.
37	....	Numeral ೧೯ (19): encircled by a ring of dots.	Same.
38	....	Numeral ೨೦ (20): encircled by a ring of dots.	Same.
39	....	Numeral ೨೧ (21): encircled by a ring of dots.	Same.
40	....	Numeral ೨೨ (22): encircled by a ring of dots.	Same.
41	....	Numeral ೨೩ (23): encircled by a ring of dots.	Same.

COPPER: CHEQUERED REVERSE—*continued.*

No.	Mint: Date.	Obverse.	Reverse.
		COINS WITH KANARESE NUMERALS—*cont.*	
42	....	Numeral ೨೪ (24): encircled by a ring of dots.	Same.
43	....	Numeral ೨೮ (28): encircled by a ring of dots.	Same.
44	....	Numeral ೩೦ (30): encircled by a ring of dots.	Same.
45	....	Numeral ೩೧ (31): encircled by a ring of dots.	Same.
		ELEPHANT CASH.[1]	
46	....	Elephant r.	Same. [Pl. IV, 20.]
47	....	Elephant r.	Same.
48	....	Elephant l, with trunk elevated, as in the act of saluting.	Same. [Pl. IV, 19.]
49	....	Same.	Same.
50	....	Elephant l: encircled by a ring of dots.	Same. [Pl. IV, 18.]
51	....	Elephant l, with moon above: encircled by dots.	Same. [Pl. IV, 21.]
52	....	Same.	Same.
53	....	Elephant l, with sun and moon above: surrounded by lined circle and ring of dots.	Same. [Pl. IV, 22.]
54	....	Same.	Same.

[1] Sir Walter Elliot says (Numismat. Orient., 1885. p. 105): "The princes of this dynasty (Wodeiyar of Mysore) seem to have inherited the cognizance of the elephant from the Kongus and the Chéras, for it appears on numerous copper which coins are still current in the form of the *áne paisa* or small elephant cash."

COPPER: MUHAMMADAN USURPATION.

No.	Mint: Date.	Observe.	Reverse.
		COINS WITHOUT DATE.	
		TIGER CASH.[1]	
1	....	Tiger r: surrounded by lined circles and ring of dots.	Battle-axe: surrounded by lined circles and ring of dots. [Pl. X, 8.]
		SINGLE PAISAH.	
2	Seringapatam.	Elephant r: surrounded by lined circle and ring of dots.	ضرب پٹن "Struck at *Puttun*:" surrounded by lined circle and ring of dots. [Pl. V, 1.]
3	Seringapatam.	Same as 2: but wanting the ring of dots.	Same as 2.
		COINS WITH DATE.	
		SINGLE PAISAH.	
4	Calicut, 1199.	Elephant r: encircled by ring of dots.	۹۹ ضرب کلیکوت "..99. Struck at *Kalikút*:" encircled by a ring of dots.
5	Bednur, 1199.	Elephant r.	۱۱۹۹ ضرب نگر "1199. Struck at *Nuggur*." [Pl. VIII, 1.]
6	Calicut, 1200.	Elephant r: date 1200 above: surrounded by lined circles.	ضرب کلیکوت "Struck at *Kalikut*:" surrounded by lined circles and ring of dots.
		HALF PAISAH.	
7	Seringapatam, 1200.	Elephant l: date 1200 above: surrounded by lined circles and ring of dots.	ضرب پٹن "Struck at *Puttun*:" surrounded by lined circles and ring of dots.
		SINGLE PAISAH.	
8	Seringapatam, 1215.	Elephant l: date 1215 above: surrounded by lined circles and ring of dots.	Same as 7.

[1] There is in the collection of Mr. R. Sewell a larger coin of the same type, but differing as regards the figure of the tiger.

COPPER: Muhammadan usurpation—*continued.*

No.	Mint: Date.	Observe.	Reverse.
		COINS WITH DATE—*cont.*	
		QUARTER PAISAH.	
9	Seringapatam, 1215.	Elephant l: date 1215 above: surrounded by lined circles and ring of dots.	Same as 8.
		HALF PAISAH.[1]	
10	Gooty, 1215.	Elephant l: date 1215 above: surrounded by lined circle and dots.	ضرب فیض حصار "Struck at *Feiz Hisár*:[2]" surrounded by lined circle and ornamental border.
		SINGLE PAISAH.	
11	Chittledroog, 1216.	Elephant l: date 1216 above: surrounded by lined circle.	ضرب فرخباب حصار "Struck at *Farakh-báb-hisár*:[3] surrounded by lined circle.
		HALF PAISAH.	
12	*Nazarbar*, 1216.	Elephant l: date 1216 above: surrounded by lined circles and ring of dots.	ضرب نظر بار "Struck at *Nazarbár*:" surrounded by lined circles and ring of dots. [Pl. V, 2.]
13	Bangalore, 1216.	Elephant l: date 1216 above: surrounded by lined circles.	ضرب بنگلور "Struck at *Bangalúr*:" surrounded by lined circle and ring of dots. [Pl. V, 3.]
14	Seringapatam, 1216.	Elephant l: date 1216 above: surrounded by lined circles and ring of dots.	ضرب پٹن "Struck at *Puttun*:" surrounded by lined circles and ring of dots.
		SINGLE PAISAH.	
15	New Calicut, 1217	Elephant l: date 1217 above: surrounded by lined circles and ring of dots.	ضرب فرخی "Struck at *Farakhi*:" surrounded by lined circles and ring of dots. [Pl. V, 5.]
16	New Calicut, 1217	Same as 15.	Same as 15.
17	New Calicut, 1217	Same as 15.	Same.

[1] "This coin was struck at a place called Gúti, a fortress near the Pennar river, by the Sultan named *Feiz Hisár*." Marsden, op. cit., p. 722.

[2] "Cuditur in castello abundantiæ." Marsden, op. cit., p. 721.

[3] Probably Chittledroog. Marsden, op. cit., p. 722.

COPPER : MUHAMMADAN USURPATION—*continued.*

No.	Mint : Date.	Obverse.	Reverse.
		COINS WITH DATE—*cont.* HALF PAISAH.	
18	New Calicut, 1217	Same.	Same as 15. [Pl. V, 6.]
19	Chittledroog.	Elephant l : date 1217 above : surrounded by lined circle and ornamental border.	ضرب فرخباب حصار "Struck at *Farakh-báb-hisár*:" surrounded by lined circle and ornamental border. [Pl. V, 7.]
20	Bednur, 1217.	Elephant l : date 1217 above : surrounded by lined circle.	ضرب نگر "Struck at *Nuggur* :" surrounded by lined circle and ring of dots. [Pl. V, 8.]
		SINGLE PAISAH.	
21	*Islamabád*, 1217.	Elephant l : date 1217 above : surrounded by ornamental border.	ضرب اسلام آباد "Struck at *Islamabád* :" surrounded by ornamental border. [Pl. V, 9.]
22	Calicut, 1215.	Elephant r : date 1215 above : surrounded by lined circle.	ضرب کلیکوٹ "Struck at *Kalikút* :" surrounded by lined circle and ring of dots. [Pl. VIII, 2.]
		QUATER PAISAH.	
23	Bangalore, 1218.	Elephant l : date 1218 above : surrounded by lined circles.	ضرب بنگلور "Struck at *Bangalúr* :" surrounded by lined circle and ring of dots. [Pl. V, 4.]
		EIGHTH OF PAISAH.	
24	Bangalore, 1218.	Elephant l : date 1218 above : surrounded by lined circle.	Same as 23.

COPPER: Muhammadan usurpation—*continued.*

No.	Mint: Date.	Obverse.	Reverse.
		COINS WITH DATE—*cont.*	
		HALF PAISAH.	
25	Chittledroog, 1218	Elephant l: date 1218 above: surrounded by lined circle and ornamental border.	ضرب فرخباب حصار "Struck at *Farakh-báb-hisár*:" surrounded by lined circle and ornamental border.
26	Chittledroog, 1218	Same as 25.	Same as 25.
		SINGLE PAISAH.	
27	New Calicut, 1218	Elephant l: date 1218 above. surrounded by lined circles and ring of dots.	ضرب فرخی "Struck at *Farakhi*:" surrounded by lined circles and ring of dots.
		EIGHTH OF PAISAH.	
28	Islamabád, 1218.	Elephant l: date 1218 above: surrounded by an ornamental circle.	ضرب اسلام آباد "Struck at *Islamabád*:" surrounded by an ornamental circle. [Pl. V, 10.]
		HALF PAISAH.	
29	Gooty, 1218.	Elephant l: date 1218 above: surrounded by lined circle and ring of dots.	ضرب فیض حصار "Struck at *Feiz Hisár*:" surrounded by lined circle and ring of dots.
		DOUBLE PAISAH.	
30	Seringapatam, 1219.	Elephant l, with trunk elevated as in the act of saluting and carrying a flag marked with a star: date 1219 behind the elephant: surrounded by lined circle and ring of dots.	عثمانی ضرب دارالسلطنت پٹن "*Usmání*. Struck at the capital, *Puttun*:" surrounded by lined circle and ring of dots. [Pl. VI, 1.]

COPPER : Muhammadan usurpation—*continued.*

No.	Mint : Date.	Obverse.	Reverse.
		COINS WITH DATE—*cont.*	
		Double Paisah—*cont.*	
31	Chittledroog, 1219	Same as 30.	ضرب دارالسلطنت فرخباب حصار " . . . . . Struck at the capital *Farakh-báb-hisár.*"
		Single Paisah.	
32	Seringapatam, 1219.	Elephant l : date 1219 above : surrounded by lined circles and ring of dots. [Pl. V, 11.]	ضرب پٹن " Struck at *Puttun* :" surrounded by lined circles and ring of dots.
		Half Paisah.	
33	Bangalore, 1219.	Elephant l : date 1219 above : surrounded by lined circles.	ضرب بنگلور " Struck at *Bangalúr* :" surrounded by lined circles and ring of dots.
		Single Paisah.	
34	Seringapatam, 1221.	Elephant l : date 1221 above : surrounded by lined circles and ring dots.	ضرب پٹن " Struck at *Puttun* :" surrounded by lined circles and ring of dots.
		Half Paisah.	
35	Seringapatam, 1221.	Elephant l : date 1221 above : surrounded by lined circles and ring of dots.	ضرب پٹن " Struck at *Puttun* :" surrounded by lined circles and ring of dots.
		Quarter Paisah.	
36	Seringapatam, 1221.	Elephant r : date 1221 above : surrounded by lined circles and ring of dots.	ضرب پٹن " Struck at *Puttun* :" surrounded by lined circles and ring of dots. [Pl. VI, 2.]

COPPER : MUHAMMADAN USURPATION—*continued.*

No.	Mint : Date.	Obverse.	Reverse.
		COINS WITH DATE—*cont.*	
		DOUBLE PAISAH.	
37	Seringapatam, 1222.	Elephant r, with trunk elevated as in making a salute and carrying a flag with a star in its centre : below the flag مولودی (*Múlúdi*) : behind the elephant date, 1222 : surrounded by lined circle and ring of dots.	مشتری ضرب دارالسلطنت پٹن "*Mushtarí*. Struck at the capital *Puttun*:" surrounded by lined circle and ring of dots. [Pl. VI, 3.]
		SINGLE PAISAH.	
38	Seringapatam, 1222.	Elephant l : date 1222, and inscription مولودی محمد (*Múlúdi Muhammad*)[1] : surrounded by lined circle and ring of dots. [Pl. VIII, 10.]	زهره ضرب پٹن "*Zahra*.[2] Struck at *Puttun* :" surrounded by lined circle and ring of dots.
		HALF PAISAH.	
39	Seringapatam, 1222.	Elephant r : date 1222 above : surrounded by lined circle and ring of dots.	بهرام ضرب پٹن "*Bahrám*.[3] Struck at *Puttun* :" surrounded by lined circle and ring of dots. [Pl. VI, 5.]
		SINGLE PAISAH.	
40	Bednur, 1222.	Elephant l : date 1222 above : surrounded by lined circle.	زهرا ضرب نگر "*Zahrá*. Struck at *Nuggur* :" surrounded by lined circle and ring of dots. [Pl. VI, 4.]
41	Bednur, 1222.	Same as 40.	Same as 40.

[1] V. ant. p. 11.
[2] زهره (*Zahra*), the planet Venus.
[3] بهرام (*Bahrám*), the planet Mars.

COPPER : MUHAMMADAN USURPATION—*continued.*

No.	Mint : Date.	Obverse.	Reverse.
		COINS WITH DATE—*cont.*	
		QUARTER PAISAH.	
42	1222.	Elephant r : letter ب (*be*) above : surrounded by lined circle.	١٢٢٢ بهرام ضرب حصار " *Bahrám.* Struck at . . . . *hisár*:" date 1222 above : surrounded by lined circle and ring of dots. [Pl. VI, 6.]
		SINGLE PAISAH.	
43	Seringapatam, 1223.	Elephant r : date 1223 above : surrounded by lined circles and ring of dots. [Pl. VI, 7.]	ضرب پٹن " Struck at *Puttun* :" surrounded by lined circle and ring of dots.
		HALF PAISAH.	
44	Seringapatam, 1223.	Elephant l : date 1223 above : surrounded by lined circle and ring of dots.	بهرام ضرب پٹن " *Bahrám.* Struck at *Puttun* :" surrounded by lined circle and ring of dots. [Pl. VI, 8.]
		QUARTER PAISAH.	
45	Seringapatam, 1223.	Elephant r : date 1223 above : surrounded by lined circle and ring of dots.	اختر ضرب پٹن " *Akhter.*[1] Struck at *Puttun* :" surrounded by lined circle and ring of dots.
		SINGLE PAISAH.	
46	Seringapatam, 1223.	Elephant l : date 1223 مولودی (*Múlúdi*) above : surrounded by lined circle and ring of dots.	زهره ضرب پٹن " *Zahra.* Struck at *Puttun* :" surrounded by lined circles and ring of dots. [Pl. VII, 1.]

[1] اختر *Akhter*, a star.

COPPER: Muhammadan usurpation—*continued.*

No.	Mint: Date.	Obverse.	Reverse.
		COINS WITH DATE—*cont.*	
		Double Paisah.	
47	Seringapatam, 1224.	Elephant r: carrying a flag marked with the letter ا (*alif*): surrounded by lined circle and ring of dots.	ضرب دارالسلطنت پٹن مشتری سنه ۴۲۲۱ مولودی "Struck at the capital *Puttun Mushtarí*: year 1224, *Múlúdi*:" surrounded by lined circle and ring of dots. [Pl. VII, 2.]
		Single Paisah.	
48	Seringapatam, 1224.	Elephant r: letter ا (*alif*) above: double stamped with lined circle and ring of dots.	زهره ۴۲۲۱ مولودی ضرب پٹن "*Zahra*. Struck at *Puttun*: year 1224, *Múlúdi*:" double stamped with lined circles and ring of dots.
49	Seringapatam, 1224.	Same as 48.	Same as 48. [Pl. VII, 3.]
		Half Paisah.	
50	Seringapatam, 1224.	Elephant r: letter ا (*alif*) above: surrounded by lined circle and ring of dots.	بهرام ۴۲۲۱ ضرب پٹن "*Bahrám*, 1224. Struck at Puttun:" surrounded by lined circle and ring of dots. [Pl. VII, 4.]
		Double Paisah.	
51	Seringapatam, 1225.	Elephant r: carrying a flag marked with the letter ب (*be*): surrounded by lined circle and ring of dots.	ضرب دارالسلطنت پٹن مشتری ۵۲۲۱ مولودی "Struck at the capital *Puttun Mushtarí*: year 1225, *Múlúdi*:" surroundedby lined circle and ring of dots. [Pl. VII, 5.]

COPPER : MUHAMMADAN USURPATION—*continued.*

No.	Mint : Date.	Obverse.	Reverse.
		COINS WITH DATE—*cont.*	
		DOUBLE PAISAH—*cont.*	
52	Seringapatam, 1225.	Same as 51.	Same as 51.
		SINGLE PAISAH.	
53	Seringapatam, 1225.	Elephant r : letter ب (*be*) above : surrounded by lined circle and ring of dots. [Pl. VII, 6.]	ضرب پتن مولودی ١٢٢٥ زهرة "*Zahrá.* Struck at *Puttun.* Year 1225, *Múládi* :" surrounded by lined circle and ring of dots.
		HALF PAISAH.	
54	Seringapatam, 1225.	Elephant r : letter ب (*be*) above : surrounded by lined circle and ring of dots. [Pl. VII, 7.]	بهرام ١٢٢٥ ضرب پتن "*Bahrám,* 1225. Struck at *Puttun* :" surrounded by lined circle and ring of dots.
		QUARTER PAISAH.	
55	Seringapatam, 1225.	Elephant r : letter ب (*be*) above : surrounded by lined circle and ring of dots.	اختر ضرب پتن ١٢٢٥ "*Akhter.* Struck at *Puttun,* 1225 :" surrounded by lined circle and ring of dots. [Pl. VII, 8.]
		SINGLE PAISAH.	
56	Bednur, 1225.	Elephant r : letter ب (*be*) above : surrounded by lined circle and ring of dots.	زهرا ضرب نگر سنه ١٢٢٥ مولودی "*Zahrá.* Struck at *Nuggur.* Year 1225. *Múládi* :" surrounded by lined circle and ring of dots.
57	Bednur, 1226.	Elephant r : letter ت (*te*) above : surrounded by lined circle and ring of dots.	زهرا ضرب نگر سنه ١٢٢٦ مولودی "*Zahrá.* Struck at *Nuggur.* Year 1226. *Múládi* :" surrounded by lined circles and ring of dots. [Pl. IX, 1.]

COPPER : MUHAMMADAN USURPATION—*continued.*

No.	Mint : Date.	Obverse.	Reverse.
		COINS WITH DATE—*cont.*	
		HALF PAISAH.	
58	Bednur, 1226.	Elephant r: letter ت (*te*) above: surrounded by lined circle and ring of dots.	بهرام ضرب نگر ۱۲۲۶ مولودی "*Bahrám.* Struck at *Nuggur*, 1226. *Múládi.*" [Pl. X, 9.]
		SINGLE PAISAH.	
59	Seringapatam, 1226.	Elephant r: letter ت (*te*) above.	زهرة ضرب پتن مولودی ۱۲۲۶ "*Zahra* Struck at *Puttun*, 1226. *Múládi*:" surrounded by lined circle and ring of dots.
		QUARTER PAISAH.	
60	Seringapatam, 1226.	Elephant r: letter ت (*te*) above: surrounded by lined circle and ring of dots.	اختر ۱۲۲۶ ضرب پتن "*Akhter*, 1226. Struck at *Puttun* :" surrounded by lined circle and ring of dots.
		SINGLE PAISAH.	
61	Seringapatam, 1260.	Elephant r: date 1260 above: surrounded by lined circle and ring of dots. [Pl. IX, 2.]	ضرب پتن "Struck at Puttun:" surrounded by lined circle and ring of dots.
		COINS WITH DOUBTFUL DATE.	
		DOUBLE PAISAH.	
62	Seringapatam.	Elephant r, with trunk elevated as in the act of saluting, and carrying a flag marked with a star and the word مولودی (*Múládi*), date.... : surrounded by lined circles and ring of dots. [Pl. X, 10.]	پتن ضرب مشتری دارالسلطنت "*Mushtarí.* Struck at the capital *Puttun*:" surrounded by lined circle and ring of dots.

COPPER : Muhammadan usurpation—*continued.*

No.	Mint : Date.	Obverse.	Reverse.
		COINS WITH DOUBTFUL DATE—*cont.*	
		Single Paisah.	
63	Calicut.	Elephant r: encircled by a ring of dots.	ضرب كليكوت بندر "Struck at the seaport *Kalikút* :" encircled by a ring of dots.
		Quarter Paisah.	
64	Chandagál.	Elephant r: surrounded by an ornamental border.	ضرب خالق آباد "Struck at *Khálakhábád* :" surrounded by an ornamental border.
		Single Paisah.	
65	Gooty.	Elephant r: surrounded by lined circle and ring of dots.	ضرب فيض حصار "Struck at *Feiz hisár* :" surrounded by lined circle and ring of dots. [Pl. VIII, 3.]
		Half Paisah.	
66	Gooty.	Elephant r: encircled by lined circle and ring of dots.	Same as 65. [Pl. VIII, 4.]
67	Gooty.	Elephant l: encircled by a ring of dots.	Same as 65.
		Quarter Paisah.	
68	Gooty.	Elephant r: surrounded by lined circle.	Same as 65. [Pl. VIII, 5.]

COPPER : MUHAMMADAN USURPATION—*continued.*

No.	Mint : Date.	Obverse.	Reverse.
		COINS NOT IN MUSEUM COLLECTION.[1] SINGLE PAISAH.	
1	Hole Honnur, 1217.	Elephant l : date 1217 above : surrounded by lined circles and ring of dots.	ضرب بی نظیر "Struck at *Bi-nazír*:"[2] surrounded by lined circles and ring of dots. [Pl. VIII, 6.]
2	Seringapatam, 1222.	Elephant r : date 1222, مولودی (*Múlúdi*) above : surrounded by lined circle and ring of dots. [Pl. VIII, 7.]	زهره ضرب پتن "*Zahra*. Struck at Puttun :" surrounded by lined circle and ring of dots. Marsden [Pl. XLVI, Fig. MXLI.]
3	Bednur, 1201.	Elephant r : date 1201 above : surrounded by lined circles.	ضرب نگر "Struck at *Nuggur* :" surrounded by lined circle and ring of dots. [Pl. VIII, 8.]
4	Dharwar, 1217.	Elephant l : date 1217 above : surrounded by lined circles and ring of dots.	ضرب خورشید سواد "Struck at *Khorshíd-suád* :" surrounded by lined circle and ring of dots. [Pl. VIII, 9.]

[1] Copper coins struck at *Selám-abád* or *Sati-mangalam* in 1217, and at *Zafarabád* or *Gurrumcondah* in 1218, are mentioned by Marsden (op. cit. p. 722).

[2] On Pl. II, No. 6, we find another of his (Tippu's) new names, which we learned on the spot, was given to Hooly Honore; but why Tippu should call Hooly Honore بی نظیر. "'*Incomparable*' is, to us, incomprehensible." Moor, op. cit. app., p. 476; Pl. II, Fig. 6.

COPPER : KṚISHṆA RÁJA WOḌEYAR.

No.	Mint : Date.	Obverse.	Reverse.
		COINS WITHOUT DATE. FIVE CASH.	
1	Mysore.	Elephant l : sun and moon above: surrounded by lined circle and ring of dots.	"*Śri Kṛishṇa Rája*" (Nág.) : surrounded by lined circle and ring of dots. [Pl. IX, 3.]
2	Mysore.	*Śri*. (Kan.)	"V Cash" (Eng.) "*Mayili kásu 5*" (Kan.) [Pl. IX, 4.]

COPPER: Kṛishṇa Rája Woḍeyar—*continued.*

No.	Mint : Date.	Obverse.	Reverse.
		ELEPHANT CASH.	
		Twenty Cash.	
3	Mysore.	Elephant l: *Śrí* (Kan.), sun and moon above: encircled by a ring of dots.	"*Mayili kásu 20*" (Kan.), "XX cash" (Eng.): encircled by a ring of dots. [Pl. IX, 5.]
4	Mysore.	Same as 3.	Same as 3.
		Ten Cash.	
5	Mysore.	Elephant l: *Śrí* (Kan.), sun and moon above: surrounded by lined circle and ring of dots. [Pl. IX, 6.]	"*Chá*[1] *Mayili kásu 10*" (*Kan.*), "*X cash*" (Eng.): surrounded by lined circle and ring of dots.
		Five Cash.	
6	Mysore.	Elephant l: *Śrí* (Kan.), sun and moon above: surrounded by lined circle and ring of dots. [Pl. IX, 7.]	"*Chá Mayili kásu 5*" (Kan.), "V cash" (Eng.): surrounded by lined circle.
		Twenty Cash.	
7	Mysore.	Elephant l: *Śrí Chámundi*[2] (Kan.), and sun and moon above: surrounded by lined circle and ring of dots.	"*Kṛishṇa Mayili kásu ippattu*"[3] (Kan.), "XX cash" (Eng.): surrounded by lined circle and ring of dots.
8	Mysore.	Same as 7.	Same as 7. [Pl. IX, 8.]
		Five Cash.	
9	Mysore.	Elephant l: *Śrí Chámundi* (Kan.), and sun and moon above: surrounded by lined circle and ring of dots.	"*Kṛishṇa Mayili kásu 5*"[4] (Kan.), "V cash" (Eng.): surrounded by lined circle and ring of dots. [Pl. IX, 9.]
10	Mysore.	Same as 9.	Same as 9.

[1] Abreviation for Chámundi.
[2] ಚಾಮುಂಡಿ = Chámundi.
[3] ಯಿಪತು = ippattu = twenty.
[4] ಕೃಷ್ಣ ಮಯಿಲಿ ಕಾಸು ೫

COPPER : Kṛishṇa Rája Woḍeyar—*continued.*

No.	Mint : Date.	Obverse.	Reverse.
		LION CASH.	
		(*a*) COINS WITHOUT DATE.	
		TEN CASH.	
11	Mysore.	Lion of Chámundi l: *Śrí* (Kan.), sun and moon above: surrounded by lined circle and ring of dots.	"*Kṛishṇa*" (Kan.) "مهیسور ضرب":[1] surrounded by lined circle and ring of dots.
12	Mysore.	Same as 11.	Same as 11. [Pl. IX, 10.]
		FIVE CASH.	
13	Mysore.	Same.	Same as 11.
14	Mysore.	Same.	Same as 11. [Pl. IX, 11.]
		TWENTY-FIVE CASH.	
15	Mysore.	Lion of Chámundí l: *Śrí Chámundí* (Kan.), and sun and moon above: surrounded by lined circle and ring of dots.	Inscription in a circle "*Mayili kásu 25*" (Kan.) "ضرب مهیسور" "XXV cash" (Eng.): within the circle "*Kṛishṇa*" (Kan.): surrounded by lined circle and ring of dots. [Pl. X, 1.]
16	Mysore.	Same as 15.	Same as 15.
		(*b*) COINS WITH DATE.	
		FIVE CASH.	
17	Bangalore, 1833.	Lion of Chámundí l: *Śrí* (Kan.), sun and moon above: date 1833 below: surrounded by lined circle and ring of dots.	"*Kṛishṇa*" (Kan.) "مهیسور ضرب": surrounded by lined circle and ring of dots.
18	Bangalore, 1833.	Same as No. 17.	"*Kṛishṇa* [2]" (Kan.), "ضرب مهیسور," numeral 5: surrounded by lined circle and ring of dots. [Pl. X, 2.]

[1] "Struck at *Mahisur*.

[2] ಕೃಷ್ಣ

COPPER : KṚISHṆA RÁJA WOḌEYAR—*continued.*

No.	Mint : Date.	Obverse.	Reverse.
		LION CASH—*cont.*	
		(*b*) COINS WITH DATE—*cont.*	
		TWENTY CASH.	
19	Bangalore, 1834.	Lion of Chámundí l: *Śrí Chámundi* (Kan.), sun and moon above: date 1834 below: surrounded by lined circle and ring of dots.	Inscription in a circle "*Mayili kásu 20*"[1] (Kan.) "Milay XX cash" (Eng.): within the circle "*Krishna*" (Kan.). "ضرب مہیسور": surrounded by lined circle and ring of dots. [Pl. X, 3.]
20	Bangalore, 1834.	Same as 19.	Same as 19.
21	Bangalore, 1834.	Same.	Same, except the word Meilee instead of Milay.
22	Bangalore, 1835.	Same.	Same as 21.
		TEN CASH.	
23	Bangalore, 1835.	Lion of Chámundi l: *Śrí* (Kan.), sun and moon above: encircled by a ring of dots.	"*Kṛishṇa*"(Kan). "مہیسور ضرب," numeral 10. [Pl. X, 4.]
		FIVE CASH.	
24	Bangalore, 1835.	Same as 23.	"*Krishṇa*"(Kan.) "مہیسور ضرب," numeral 5.
		TWENTY CASH.	
25	Bangalore, 1836.	Lion of Chámundi l: *Śrí Chámundi* (Kan.), sun and moon above, date 1836 below: encircled by a ring of dots. [Pl. X, 5.]	Inscription in a circle "*Mayili kásu 20*" (Kan.), "Meilee XX cash" (Eng.): within the circle "*Kṛishṇa*" (Kan.). "ضرب مہیسور": encircled by a ring of dots.
		FIVE CASH.	
26	Bangalore, 1836.	Lion of Chámundi l: "*Śrí*" (Kan.), sun and moon above: date 1836 below.	"*Kṛishṇa*"(Kan.), "مہیسور ضرب," numeral 5: encircled by a ring of dots.
27	Bangalore, 1836.	Same as 26.	Same as 26.

1 ಮೈಲಿ ಕಾಸು ೨೦

COPPER : KṚISHṆA RÁJA WOḌEYAR—*continued.*

No.	Mint : Date.	Obverse.	Reverse.
		LION CASH—*cont.*	
		(*b*) COINS WITH DATE—*cont.*	
		TWENTY CASH.	
28	Bangalore, 1837.	Lion of Chámundi l: *Śrí Chámundi* (Kan.), sun and moon above: date 1837 below: encircled by a ring of dots.	Inscription in a circle "*Mayili kásu 20*" (Kan), "Meilee XX cash" (Eng.): within the circle "*Kṛishṇa*" (Kan.), "ضرب مهيسور": encircled by a ring of dots.
29	Bangalore, 1837.	Same as 28.	Same as 28.
		FIVE CASH.	
30	Bangalore, 1837.	Lion of Chámundi l: *Śrí* (Kan.), sun and moon above: date 1837 below.	"*Kṛishṇa*" (Kan.), "ضرب مهيسور," numeral 5: encircled by a ring of dots.
		TWENTY CASH.	
31	Bangalore, 1838.	Lion of Chámundi l: *Śrí Chámundi* (Kan.), sun and moon above: date 1838 below: encircled by a ring of dots.	Inscription in a circle "*Mayili kásu 20*" (Kan.), "Meillee XX cash." (Eng.): within the circle "*Kṛishṇa*" (Kan.). "ضرب مهيسور": encircled by a ring of dots.
32	Bangalore, 1838.	Same as 31.	Same as 31.
		TEN CASH.	
33	Bangalore, 1838.	Lion of Chámundi l: *Śrí* (Kan.), sun and moon above: date 1838 below: encircled by a ring of dots.	"*Kṛishṇa*" (Kan.), "ضرب مهيسور," numeral 10: encircled by a ring of dots. [Pl. X, 6.]

COPPER : KṚISHṆA RÁJA WOḌEYAR—*continued.*

No.	Mint : Date.	Obverse.	Reverse.
		LION CASH—*cont.*	
		(*b*) COINS WITH DATE—*cont.*	
		TWENTY CASH.	
34	Bangalore, 1839.	Lion of Chámundi l: *Śrí Chámundi* (Kan.), sun and moon above: date 1839 below.	Inscription in a circle "*Mayili kásu 20*" (Kan.), "Meilee XX cash" (Eng.), within the circle "*Kṛishṇa*" (Kan.), "ضرب مہیسور": encircled by a ring of dots.
35	Bangalore, 1839.	Same as 34.	Same as 34.
		TEN CASH.	
36	Bangalore, 1839.	Lion of Chámundi l: *Śrí* (Kan.), sun and moon above: date 1839 below.	"*Kṛishṇa*" (Kan.), "ضرب مہیسور," numeral 10: encircled by a ring of dots.
37	Bangalore, 1839.	Same as 36.	Same as 36. [Pl. X, 7.]
		TWENTY CASH.	
38	Bangalore, 1840.	Lion of Chámundi l: *Śrí Chámundi* (Kan.), sun and moon above: date 1840 below.	Inscription in a circle "*Mayili kásu 20*" (Kan.), "Meilee XX cash" (Eng.), within the circle "*Kṛishṇa*" (Kan.), "ضرب مہیسور": encircled by a ring of dots.
39	Bangalore, 1841.	Same as 38, but date 1841.	Same as 38.
		TEN CASH.	
40	Bangalore, 1841.	Lion of Chámundi l: *Śrí* (Kan.), sun and moon above: date 1841 below: encircled by a ring of dots.	"*Kṛishṇa*" (Kan.), "ضرب مہیسور," numeral 10: encircled by a ring of dots.
41	Bangalore, 1841.	Same as 40.	Same as 40.

COPPER: KṚISHṆA RÁJA WOḌEYAR—*continued.*

No.	Mint : Date.	Obverse.	Reverse.
		LION CASH—*cont.*	
		(*b*) COINS WITH DATE—*cont.*	
		FIVE CASH.	
42	Bangalore, 1841.	Same.	"*Kṛishṇa*" (Kan.), "ضرب مهيسور," numeral 5 : encircled by a ring of dots.
43	Bangalore, 1841.	Same.	Same.
		TEN CASH.	
44	Bangalore, 1842.	Same.	"*Kṛishṇa*" (Kan.), "ضرب مهيسور," numeral 10 : encircled by a ring of dots.
		FIVE CASH.	
45	Bangalore, 1842.	Same.	"*Kṛishṇa*" (Kan.), "ضرب مهيسور," numeral 5.
		TWENTY CASH.	
46	Bangalore, 1843.	Lion of Chámundi l : *Śrí Chámundi* (Kan.), sun and moon above : date 1843 below.	Inscription in a circle "*Mayili kásu 20*" (Kan.), "Meillee XX cash" (Eng.), within the circle "*Kṛishṇa*" (Kan.), "ضرب مهيسور."
		TEN CASH.	
47	Bangalore, 1843.	Lion of Chámundi l : *Śrí* (Kan.), sun and moon above : date 1843 below.	"*Kṛishṇa*," (Kan.). "ضرب مهيسور," numeral 10.

ADDENDA.

No.	Date.	Obverse.	Reverse.
		p. 21.	
		SULTÁNÍ PAGODA. TIPPOO.	
9.1	1198	اح Haidar's initial and letter *alif*, on a granulated surface, surrounded by lined circles and ring of dots.	هوالسلطان العادل سنه ۱۱۹۸ هجری "He is the just Sultan. Year hejirah 1198:" surrounded by lined circle and ring of dots.
		p. 21.	
11.1	1215	پٹن ح ۵ Haidar's initial joined to the word *Puttun*, and numeral ۵ (5) on a granulated surface, surrounded by lined circles and ring of dots.	محمد هوالسلطان العادل سنه ۱۲۱۵ "Muhammad. He is the just Sultan. Year 1215:" surrounded by lined circle and ring of dots.
		p. 23.	
		DHOTIE FANAM. TIPPOO.	
26.1		Illegible.	فرخ "*Furrokh.*"
		p. 25.	
		NOKÁRA. TIPPOO.	
1.1	1198	دین احمد در جهان روشن است زفتح حیدر ح ضرب پٹن . سال ازل سنه هجری ۱۱۹۸ "The religion of Muhammad is made illustrious in the world by the victory of Haidar. H. Struck at *Puttun* in the year of the cycle *Ázal*; hejirah 1198:"[1] surrounded by lined circle and ring of dots.	هوالسلطان الوحید العادل سیوم بهاری سال ازل سنه جلوس ۲ "He is the only just Sultan. Third (day of the month) *Bahárí*; year of the cycle *Ázal*; year of the reign 2:" surrounded by lined circle and ring of dots. [Pl. XI, 1.]

[1] "This," Marsden says (Numismat. Orient., 1825, Pl. II, p. 709), "is the earliest date that occurs of any coin struck by this Sultan, and as neither Major Moor's nor the Göttingen collection contains one of 1197, it is probable that he did not coin money during the first year of his reign. He was then still engaged in war, and not having arranged his systematic plan for the mint, might, as was done by his father, issue for a time the *Kanter'râya* and *Virârâya* or swâmî pagodas of Mysore and Kûrga.

As the year 1198 of the *hejrah*, in which this double rupih was struck, began in November 1783 and ended in November 1784, it answers to the second year of the reign, whether we reckon from the death of *Heider Ali* in December 1782, or, with more correctness, from the epoch of *Tipû's* accession in the following year. But besides these two dates there is superadded the year of the cycle of sixty, which it thus appears he adopted from the Hindûs, some time before the introduction of his new era. This year is named ازل *azal* 'eternity,' and upon reference to the *abjed* table (the *abtas* not being yet in use) we shall find that ا , ز, and ل, 30, express, when added together, 38, the proper number of the current year, which commenced on the 22nd March 1784.

No.	Date.	Obverse.	Reverse.
		p. 42. **SINGLE PAISAH. TIPPOO.**[1]	
60.1	1227	Elephant r: letter ث (*sé*) above: surrounded by lined circle and ring of dots.	زهرا ضرب نگر سنه ۱۲۲۷ مولودی "Zahrá. Struck at *Nuggur*. Year 1227, *Múlúdi*:" surrounded by lined circle and ring of dots. [Pl. XI, 2.]
		COINS OF KRISHNA RÁJA.	
		p. 45. **ELEPHANT. TWENTY-FIVE CASH.**	
10.1		Elephant l: "*Śrí Chámundi*" (Kan.), and sun and moon above: surrounded by lined circles.	Inscription in a circle "*Mayili kásu* 25" (Kan.) "XXV VAUH" (Eng.): within the circle "*Krishna*" (Kan.): surrounded by a lined circle. [Pl. XI, 3.]
		p. 45. **ELEPHANT. TWENTY-FIVE CASH.**	
10.2		Caparisoned elephant l: "*Śrí Chámundi*" (Kan.), sun and moon and symbol of rose above: surrounded by lined circles and ring of dots.	Inscription in a circle "*Mayili kásu* XXV" (Kan.), XXV cash (Eng.): within the circle "*Krishna*" (Kan.): surrounded by lined circles and ring of dots. [Pl. XI, 4.]
		p. 46. **LION. TWENTY-FIVE CASH.**	
16.1		Lion of Chámundi l: "*Śrí Chámundi*" (Nag.), sun and moon above, مہیسور ضرب below: surrounded by lined circle and ring of dots.	Inscription in a circle "*Mayili kásu* XXV" (Kan.), XXV UAUH (Eng.): within the circle "*Krishna*" (Kan.): surrounded by lined circle and ring of dots. [Pl. XI, 5.]

[1] Concerning this coin Marsden says, (Op. cit., vol. II, p. 724) "a *peisah* or *zahrá* of 1227, from the mint of *Nagar* or Bednore, has in like manner a ث, the fourth and last letter of the word ابتث given by the Sultan as a name to his numerical system on which he appears to have wasted no small share of ingenuity.

This is probably the last specimen of his coinage that has been preserved, and must have been struck within a month of his death; the year 1227 of his era having begun on the 6th April 1799, and the storming of Seringapatam, on which occasion he fell, having happened on the 4th May of that year, being the anniversary of his accession."

SUPPLEMENT.

Note by Marsden on the Abjed and Abtas. "Numismata Orientalia," 1825, Pt. II. pp. 701–7.

"Many eastern nations, as well as the Greeks and Romans, have been in the practice of expressing numbers, and dates in particular, by means of the letters of the alphabet, to each of which a certain value is assigned. These may be either employed simply like other ciphers, or, being distributed among the words of a sentence, may constitute what is termed a chronogram. It must at the same time be noticed, that in forming their system the Arabians did not adhere to the direct order of the letters in their own alphabet (such at least as it now exists), but followed that of the Hebrews, from which they acquired much of their learning, calling ا 1, ب 2, ج 3, د 4, &c., and from thence names the scheme ابجد *abjd*, or, as pronounced *abjed*. With this antiquated system of notation the Sultan was dissatisfied, and he determined upon making it conform to the modern Arabic alphabet. Accordingly, in his scheme, ا is 1, ب 2, ت 3, ث 4, &c., and instead of ابجد *abjd* it is consistently named ابتث *abts* or *abtas*. In the following table, the numerical powers of the letters of both alphabets are expressed, and their application to the coinage will be hereafter shown :—

The ابجد abjed or *usual mode of alphabetical numeration.*

ص	ف	ع	س	ن	م	ل	ک	ی	ط	ح	ز	و	ه	د	ج	ب	ا
٩٠	٨٠	٧٠	٦٠	٥٠	۴٠	٣٠	٢٠	١٠	٩	٨	٧	٦	٥	۴	٣	٢	١
90	80	70	60	50	40	30	20	10	9	8	7	6	5	4	3	2	1

غ	ظ	ض	ذ	خ	ث	ت	ش	ر	ق
١٠٠٠	٩٠٠	٨٠٠	٧٠٠	٦٠٠	٥٠٠	۴٠٠	٣٠٠	٢٠٠	١٠٠
1000	900	800	700	600	500	400	300	200	100

The ابتث abtas *or* Sultânî *mode.*

ع	ظ	ط	ض	ص	ش	س	ز	ر	ذ	د	خ	ح	ج	ث	ت	ب	ا
٩٠	٨٠	٧٠	٦٠	٥٠	۴٠	٣٠	٢٠	١٠	٩	٨	٧	٦	٥	۴	٣	٢	١
90	80	70	60	50	40	30	20	10	9	8	7	6	5	4	3	2	1

ی	ه	و	ن	م	ل	ک	ق	ف	غ
١٠٠٠	٩٠٠	٨٠٠	٧٠٠	٦٠٠	٥٠٠	۴٠٠	٣٠٠	٢٠٠	١٠٠
1000	900	800	700	600	500	400	300	200	100

It is proper to observe that although the late Government of Mysore was Mahometan, the population of the country is Hindu, and that amongst this ancient agricultural race, a solar or luni-solar computation of time had prevailed from the earliest ages. They had also established, for civil purposes, a cycle of sixty years, each distinguished by a particular name, and commencing about the vernal equinox. Their current cycle began in the year 1807.

Tipû being sensible of much practical utility in this system, or desirous of showing indulgence to the customs of his Hindu subjects, resolved upon adopting it into his calendar, and at the period of reforming the lunar year and era of the *hejrah*, began to reckon also by this luni-solar cycle. Instead, however, of retaining the original names of the respective years, he formed from the letters of his *abtas* above described, a new set of numerical terms, composed of such letters as would denote the progressive numbers from one to sixty. But as these letters, if taken either indiscriminately or in strict succession, might not form significant or even pronounceable words, which common use required, a latitude was admitted in the selection and arrangement of letters equally capable of forming by their combination the same number: for as the sum results from simple addition, and does not depend upon the place (of units, tens, &c.), it follows that they may be combined in any order; and that order was chosen which produced any known terms, however trifling or inapplicable their meanings.

To explain this by an example, we shall take the year 42 of the cycle, corresponding with 1788 of J.C., 1202 of the *hejrah*, 1216 of the Sultan's new era, and the sixth of his reign. The number 42 may be expressed by various combinations of the letters of the *abtas*, but if we produce it by adding together س 30, ا 1, ر 10, and again ا 1, we shall at the same time compose the word سارا sârâ 'odoriferous;' which is the name appropriated to the forty-second year of the cycle, and such we find it on the coins. Thus (for illustration) if it were required to express in the Roman method of numeration the date of 65, it might be done by combining the letters L 50, V 5, and X 10, which together would form the word LVX, light.

Names of the Sultânî *years of the cycle of sixty according to the* ابجد *abjed.*

١	احد
٢	احمد
٣	اب
٤	ابا
٥	ببا
٦	بجا
٧	ابد
٨	اباد
٩	جاه
١٠	اوج
١١	حج
١٢	جهد
١٣	جهاد
١٤	وجه
٥١	ياد
١٦	زهد
١٧	جوزاه
١٨	حی
١٩	واهد
٢٠	بدوح
٢١	طيب
٢٢	طايب
٢٣	يوز
٢٤	كد
٢٥	حاوی
٢٦	كبد
٢٧	اكاه
٢٨	وحيد
٢٩	ياحی
٣٠	كی
٣١	كيا
٣٢	كبود
٣٣	ابل
٣٤	دل
٥٣	دال
٣٦	جبال
٣٧	زكی
٣٨	ازل
٣٩	حلو
٤٠	دلو
٤١	ما
٤٢	كبك
٤٣	جم
٤٤	جام
٤٥	ادم
٤٦	ولی
٤٧	والی
٤٨	كوكب
٤٩	كواكب
٥٠	يم
٥١	دوام
٥٢	حمد
٥٣	حامد
٥٤	جان
٥٥	ادن
٥٦	همای
٥٧	مجيد
٥٨	كحل
٥٩	جهان
٦٠	مجير

Names of the Sultânî *years of the cycle of sixty according to the* ابتث *abtas.*

١	احد
٢	احمد
٣	اب
٤	ابا
٥	باب
٦	تاب
٧	تابا
٨	بها
٩	تاج
١٠	تابت
١١	ابد
١٢	اداب
١٣	بار
١٤	حاجب
١٥	جر
١٦	رجا
١٧	حار
١٨	در
١٩	دار
٢٠	راحت
٢١	بارد
٢٢	چرخ
٢٣	خراج
٢٤	تاز
٢٥	خرد
٢٦	بدرتاب
٢٧	درتاج
٢٨	دادار
٢٩	زاد
٣٠	زر
٣١	زار
٣٢	بزر
٣٣	زراب
٤٣	ستا
٣٥	زرتاب
٣٦	رختار
٣٧	سخ
٣٨	سخا
٣٩	دراز
٤٠	بسد
٤١	ها
٤٢	سارا
٤٣	سراب
٤٤	هتا
٤٥	زبرجد
٤٦	سحر
٤٧	ساحر
٤٨	راسخ
٤٩	هاد
٥٠	حراست
٥١	ساز
٥٢	هاداب
٥٣	بارش
٥٤	رستار
٥٥	بشتر
٥٦	بشارت
٥٧	هارج
٥٨	رهد
٥٩	صباح
٦٠	ارهاد

It must be observed that the terms احد *ahad* and احمد *ahmed* are arbitrarily assigned to the first and second years, because no letters besides ا or ب could, accordiug to the principle of the system, be assigned to them, and these, separately, do not constitute words, although jointly as اب *áb* 'water,' they apply well to the third year. It is thought superfluous to annex translations of the sixty names, as the knowledge of their signification, even if free from ambiguity, would add nothing to our knowledge of the subject.

To the twelve months also, of which these years consist, new and fanciful names were assigned, and as they frequently appear in the legends, it becomes necessary to specify them. The former of the two lists here given was that which Tîpû employed during the first four years of his reign. The second contains those names which, upon changing the *abjed* for the *abtas*, he found it requisite to adapt to the new system of numeration; for as the initial letters of each month denote the numerical order in which they stand, the former set of names could not be retained without confusion.

Names of the twelve months, commencing with numerical letters, according to the abjed.

٦	٥	٤	٣	٢	١
واسعی	هاشمی	دارائی	جعفری	بهاری	احمدی
١٢	١١	١٠	٩	٨	٧
بیامی	ایزدی	یوسفی	طلوعی	حیدری	زبرجدی

Names of the twelve months, commencing with numerical letters, according to the abtas.

٦	٥	٤	٣	٢	١
حیدری	جعفری	ثمری	تقی	بهاری	احمدی
١٢	١١	١٠	٩	٨	٧
ربانی	رازی	رحمانی	ذاکری	دینی	خسروی

In the names of the eleventh and twelfth months, it will be noticed that in the old series the letter ا denoting 1, and the letter ب denoting 2, are followed (according to the usual order of Arabic from right to left) by the letter ی denoting 10; but that in the new, the decimal *precedes* the units ا and ب. To explain the principle of this inversion it must be considered that the Arabians, who in all their early inscriptions expressed numbers in words, at length, borrowed in later times the arithmetical notation of the Indians, by whom the figures are placed (as with us, who borrowed them at second hand from the Arabians) in the order of from left to right; and, consequently, that the arrangement of numeral figures in Arabic and Persian manuscripts is at variance with the mode of writing. To the Sultan this incongruity was offensive, and he determined upon correcting it throughout his dominions, by causing the numerals in all public documents, and especially on his coinage, to proceed, in conformity with the words, from right to left. There are occasional instances, however, of the engravers forgetting his master's commands and relapsing into the ancient practice."

INDEX OF MINTS.

Mint.	Metal.	Date.	Name of Coin.	Prince.	No.	Page.
Mysore.	Ar.	..	Rája Rupee.	Krishṇa Rája.	12	28
,,	,,	..	,, ½ ,,	,,	13	,,
,,	,,	..	,, ,,	,,	13·1	,,
,,	,,	..	,, ¼ ,,	,,	14	,,
,,	,,	..	,, ,,	,,	14·1	,,
,,	,,	..	Chámundi ,,	,,	15	,,
,,	,,	..	,,	,,	16	,,
,,	,,	..	Aḍḍa ½ Fanam.	,,	17	,,
,,	,,	..	,, ,,	,,	17·1	,,
,,	,,	..	Hágá ¼ ,,	,,	18	,,
,,	,,	..	,, ,,	,,	18·1	,,
....	Ae.	..	Tiger Cash.	Tippoo.	1	33
Seringapatam.	,,	..	Single Paisah.	,,	2	,,
,,	,,	..	,,	,,	3	,,
Calicut.	,,	1199	,,	,,	4	,,
Bednur.	,,	1199	,,	,,	5	,,
Calicut.	,,	1200	,,	,,	6	,,
Seringapatam.	,,	1200	Half Paisah.	,,	7	,,
,,	,,	1215	Single ,,	,,	8	,,
,,	,,	1215	Quarter ,,	,,	9	34
Gooty.	,,	1215	Half ,,	,,	10	,,
Chittledroog.	,,	1216	Single ,,	,,	11	,,
Nazarbár.	,,	1216	Half ,,	,,	12	,,
Bangalore.	,,	1216	,, ,,	,,	13	,,
Seringapatam.	,,	1216	,, ,,	,,	14	,,
New Calicut.	,,	1217	Single ,,	,,	15	,,
,,	,,	1217	,, ,,	,,	16	,,
,,	,,	1217	,, ,,	,,	17	,,
,,	,,	1217	Half ,,	,,	18	35
Chittledroog.	,,	1217	,, ,,	,,	19	,,
Bednur.	,,	1217	,, ,,	,,	20	,,
Islamabád.	,,	1217	Single ,,	,,	21	,,
Calicut.	,,	1217	,, ,,	,,	22	,,
Bangalore.	,,	1218	Quarter ,,	,,	23	,,
,,	,,	1218	Eighth ,,	,,	24	,,
Chittledroog.	,,	1218	Half ,,	,,	25	36
,,	,,	1218	,, ,,	,,	26	,,
New Calicut ?	,,	..	Single ,,	,,	27	,,
Islamabád.	,,	1218	Eighth ,,	,,	28	,,
Gooty.	,,	1218	Half ,,	,,	29	,,
Seringapatam.	,,	1219	Double ,,	,,	30	,,
Chittledroog.	,,	1219	,, ,,	,,	31	37

Mint.	Metal.	Date.	Name of Coin.	Prince.	No.	Page.
Seringapatam.	Ae.	1219	Single Paisah.	Tippoo.	32	37
Bangalore.	,,	1219	Half ,,	,,	33	,,
Seringapatam.	,,	1221	Single ,,	,,	34	,,
,,	,,	1221	Half ,,	,,	35	,,
,,	,,	1221	Quarter ,,	,,	36	,,
,,	,,	1222	Double ,,	,,	37	38
,,	,,	1222	Single ,,	,,	38	,,
,,	,,	1222	Half ,,	,,	39	,,
Bednur.	,,	1222	Single ,,	,,	40	,,
,,	,,	1222	,, ,,	,,	41	,,
....	,,	1222	Quarter ,,	,,	42	39
Seringapatam	,,	1223	Single ,,	,,	43	,,
,,	,,	1223	Half ,,	,,	44	,,
,,	,,	1223	Quarter ,,	,,	45	,,
,,	,,	1223	Single ,,	,,	46	,,
,,	,,	1224	Double ,,	,,	47	40
,,	,,	1224	Single ,,	,,	48	,,
,,	,,	1224	,, ,,	,,	49	,,
,,	,,	1224	Half ,,	,,	50	,,
,,	,,	1225	Double ,,	,,	51	,,
,,	,,	1225	,, ,,	,,	52	41
,,	,,	1225	Single ,,	,,	53	,,
,,	,,	1225	Half ,,	,,	54	,,
,,	,,	1225	Quarter ,,	,,	55	,,
Bednur.	,,	1225	Single ,,	,,	56	,,
,,	,,	1226	,, ,,	,,	57	,,
,,	,,	1226	Half ,,	,,	58	42
Seringapatam	,,	1226	Single ,,	,,	59	,,
,,	,,	1226	Quarter ,,	,,	60	,,
,,	,,	1260	Single ,,	,,	61	,,
,,	,,	..	Double ,,	,,	62	,,
Calicut.	,,	..	Single ,,	,,	63	43
Chandagál.	,,	..	Quarter ,,	,,	64	,,
Gooty.	,,	..	Single ,,	,,	65	,,
,,	..	..	Half ,,	,,	66	,,
,,	..	..	,, ,,	,,	67	,,
,,	,,	..	Quarter ,,	,,	68	,,
Hole Honnur.	,,	1217	Single ,,	,,	1	44
Seringapatam.	,,	1222	,, ,,	,,	2	,,
Bednur.	,,	1201	,, ,,	,,	3	,,
Dharwar.	,,	1217	,, ,,	,,	4	,,
Mysore.	..	..	Five Cash.	Kṛishṇa Rája.	1	,,
....	..	..	,,	,,	2	,,
Mysore.	,,	..	Elephant xx Cash.	,,	3	45
,,	,,	..	,, ,, ,,	,,	4	,,
,,	,,	..	,, x ,,	,,	5	,,
,,	,,	..	,, v ,,	,,	6	,,
,,	,,	..	,, xx ,,	,,	7	,,
,,	,,	..	,, ,, ,,	,,	8	,,
,,	,,	..	,, v ,,	,,	9	,,

Mint.	Metal.	Date.	Name of Coin.	Prince.	No.	Page.
Mysore.	Ae.	..	Elephant Cash.	Krishṇa Rája.	10	45
,,	,,	..	Lion x ,,		11	46
,,	,,	..	,, x ,,	,,	12	,,
,,	,,	..	,, v ,,	,,	13	,,
,,	,,	..	,, v ,,	,,	14	,,
,,	,,	..	,, xxv ,,	,,	15	,,
,,	,,	..	,, xxv ,,	,,	16	,,
Bangalore.	,,	1833	,, v ,,	,,	17	,,
,,	,,	1833	,, v ,,	,,	18	,,
,,	,,	1824	,, xx ,,	,,	19	47
,,	,,	1834	,, xx ,,	,,	20	,,
,,	,,	1834	,, xx ,,	,,	21	,,
,,	,,	1835	,, xx ,,	,,	22	,,
,,	,,	1835	,, x ,,	,,	23	,,
,,	,,	1835	,, v ,,	,,	24	,,
,,	,,	1836	,, xx ,,	,,	25	,,
,,	,,	1836	,, v ,,	,,	26	,,
,,	,,	1836	,, v ,,	,,	27	,,
,,	,,	1837	,, xx ,,	,,	28	48
,,	,,	1837	,, xx ,,	,,	29	,,
,,	,,	1837	,, v ,,	,,	30	,,
,,	,,	1838	,, xx ,,	,,	31	,,
,,	,,	1838	,, xx ,,	,,	32	,,
,,	,,	1838	,, x ,,	,,	33	,,
,,	,,	1839	,, xx ,,	,,	34	49
,,	,,	1839	,, xx ,,	,,	35	,,
,,	,,	1839	,, x ,,	,,	36	,,
,,	,,	1839	,, x ,,	,,	37	,,
,,	,,	1840	,, xx ,,	,,	38	,,
,,	,,	1841	,, xx ,,	,,	39	,,
,,	,,	1841	,, x ,,	,,	40	,,
,,	,,	1841	,, x ,,	,,	41	,,
,,	,,	1841	,, v ,,	,,	42	50
,,	,,	1841	,, v ,,	,,	43	,,
,,	,,	1842	,, x ,,	,,	44	,,
,,	,,	1842	,, v ,,	,,	45	,,
,,	,,	1843	,, xx ,,	,,	46	,,
,,	,,	1843	,, x ,,	,,	47	,,

INDEX OF PLATES.

PLATE I.

Name of Coin.	Metal.	Date.	Prince.	Page.	Plate.	Fig.
Kanteroy Fanam.	Au.	..	Kanṭhirava.	19	I	1
,, ,,	,,	..	,,	,,	,,	2
Baháduri Pagoda.	,,	..	Haidar.	,,	,,	3
,, ,,	,,	..	,,	,,	,,	4
,, ,,	,,	..	,,	,,	,,	5
Fárúkhí Pagoda.	,,	1217	Tippoo.	22	,,	6
Baháduri Fanam.	,,	..	Haidar.	19	,,	7
Ahmedi Mohur.	,,	1219	Tippoo.	20	,,	8
Sultání Pagoda.	,,	1198	,,	21	,,	9
,, ,,	,,	1200	,,	,,	,,	10
,, ,,	,,	1216	,,	,,	,,	11
Fárúkhí Pagoda.	,,	1216	,,	,,	,,	12
,, ,,	,,	1221	,,	22	,,	13
Sultání Fanam.	,,	1217	,,	,,	,,	14
,, ,,	,,	1199	,,	23	,,	15
Calicut Fanam.	,,	1215	,,	,,	,,	16
,, ,,	,,	1215	,,	,,	,,	17
Dhotie Fanam.	,,	1216	,,	,,	,,	18
Kṛishṇa Rája Pagoda.	,,	1216	Kṛishṇa Rája.	24	,,	19
Half Ptomán.[1]	,,	1271	....	..	,,	20

[1] This gold coin is said to have been formerly current in Mysore.

PLATE II.

Name of Coin.	Metal.	Date.	Prince.	Page.	Plate.	Fig.
Nokára double rupee.	Ar.	1200	Tippoo.	25	II	1
,,	,,	1216	,,	,,	,,	2
,,	,,	1217	,,	,,	,,	3
Imámí single rupee.	,,	1216	,,	26	,,	4
Ábidí half rupee.	,,	..	,,	,,	,,	5

PLATE III.

Name of Coin.	Metal.	Date.	Prince.	Page.	Plate.	Fig.
Ábidí half rupee.	Ar.	..	Tippoo.	26	III.	1
Bákhrí quarter rupee.	,,	1217	,,	,,	,,	2
,,	,,	1218	,,	27	,,	3
Jazri two annas.	,,	1221	,,	,,	,,	4
Kázmí one anna.	,,	,,	,,	,,	,,	5
Rája rupee.	,,	..	Kṛishṇa Rája.	,,	,,	6
,,	,,	..	,,	28	,,	7
Rája half rupee.	,,	..	,,	,,	,,	8
Rája quarter rupee.	,,	..	,,	,,	,,	9
Chámundi quarter rupee.	..	..	,,	,,	,,	10
,,	,,	..	,,	,,	,,	11
Aḍḍa half fanam.	,,	..	,,	,,	,,	12
Hága quarter fanam.	,,	..	,,	,,	,,	13

PLATE IV.

Name of Coin.	Metal.	Date.	Prince.	Page.	Plate.	Fig.
Chequered Reverse.	Ae.	..	....	29	IV	1
,,	,,	..	....	,,	,,	2
,,	,,	..	....	,,	,,	3
,,	,,	..	....	,,	,,	4
,,	,,	..	....	30	,,	5
,,	,,	..	....	29	,,	6
,,	,,	..	....	,,	,,	7
,,	,,	..	....	,,	,,	8
,,	,,	..	....	,,	,,	9
,,	,,	..	....	30	,,	10
,,	,,	..	....	29	,,	11
,,	,,	..	....	,,	,,	12
,,	,,	..	....	30	,,	13
,,	,,	..	....	,,	,,	14
,,	,,	..	....	,,	,,	15
,,	,,	..	....	31	,,	16
,,	,,	..	....	30	,,	17
,,	,,	..	....	32	,,	18
,,	,,	..	....	,,	,,	19
,,	,,	..	....	,,	,,	20
,,	,,	..	....	,,	,,	21
,,	,,	..	....	,,	,,	22

PLATE V.

Name of Coin.	Metal.	Date.	Prince.	Page.	Plate.	Fig.
Single Paisah	Ae.	..	Tippoo	33	V	1
Half ,,	,,	1216	,,	34	,,	2
,, ,,	,,	,,	,,	,,	,,	3
Quarter ,,	,,	1218	,,	35	,,	4
Single ,,	,,	1217	,,	34	,,	5
Half ,,	,,	,,	,,	35	,,	6
,, ,,	,,	,,	,,	,,	,,	7
,, ,,	,,	,,	,,	,,	,,	8
Single ,,	,,	,,	,,	,,	,,	9
Eighth ,,	,,	1218	,,	36	,,	10
Single ,,	,,	1219	,,	37	,,	11

PLATE VI.

Name of Coin.	Metal.	Date.	Prince.	Page.	Plate.	Fig.
Double Paisah	Ae.	1219	Tippoo	36	VI	1
Quarter ,,	,,	1221	,,	37	,,	2
Double ,,	,,	1222	,,	38	,,	3
Single ,,	,,	,,	,,	,,	,,	4
Half ,,	,,	,,	,,	,,	,,	5
Quarter ,,	,,	,,	,,	39	,,	6
Single ,,	,,	1223	,,	,,	,,	7
Half ,,	,,	,,	,,	,,	,,	8

PLATE VII.

Name of Coin.	Metal.	Date.	Prince.	Page.	Plate.	Fig.
Single Paisah	Ae.	1223	Tippoo	39	VII	1
Double ,,	,,	1224	,,	40	,,	2
Single ,,	,,	,,	,,	,,	,,	3
Half ,,	,,	,,	,,	,,	,,	4
Double ,,	,,	1225	,,	,,	,,	5
Single ,,	,,	,,	,,	41	,,	6
Half ,,	,,	,,	,,	,,	,,	7
Quarter ,,	,,	,,	,,	,,	,,	8

PLATE VIII.

Name of Coin.	Metal.	Date.	Prince.	Page.	Plate.	Fig.
Single Paisah	Ae.	1199	Tippoo.	33	VIII	1
,, ,,	,,	1215	,,	36	,,	2
,, ,,	,,	..	,,	43	,,	3
Half ,,	,,	..	,,	,,	,,	4
Quarter ,,	,,	..	,,	,,	,,	5
Single ,,	,,	1217	,,	44	,,	6
,, ,,	,,	1222	,,	,,	,,	7
,, ,,	,,	1201	,,	,,	,,	8
,, ,,	,,	1217	,,	,,	,,	9
,, ,,	,,	1222	,,	38	,,	10

PLATE IX.

Name of Coin.	Metal.	Date.	Prince.	Page.	Plate.	Fig.
Single Paisah.	Ae.	1226	Tippoo.	41	IX	1
,, ,,	,,	1260	,,	42	,,	2
Five Cash.	,,	..	Kṛishṇa Rája.	44	,,	3
,, ,,	,,	..	,,	,,	,,	4
Twenty ,,	,,	..	,,	45	,,	5
Ten ,,	,,	..	,,	,,	,,	6
Five ,,	,,	..	,,	,,	,,	7
Twenty ,,	,,	..	,,	,,	,,	8
Five ,,	,,	..	,,	,,	,,	9
Ten ,,	,,	..	,,	46	,,	10
Five ,,	,,	..	,,	,,	,,	11

PLATE X.

Name of Coin.	Metal.	Date.	Prince.	Page.	Plate.	Fig.
Twenty-five Cash	Ae.	..	Kṛishṇa Rája.	46	X	1
Five ,,	,,	1833	,,	,,	,,	2
Twenty ,,	,,	1834	,,	47	,,	3
Ten ,,	,,	1835	,,	,,	,,	4
Twenty ,,	,,	1836	,,	,,	,,	5
Ten ,,	,,	1838	,,	48	,,	6
Do. ,,	,,	1839	,,	49	,,	7
Tiger ,,	,,	..	Tippoo	33	,,	8
Half Paisah	,,	1226	,,	42	,,	9
Double ,,	,,	..	,,	,,	,,	10
Mark on Tippoo's cannon, &c.	..	..	....	14	,,	11

PLATE XI.

Name of Coin.	Metal.	Date.	Prince.	Page.	Plate.	Fig.
Nokára.	Ar.	1198	Tippoo.	51	XI	1
Single Paisah.	Ae.	1227	„	52	„	2
Twenty-five Cash.	„	..	Kṛishṇa Rája.	„	„	3
„ „	„	..	„	„	„	4
„ „	„	..	„	„	„	5

PLATE I.

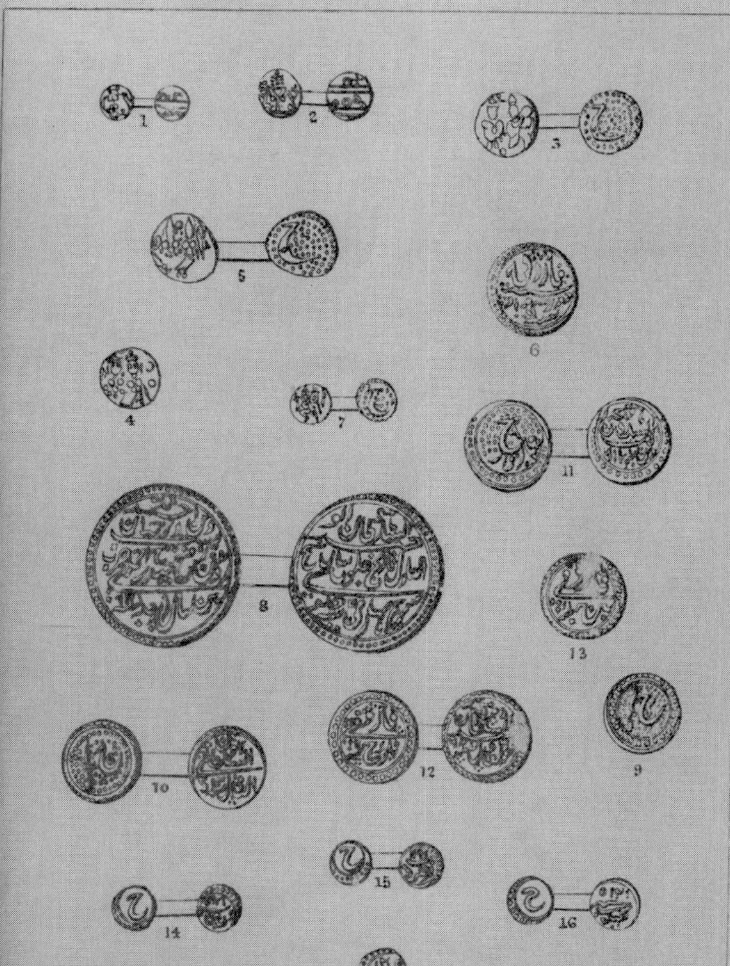

ALEX: BARREN: LITHOG: MADRAS, 1887.

GOLD. COINS.

PLATE II.

ALEX: BARREN: LITHOG: MADRAS 1887.

SILVER COINS

PLATE III.

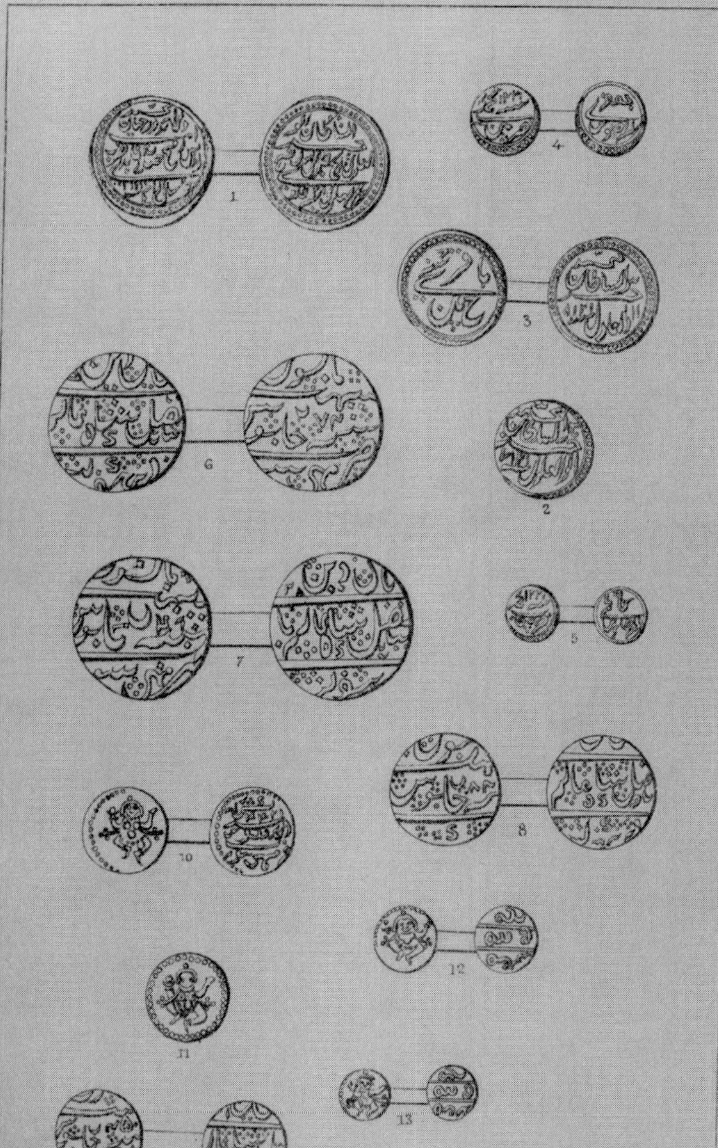

ALEX· BARKER LITOG· MADRAS 1887

SILVER COINS.

PLATE IV.

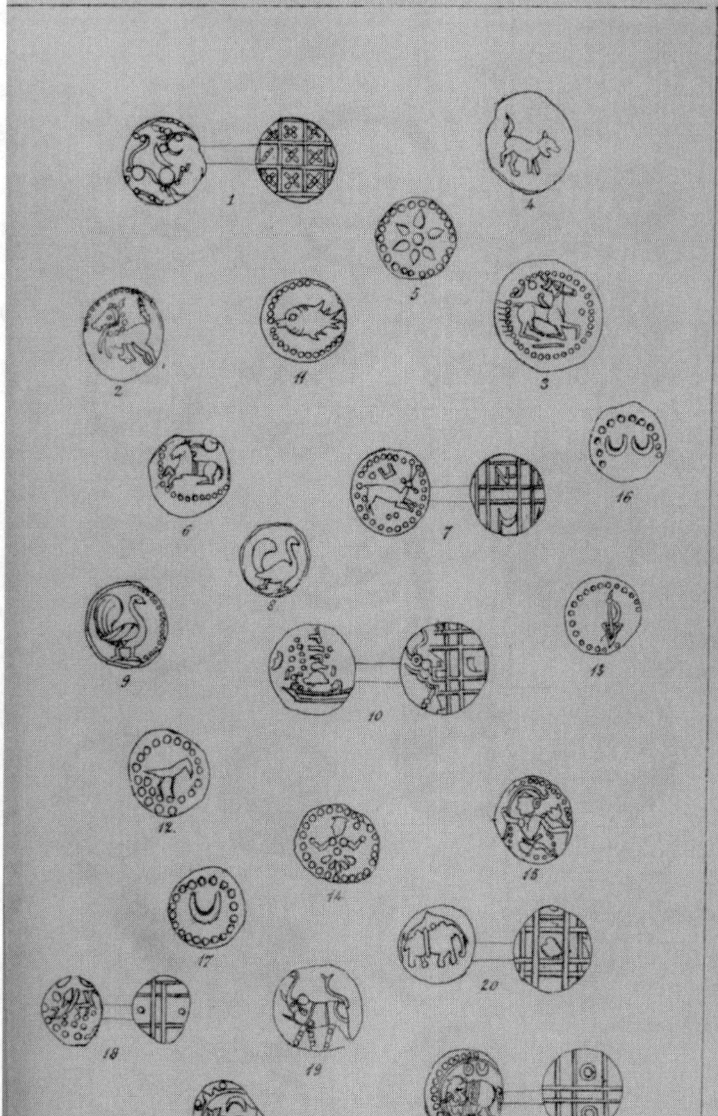

COPPER COINS.

PLATE, V.

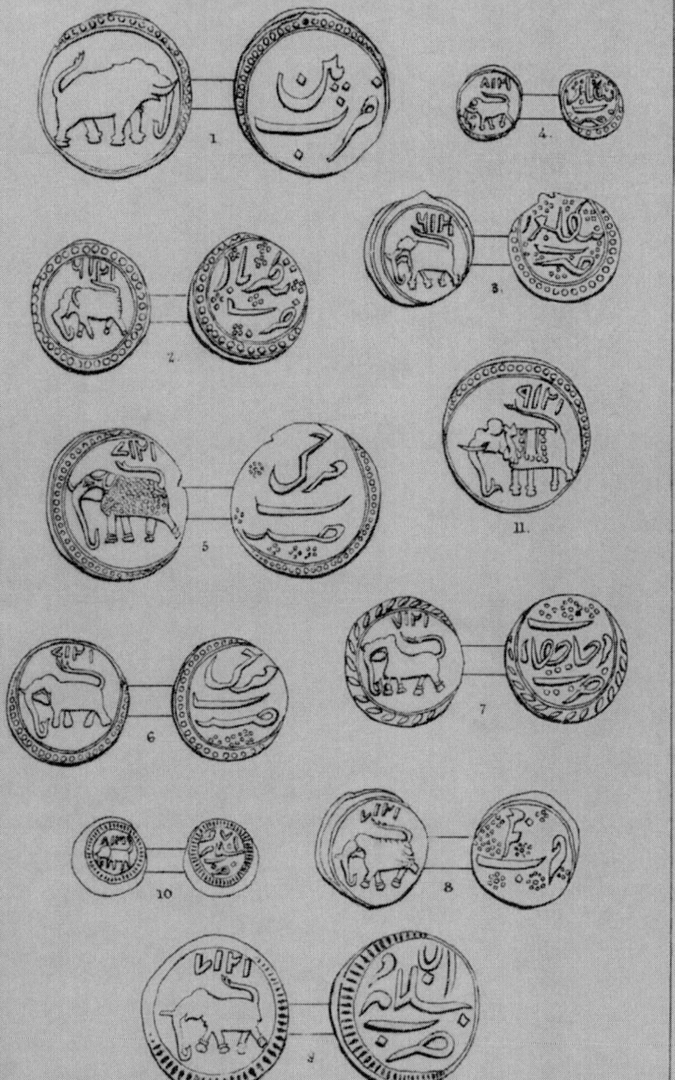

EX. BARREN. LITHOG: MADRAS

COPPER COINS.

PLATE. VI

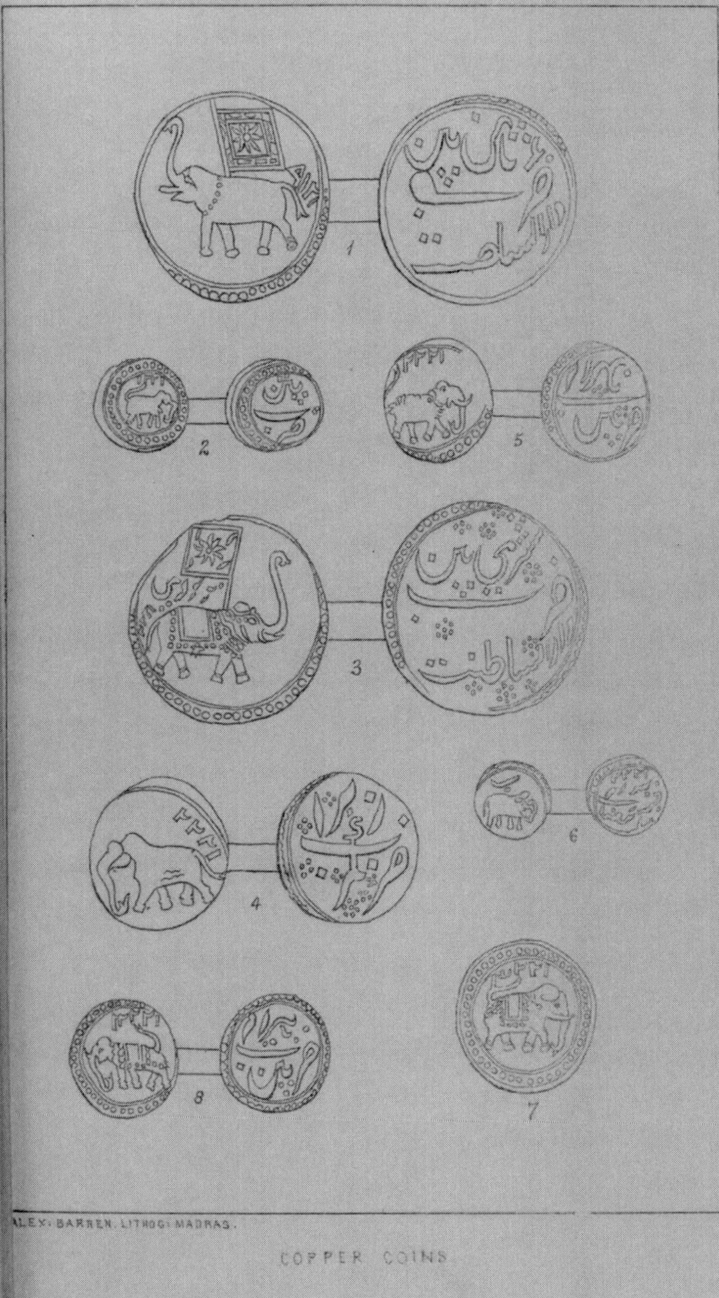

ALEX: BARREN. LITHOG: MADRAS.

COPPER COINS

PLATE. VII.

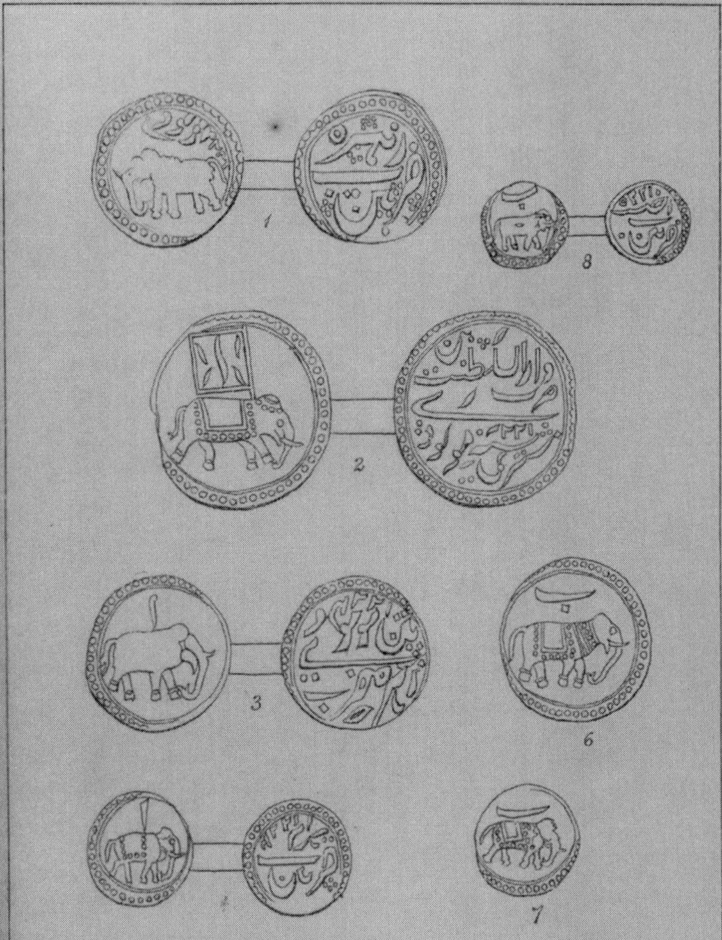

ALEX. BARREN. LITHOG. MADRAS.

COPPER COINS

PLATE VIII.

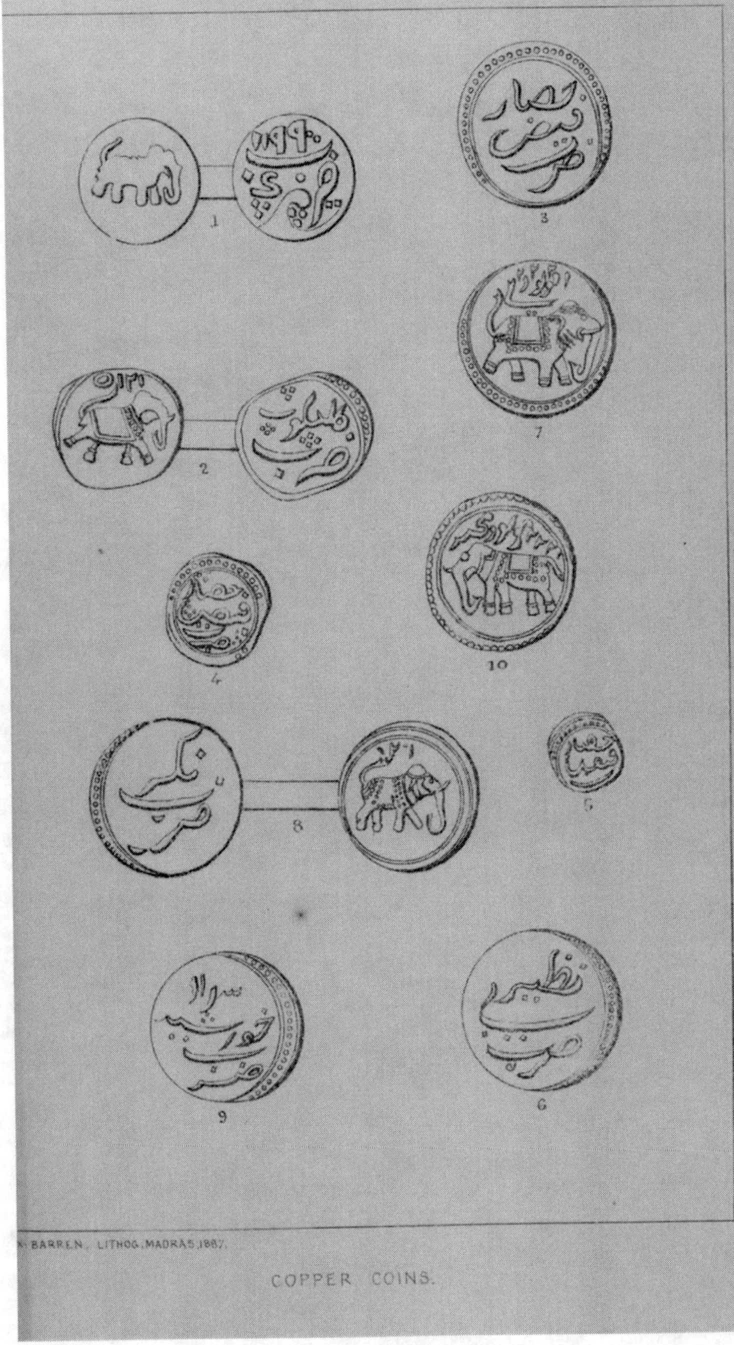

A. BARREN, LITHOG. MADRAS 1887.

COPPER COINS.

PLATE, IX.

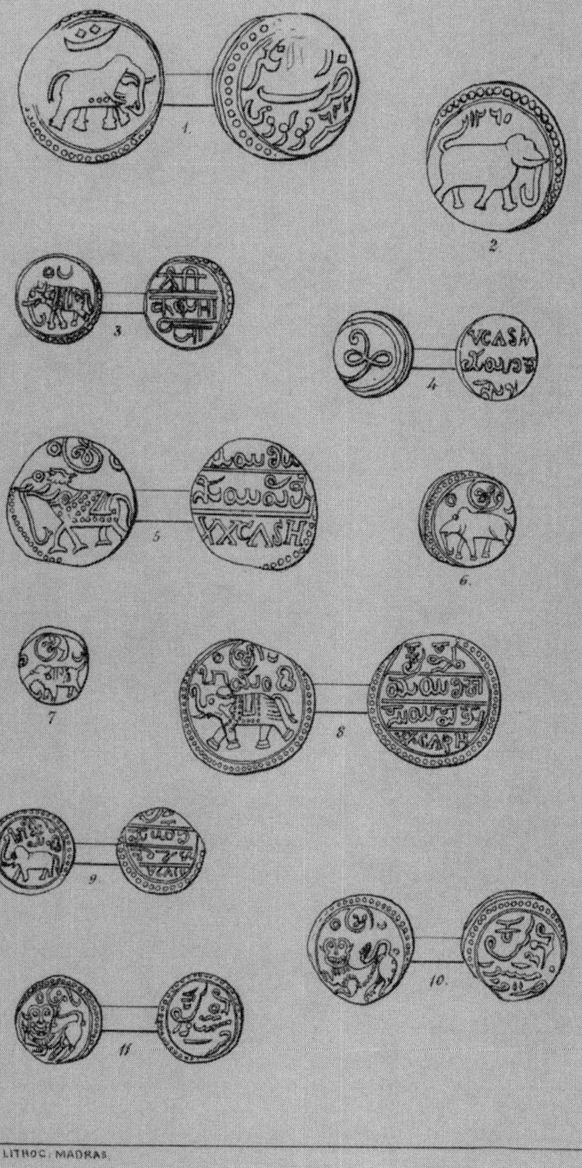

BARREN, LITHOG: MADRAS.

COPPER COINS

PLATE X.

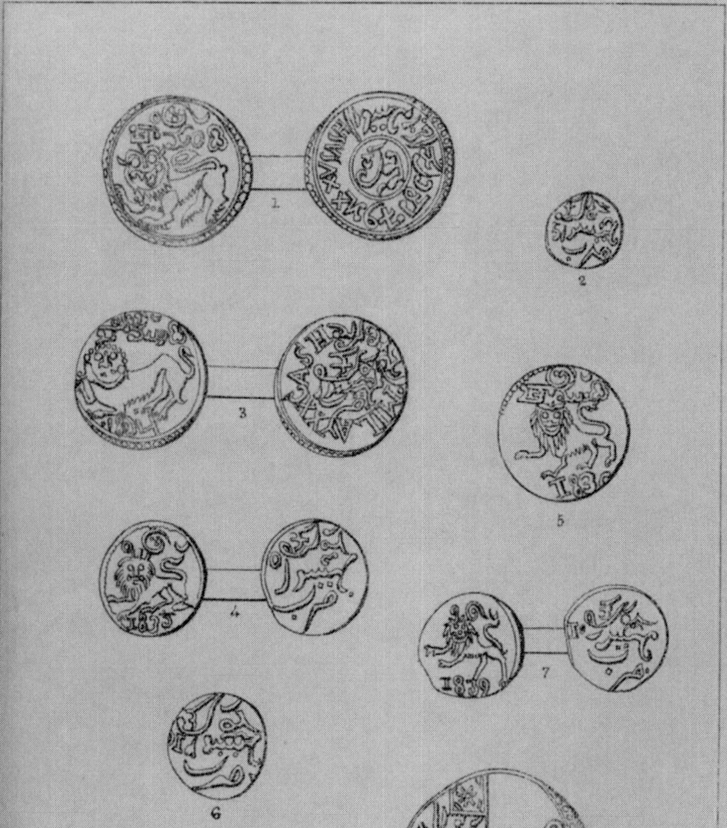

LEX: BARREN: LITHOG: MADRAS, 1887.

COPPER COINS.

PLATE XI.

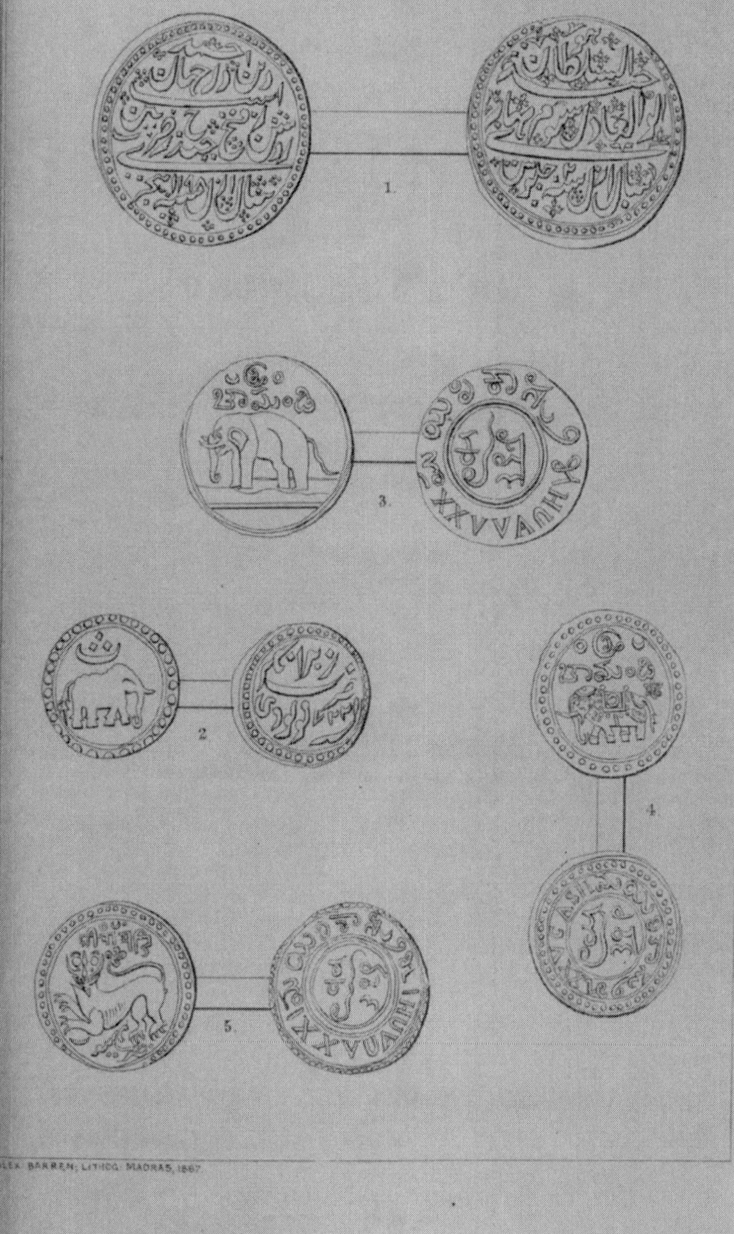

ALEX: BARREN; LITHOG: MADRAS, 1867.

GOVERNMENT CENTRAL MUSEUM.
MADRAS.

COINS.

CATALOGUE No. 2.

ROMAN, INDO-PORTUGUESE, AND CEYLON.

With One Plate.

BY

EDGAR THURSTON.
SUPERINTENDENT, MADRAS GOVERNMENT CENTRAL MUSEUM.

MADRAS:
PRINTED BY THE SUPERINTENDENT, GOVERNMENT PRESS.
1888.

CONTENTS.

I.—ROMAN COINS.

ROMAN COINS.

"What! A gold coin amid these jewelled treasures
Why send me such a relic?"—So you say.
"Good to enhance some antiquary's pleasures;
Stamped for dead people in a buried day!"

True now, but look a little! If one ponder
The legend of this piece, its gold may shine
With lustre leaving dull the gems of wonder
Which I did lay in those dear hands of thine.

An aureus of the Roman empire—See!

Edwin Arnold.

I HAVE included in the present catalogue all the types of coins of the Roman Imperial series, which are contained in the museum collection, although the majority of the copper issues were doubtless not discovered in India.

The earliest notice, so far as I am aware, of the discovery of gold Roman coins (aurei) in the Madras Presidency, is contained in a letter from Alexander Davidson, Esq., formerly Governor of Madras, dated July 12, 1787,[1] who writes as follows:—"A peasant near Nelòr, about 100 miles north-west of Madras, was ploughing on the side of a stony craggy hill; his plough was obstructed by some brickwork; he dug and discovered the remains of a small Hindu temple, under which a little pot was found with Roman coins and medals of the second century. He sold them as old gold, and many no doubt were melted, but the Nawáb Amír ul Umará recovered upwards of thirty of them. This happened while I was governor, and I had the choice of two out of the whole. I chose an Adrian and a Faustina. Some of the Trajans were in good preservation. Many of the coins could not have been in circulation; they were all of the purest gold, and many of them as fresh and beautiful as if they had come from the mint but yesterday; some were much defaced and perforated, and had probably been worn as ornaments on the arm, and others pending from the neck."

In 1800 a pot was dug up at Palachy, containing a great many coins of Augustus and Tiberius, which were all of the same weight and value, each weighing 56 grains. Concerning these coins Buchanan says:[2] "One of the kinds is of Augustus. The legend round the head is CAESAR AVGVSTVS DIVI F PATER PATRIAE, that is, *Cæsar Augustus, Divi Filius, Pater Patriæ.* Above the reverse, representing two persons standing with two bucklers and spears placed between them, the legend is AVGVSTI F COS DESIG PRINC JVVENT, that is *Augusti Filio, Consule designato, principe juventutis.* Under the figures is written CAESARIA or *Cæsaria,* at some city of which name it has been struck. The other coin is of the same weight and belongs to Tiberius. The legend round the head is TI CAESAR DIVI AVG F AVGVSTVS—*Tiberius*

[1] Asiatic Researches, 1790, vol. ii, p. 332.
[2] Journey through Mysore, Canara and Malabar, ed. ii, 1870, vol. ii, p. 31.

Cæsar Divi Augusti Filius Augustus. On the reverse, representing a person seated and holding a spear in one hand and a branch in the other is the following legend :—PONTIF MAXIM, or Pontifex Maximus."

In 1806 the following five gold coins, all of different types, were found at Caroor, figured by Colonel Mackenzie, and described some years later by Sir Walter Elliot,[3] viz., "1. AVGVSTVS DIVI F., with a very curious and apparently undescribed reverse like a dog or sow or some large quadruped with its nose to the ground and its tail over its back, below which in the exergue IMP. X; 2. the common type of Tiberius as Pontifex Maximus; 3. of Antonia, CONSTANTIÆ. AVGVSTAE. (Akerman, D.C.I., p. 148, No. 1); 4. two of Claudius, one CONSTANTIÆ. AVGVSTI (Akerman, I. p. 155, No. 2), and the other S.P.Q.R.P.P. OB. C.S. in an oak wreath."

In 1810 a pot full of well-preserved coins of Augustus and Tiberius was dug up at Poláchi in the Coimbatore district, and seven years later a silver coin of Augustus was found in one of the old tombs called *Pandu Culis*, together with a number of irregular-shaped punch-marked "Buddhist coins."[3]

Concerning finds of Roman coins in the Coimbatore district, Mr. R. Sewell says:[4] "It is evident that there was at one time a very considerable commerce between the inhabitants of this district and the Romans, for there have been numerous finds of Roman coins made here. Mr. Walhouse (Ind. Ant. v, 237) thinks that this was in great measure due to the beryl mine at Padiyúr in the Dhárápuram taluk, for the Romans set great store by the beryl, and Pliny declares that the best beryls come from India." On this subject the Rev. Henry Little writes:[5] "He (Mr. Walhouse) says that in the Kangyam taluk (near Dhárápuram) of the Coimbatore district, at a village called Padiyúr, there is an extensive dyke of crystalline porphyritic granite in the gneiss rock; the dyke abounds with masses of quartz with large crystals of the same, as well as felspar, cleavelundite and garnets; the crystals of cleavelundite are remarkably fine, and it often occurs in large masses, in the cavities of which the aqua marina is found in six-sided prisms. Mr. Walhouse gives an account of the enlargement of a well in 1798 and the discovery of these gems; also of a systematic search made by a Mr. Heath in 1819-20, resulting in the securing of 2,196 stones, which weighed 60 seers and were worth £1,200." He then adds "it is highly probable that most of the best aqua marines of the true sea-green color used in modern times in Europe come from this well, and some considerations will now be offered endeavouring to show the probability, at least, that its produce reached Europe in classical times and may have been the object of Roman barter ..... Pliny first conjectured what science has proved that it is but a variety of emerald, and says especially of it (*Nat. Hist.*, Bk. XXXVII, cap. v). The best beryls are those which have the greenness of pure sea water, and come from India, seldom found elsewhere. He also remarks that they are most lustrous when artificially polished hexagonally, not being aware that they occur in six-sided crystals. Now whence came the aqua marines known to Pliny and on which the Greek and Roman engravers exercised their

[3] Madras Journal of Literature and Science, 1844, vol. xiii, p. 214.
[4] Lists of the Antiquarian Remains in the Presidency of Madras, 1881, vol. i, p. 214.
[5] Madras Christian College Magazine, December 1883, pp. 344-6.

skill? In modern times the gem besides occurring in the Indian well has been found in America (North and South), in Siberia, and at a few places scattered over Europe, particularly at Limoges in France. America and Siberia may be excluded from the sources of ancient supply. The localities in Europe are in regions little known to the Romans and unmentioned by Pliny, who had the best means of information. It is unknown in Ceylon. Its ancient origin seems therefore limited, as Pliny says it was, to India, and there it is only known to occur at the locality in Coimbatore described in this note, where moreover the gem is distinguished by the true sea-green color specified by Pliny; elsewhere it is bluish or muddy in tint. It must be added too that most of the finds of Roman coins have been within a radius of 30 miles of this well, and it has been stated to me that between that locality and the west coast there are plenty of Roman coins, both silver and gold, owned by cultivators who now and then dispose of one or two of them when they go to any distant place to a festival."

I have been informed by Mr. Henry Sullivan, and the fact is recorded by Mr. R. Sewell[6] that, when his father, Mr. John Sullivan, was digging the foundations of the house on the hill to the south of the lake at Ootacamund, now called Bishopsdown, about the year 1827, he discovered a gold Roman coin, which passed into the possession of Sir Walter Elliot; and it is noted by Mr. Sewell that in the valley behind Bishopsdown and Fernhill, called by the natives Púnthat, are some ancient gold workings.

In 1838 an aureus of Trajan in fine preservation was picked up by a woman gathering sticks on the side of a stony hill near the village of Athiral in the Chitwail taluk of the Cuddapah district.

Obverse.—Head of Trajan. IMP. TRAIANO. AVG. GER. DAC. P.M. TR. P.

Reverse.—A soldier with a spear over his shoulder, marching to the right. COS. V. P.P. S.P.Q.R. OPTIMO. PRINC.

A solidus of Zeno was found in company with three or four of the pagodas, called Animitti, from their bearing the impression of an elephant, and with several silver coins of the type figured by Prinsep as No. 9 of his Ceylon series,[7] at the foot of an insulated hill in the Tirumangalum taluk of the province of Madura in May 1839. The type of the Roman coin, which has been pierced to be worn as an ornament, bears the armed bust of the emperor, with D.N. ZENO. PERP. AVG. and the type of Victory holding a long cross. VICTORIA. AVG.G.G. θ. In the exergue CONOB.[8]

Still more recently in June 1840 a hoard of Roman aurei was discovered at the village of Darphal, about 15 miles from Sholapoor. They were contained in a small earthen lota, and only eighteen were secured, chiefly of the reign of Severus, but a few also of Antoninus, Commodus, Lucius Verus, and Geta. Drawings of a few have been seen, and some of these prove to be rare types, such as Severus,

ADVENTVI. AVG. FELICISSIMO.
FELICITAS. SAECVLI
FORTVNAE. REDVCI.
PROVIDENTIA. Medusa's head.

[6] Op. cit., vol. i, p. 226.
[7] Journ. As. Soc., Beng., 1837, vol. vi, p. 298, pl. 20.
[8] No. 1 of Akerman's Des. Cat., ii, p. 381.

One of the emperors on horseback spearing a lion appears to refer to a type of Commodus (Akerman, No. 99), but the legend is illegible in the drawing. There is also a specimen of Lucius Verus with the type of Æsculapius, and SALVTI. AVG. V. S.P.Q.R. TR. POT. III. COS. II.[9]

"In the month of May 1842, after a heavy fall of rain, an earthen pot was discovered in a piece of waste land belonging to the village of Vellaloor, about four miles to the east of the town of Coimbatore, which on examination was found to be filled with silver coins. When brought to the Collector, they were found to be Roman Denarii, 522 in number, chiefly of the reigns of Augustus and Tiberius, with a few of Caligula and Claudius. The earthen vessel in which they had lain was like the common terra-cotta *lota* of the present time. It was broken to pieces in the scramble of the finders to possess themselves of its contents. Vellaloor is not known to be remarkable as a place of importance either in ancient or modern times.

"Only eleven different types were found to occur in the large number of coins above mentioned.

1. *Obverse.*—Head of Augustus ...... 134 examples.
   CAES. AVGVSTVS. DIVI. F. PATER. PATRIAE.
   Reverse.— The Pontifical instruments, and two bucklers between the standing figures of Caius and Lucius.
   C. L. CAESARIS. AVGVSTI. F. COS. DESIG. PRINC. JVVENT.

2. Head of Augustus .... 1 example.
   AVGVSTVS. DIVI. F.
   Diana Venetrix.
   IMP. X.

3. Head of Tiberius ..... 378 examples.
   TI. CAESAR. DIVI. AVG. F. AVGVSTVS.
   The emperor seated in a chair.
   PONTIF. MAXIM.

4. Head of Drusus senior ... 1 example.
   NERO. CLAVDIUS. DRVSVS. GERMANICUS. IMP.
   A triumphal arch; on the frieze, DE. GERMANIS.

5. Head of Germanicus (son of the above) .... 1 example.
   GERMANICUS. CAES. P.C. CAES. AVG. GERM.
   Head of Caligula.
   C. CAES. AVG. GERM. P.M. TR. POT. III. COS. II.

6. Head of Agrippina ...... 1 example.
   AGRIPPINA. MAT. CAES. AVG. GERM.
   Head of Caligula.
   C. CAESAR. AVG. GERM. P.M. TR. POT.

7. Head of Caligula ..... 1 example.
   C. CAES. AVG. GERM. P.M. TR. POT.
   Radiated head between two stars.

8. Head of Claudius ... 1 example.
   TI. CLAVD. CAES. AVG. GERM. P.M. TR. P.
   Female seated.
   CONSTANTIAE. AVGVSTI.

---

[9] Madras Journal of Literature and Science, 1844, vol. xiii, p. 215.

9. Head of Claudius . . . . . 1 example.
DIVVS. CLAVDIVS. AVGVSTVS.
A carpentum drawn by four horses.
In the exergue EX. S.C.

10. Head of Claudius . . . 2 examples.
TI. CLAVD. CAESAR. AVG. P.M. TR. VI. IMP. XI.
Victory pointing with a caduceus to a serpent.
PACI. AVGVSTAE.

11. Head of Claudius. . . . 1 example.
CLAVD. CAESAR. AVG. P.M. TR. POT. IMP. X.
An oak wreath, within which. S.P.Q.R. P.P. OB. C.S." [10]

As regards the same find of coins Mr. M. J. Walhouse says: [11] "This discovery took place just before I joined the district. I took casts of some of the coins, which by order of Government were sent to Madras—whether there melted in the mint or reserved in the museum I know not. The coins were doubtless all of well-known and 'edited' types; a short description may, however, be archæologically interesting. Of the 522, there were 134 bearing the head of Augustus with inscription CAES. AVGVSTVS. DIVI. F. PATER. PATRIAE, on the reverse a trophy of arms between two standing figures and legend C.L. CAESARIS. AVGVSTI. F. COS. DESIG. PRINC. JVVENT; and 378 bore the head of Tiberius with inscription TI. CAESAR. DIVI. AVG. F. AVGVSTVS, on the reverse the emperor seated, with PONTIF. MAXIM. Of the remainder, two bore the head of Claudius and legend TI. CLAVD. CAESAR. AVG. P.M. TR. VI. IMP. XI, on the reverse a winged figure pointing with a wand to a snake, and inscription PACI. AVGVSTAE; another bore the head of Claudius with DIVVS. CLAVDIVS. AVGVSTVS, on the reverse a chariot drawn by four horses abreast, with letters EX. S. C. There were two other types of Claudius, one bearing on the reverse a female seated, the other a wreath enclosing letters; and two coins of Caligula bearing the emperor's head, on the reverse of one a head surrounded with rays. A single example bore a head of Augustus with AVGVSTVS. DIVI. F. and on the reverse Diana carrying a spear, accompanied by a deer or hound, and legend IMP. X. Two remaining types were indistinct, one bearing a sort of arch."

In his *Remarks on some lately discovered Roman gold coins* (1851), Captain Drury says: [12] "A most interesting discovery of a large quantity of ancient Roman gold coins has lately been made in the neighbourhood of Cannanore on the Malabar coast, not only remarkable for the numbers found (amounting to some hundreds) but also for their wonderful state of preservation. Many appear almost as fresh as on the day they were struck—the outline of the figures is so sharp and distinct, and the inscriptions so clear and legible. With very few exceptions, they are all of gold, and of the age of Imperial Rome from Augustus downwards, several of them being coeval with the earliest days of the Christian era. From what we have been able to learn regarding their first appearance, it seems that a few were brought into the town of Calicut and offered for sale in the bazaar by some poor natives, who, naturally supposing from their shining appearance, that they were worth perhaps some trifle, gladly bartered them away for a

---

[10] Madras Journal of Literature and Science, 1844, vol. xiii, p. 212.
[11] Indian Antiquities, 1876, vol. v, p. 239, foot-note.
[12] Journ. As. Soc., Beng., 1852, vol. xx, pp. 371–387.

day's feed of rice. The coins, however, speedily found their way among those who were not long in estimating their real value, and the natives, finding that some importance was attached to the glittering metal, began to rise in their demands, and at length sold them for one, five, ten, and subsequently, for fourteen rupees the coin. The purity of the gold especially attracted the notice of the jewellers and the wealthier natives, who purchased them for the purpose of having them melted down for trinkets and ornaments, and many, it is to be regretted, have been irretrievably lost in this way. The secrecy at first so carefully maintained by the natives in respect to the spot whence they brought them rose in proportion to the eagerness with which the coins were bought up, and for a long time all endeavours proved fruitless in ascertaining the precise locality wherein they were found. It now appears that they were accidentally discovered in the search for gold dust by the gradual clearing away of the soil on the slope of a small hill in the neighbourhood of Kottayem, a village about ten miles to the eastward of Cannanore. A brass vessel was also found, in which many of the coins were deposited. For a length of time the numbers appear to have been very great, and it has been stated that no less than five cooly-loads of gold coins were dug out of the same spot.........It is impossible to make any correct calculation as to the numbers which have actually been found, but it might be mentioned that about eighty or ninety have come into the possession of His Highness the Rajah of Travancore, and still a greater quantity has been collected and preserved by General Cullen, Resident in Travancore, while even after the lapse of more than a year from their first discovery they are still procurable from the natives in the neighbourhood of Tellicherry and Calicut. The most numerous examples which occur are those of the reign of Tiberius, and next to that emperor, those of Nero. It is not a little remarkable that both among these aurei as well as among the denarii alluded to as discovered at Coimbatore, 1842, the examples of coins of the Emperor Tiberius should in both instances have been more frequent than any other, although this may in some manner be accounted for when we consider that the reign of Tiberius extended over a period of twenty-three years—a long time in comparison with that of the other emperors except Augustus."

Translation of a native letter, descriptive of the locality, and first discovery of the coins.

Tellicherry, December 16, 1850.

"Agreeably to my last note, I now beg to furnish you with the information of the discovery of gold coins here. About three years ago certain Syrians residing at Keelaloor Dashom in Palashy Amsham of the Cotiacum taluk were in the habit of collecting gold from the bed of the river Vanienoudavoo (by taking the sand and sifting it), which was between Keelaloor Dashom and Vengador. One day, whilst they were engaged in digging the bed of the river, a number of gold coins was found in a part where there was a mixture of sand and mud. These were lying buried in the ground, but not in a vessel. A great quantity was taken, but nobody knows how many. Some suppose that these might have been buried here in bags, which have been destroyed. At a distance of ten koles east of this, there is a garden belonging to some low caste people who always reside there. During the hot season there is water to a man's depth, whilst in the monsoon there is depth equal to four or five men. The stream runs through one side of the dry bed of the river, whilst the other is so filled up with sand that it is like an island. Below this island on the other side there is another current resembling a small canal, which is the place whence the coins are taken. Certain Maplamars of Curvoye taluk hearing of the discovery of gold at this canal proceeded thither and tried to collect some, and it is said that they also got some coins. Although what these people got is not so much as taken formerly by others, nobody knows what was the exact quantity. About the year 964 (1788 A.D.) it is supposed that certain Gentoo inhabitants of Coorg or Mysore were in the habit of trading in these parts. This being the time of war, some wealthy merchants might have, from competent reasons, cast their gold coins into the river. There is no story of a wealthy man having ever resided in any of the adjacent villages."

DESCRIPTION OF THE COINS.

Augustus born 63 B.C., died 14 A.D.; reigned 58 years.

1. *Obverse.*—AVGVSTVS. DIVI. F. Head of emperor.
   Reverse.—IMP. XIII. Two figures, one seated.
2. *Obverse.*—Head of emperor. No inscription.
   Reverse.—CAESAR. AVGVS. Triumphal quadriga.
3. *Obverse.*—AVGVSTVS. DIVI. F. Head of emperor.
   Reverse.—AVGVS.; rest illegible. Equestrian figure galloping.
4. *Obverse.*—CAESAR. AVGVSTVS. DIVI. F. PATER. PATRIAE. Head of emperor.
   Reverse.—AVGVSTI. F. COS. DESIG. PRINC.
   JVVENT. L. CAESARIS. Two figures of Caius and Lucius; standing between them are two shields on the ground.

The inscription on the reverse of this coin would run thus: *Caius et Lucius Cæsares Augusti filii, Consules designati, principes juventutis.* Caius and Lucius were the grandsons of Augustus, upon whom was bestowed the title of *Principes juventutis*, and it was subsequently conferred upon the probable successor to the throne when he first entered upon public life. Tacitus explains this when he says: "Nam genitos Agrippâ, Caium ac Lucium, in familiam Cæsarum induxerat; nec dum positâ puerili prætextâ, *Principes juventutis* appelari, destinari consules," &c.,—Tac. Ann., 1, 3. See also Suet. in Aug. Cap. 64 et seqq. The origin of the designation "Pater Patriæ" given to Augustus by universal consent is thus described by Suetonius (in Aug. Cap. 58). Valerius Messala leaving the Senate House, said "bonum faustumque sit tibi, domuique tuæ, Cæsar Auguste, Senatus te consentiens cum populo Romano consalutat Patriæ Patrem."

Tiberius born 42 B.C., died 38 A.D.; reigned 23 years.

5. *Obverse.*—TI. CAES. DIVI. AVG. F. AVGVSTVS. PONTIF. MAX. Head of emperor.
   Reverse.—Figure of Clemency. A spear in one hand and olive branch in the other.
6. *Obverse.*—TI. CAESAR. DIVI. AVG. F. AVGVSTVS. Head of emperor.

Reverse.—DIVVS. AVGVST. DIVI. F. Head of emperor surmounted with a star. The star was used as a symbol of the protection of heaven.

Claudius born 10 B.C., died 54 A.D.; reigned 14 years.

7. *Obverse.*—DIVVS. CLAVDIVS AVGVSTVS. Head of emperor.
Reverse.—EX. S.C. A triumphal quadriga.

[13] 8. *Obverse.*—TI. CLAVD. CAESAR. AVG. GERM. P.M. TRIB. POT. P.P. Head of emperor.
Reverse.—AGRIPPINAE. AVGVSTAE. Head of Agrippina, representing a young female.

The inscription on the obverse would run thus: "Tiberius, Claudius Cæsar, Augustus, Germanicus, Pontifex Maximus, Tribunitiæ potestate, Pater Patriæ." There were two celebrated persons bearing the name of Agrippina; one was niece of Tiberius and mother of Caligula, the other was mother of Nero. The image on this coin is that of the former.

9. *Obverse.*—TI. CLAVD. CAESAR. AVG. P.M. TR. P. IV. Head of emperor.
Reverse.—IM.; rest illegible. A bridge, and figure seated.

May not this coin commemorate the building of the celebrated Claudian aqueduct, which bears the emperor's name to this day, and is yet in use at Rome, though partly in ruins?

10. *Obverse.*—TI. CLAVD. CAESAR. AVG. P.M. TR. P. XI. IMP. P.P. COS. V. Head of emperor.
Reverse.—S.P.Q.R. P.P. OB. C.S. The former is enclosed in a wreath or garland.

This would run: "Tiberius, Claudius, Cæsar, Augustus, Pontifex Maximus, Tribunitiæ potestatis undecimo (anno), Imperator, Pater Patriæ, Consulatûs quinto (anno). Senatus, Populusque Romanus, Pater Patriæ, ob cives servatos." The device of a civic crown is very frequently met with. This was usually bestowed upon those who had saved the life of a Roman citizen. The senate in bestowing honors upon Augustus decreed that a civic crown should be hung from the top of his house, and this honor having been assumed by the later emperors, a crown of oak leaves with *ob cives servatos* in the centre is often found on the reverse of coins in those Imperial times.

11. *Obverse.*—TI. CLAVD. CAESAR. AVG. GERM. P.M. TR. P. Head of emperor.
Reverse.—EX. S.C. OB. C.S. Enclosed in wreath as above.

"Ex Senatus consulto" began to be invariably used on coins in the reign of Augustus. A few republican coins are found with the same initials.

12. *Obverse.*—TI. CLAVD. CAESAR. AVG. P.M. TR. P. VI. IMP. XI. Head of emperor.
Reverse.—S.P.Q.R. P.P. OB. C.S. Encircled with wreath.

13. *Obverse.*—TI. CLAVD. CAESAR. AVG. P.M. TR. P.X. IMP. P.P. Head of emperor.
Reverse.—PACI. AVGVSTAE. Winged figure of Victory.

14. *Obverse.*—TI. CLAVD. CAESAR. AVG. P.M. TR. P. Head of emperor.
Reverse.—PRAETOR. RECEPT. Emblem of concord representing two figures joining hands.

15. *Obverse.*—TI. CLAVD. CAESAR. AVG. P.M. TR. P. VI. IMP. XI. Head of emperor.

[13] Now in the cabinet of Captain Tufnell.

Reverse.—DE. BRITANN. Triumphal arch. Emperor mounted, with trophies.[14]

A most interesting coin representing the arch erected by a decree of the Senate to the Emperor Claudius on the final subjugation of Britain. It was in the year 43 A.D. that the Emperor Claudius sent over a large force to conquer the island, which he subsequently joined himself, Vespasian, afterwards emperor, being his second in command. This triumphal arch no longer exists, and, were it not for the representation of it on coins, we should have remained in ignorance of its ever having been erected.

Caligula born 12 A.D., died 41 A.D.; reigned 3 years 10 months:

16. *Obverse.*—C. CAESAR. AVG. GERM. P.M. TR. POT. Head of emperor.
Reverse.—AGRIPPINAE. MAT. CAES. AVG. GERM. Head of Agrippina.
The name of Caligula never appears on his coins and Caius is always expressed by C.

The above coin was struck in honor of his mother, Agrippina.

17. *Obverse.*—C. CAESAR. AVG. PON. M. TR. POT. III. COS. III. Head of emperor.
Reverse.—GERMANICVS. CAES. P.C. CAES. AVG. GERM. Head of Germanicus.

A coin struck in honor of his father, Germanicus.

Drusus born 38 B.C., died 8 B.C.

18. *Obverse.*—NERO. CLAVDIVS. DRVSVS. GERM. AVGVSTVS. IMP. Head of Drusus.
Reverse.—DE GERMAN. Triumphal arch, surmounted with equestrian figure commemorative of the victories of Drusus in Germany.

19. *Obverse.*—NERONI. CLAVDIO. DRVSO. GERM. COS. DESIGN. Head of the young Drusus.
Reverse.—EQVESTER. ORDO. PRINCIPI. JVVENT.

Drusus was made consul 9 B.C. The "ordo equestris" established 123 B.C. Those who were admitted into the equestrian order enjoyed several privileges apart from the rest of the citizens, such as their distinction of seats in public assemblies, &c.

Nero born 37 A.D., died 68 A.D.; reigned 14 years.

20. *Obverse.*—NERO. CAESAR. AVG. IMP. Head of emperor.
Reverse.—PONTIF. MAX. TR. POT. ...... IV. P.P. EX. S.C. Figure holding a spear.

21. *Obverse.*—NERO. CAESAR AVG. IMP. Head of emperor.
Reverse.—PONTIF. MAX. TR. P.X. COS. IV. P.P. EX. S.C. Armed warrior.

22. *Obverse.*—NERO. CAESAR. AVG. IMP. Head of emperor.
Reverse.—PONTIF. MAX. TR. POT. IV. P.P. EX. S.C. Encircled in wreath.

23. *Obverse.*—NERO. CAESAR. AVG. IMP. Head of emperor.
Reverse.—PONTIF. MAX. TR. P.V. COS. IV. P.P. EX. S.C. Armed warrior.

---

[14] Concerning this coin Sir Edwin Arnold says ("India revisited" 1886, p. 260): "Among the curious treasures of the (Madras) Museum, which the Governor (Sir M. E. Grant Duff) has greatly developed, is a golden coin of Claudius, the Emperor, struck to commemorate the conquest of Britain, and discovered in excavating a foundation near Madras. What chapters of fancy might be written about this *aureus*, which thus strangely links the past and present of England's history, and came, perhaps, to India in the scrip of St. Thomas!"

24. *Obverse.*—NERONI. CLAVD. DIVI. F. CAES. AVG. GERM. IMP. TR. POT. EX. S.C. Encircled in wreath.

Reverse.—AGRIPP. AVG. DIVI. CLAVD. NERONIS. CAES. MAT.; rest illegible. Two heads, male and female.

25. *Obverse.*—ANTONIA AVGVSTA. Head of Antonia.

Reverse.—SACERDOS. DIVI. AVGVSTI. Two torches in upright position.

Antonia, daughter of Marc Antony, was born 38 B.C. and was married to Drusus Nero. The inscription on the reverse of this coin may allude to the custom of priestesses (sacerdotes) or flamens being appointed after the deification of the emperors to superintend their worship at Rome and elsewhere.

Antoninus Pius born 86 A.D., died 161 A.D.; reigned 23 years.

26. *Obverse.*—ANTONINVS. PIUS. AUG. GERM. Head of emperor.

Reverse.—P.M. TR. P. XVIII. COS. IV. P.P. A temple.

This temple may perhaps bear some allusion to that decreed by the senate to Antoninus' wife, Faustina, after her death.

Additional.

27. *Obverse.*—CAESAR. AVGVSTVS. DIVI. F. PATER. PATRIAE. Head of emperor.

Reverse.—TI. CAESAR. AVG. F. TR. POT. XV. Triumphal quadriga.

28. *Obverse.*—TI. CAESAR. DIVI. AVG. F. AVGVSTVS. Head of emperor.

Reverse.—IMP. VII. TR. POT. XVII. Triumphal quadriga.

29. *Obverse.*—TI. CLAVD. CAESAR. AVG. GERM. P.M. Head of emperor.

Reverse.—CONSTANTIAE. AVGVSTAE. Female figure seated."

As regards the coins referred to above as being in the possession of the Rajah of Travancore, these are described by Bishop Caldwell, who says: [15] "Of the coins described, all belong to the reigns of the first five Roman emperors.

All are in good preservation with the exception of Nos. 3 and 4, which are partially obliterated. A duplicate of No. 10 is also considerably worn. Several of the coins appear as fresh as if they had but recently issued from the mint. One cannot omit noticing the beauty of the design and execution apparent in several of them, particularly the heads of Antonia and Agrippina, and the distinct and striking individuality of all the heads.

It would be very desirable to endeavour to collect and examine the whole of the coins discovered near Calicut (of which these are a portion, and) which are said to have numbered several hundreds, all gold coins, and all, it is supposed, Roman imperial aurei. If this could be done, the number of examples of each type could be ascertained, undescribed types might be discovered, and a conjecture could be formed *at* what time, or at least, *after* what time, the coins were concealed where they have been found. As far as appears at present, they *may* have been concealed about A.D. 70. If an opinion can be formed from the worn or fresh appearance of the coins, as compared with their earlier or later date, and the absence of all coins later than the reign of Nero, it would

[15] A description of Roman Imperial aurei found near Calicut on the Malabar coast, and now in the possession of His Highness the Rajah of Travancore.—*Trevandrum Government Press*, 1851.

appear that they could not have remained in circulation after A.D. 70, and probably not so long.

From the conquest of Egypt by the Romans about B.C. 30 till the decline of their power, Roman merchants traded extensively with India, and especially with the towns on the Malabar coast, to which they learned to sail direct with the monsoon from the ports of the Red Sea.

Having few commodities that would be considered valuable in India to exchange for silks and muslins, gems and spices, ivory and steel, they were obliged to pay for the greater part of their purchases in specie. Roman coins were in consequence introduced into India so plentifully that they appear to have formed part of the ordinary currency of the country, and even the *name* of the Roman "*Denarius*" has survived to our own day in that of the Indian "*Dinar*."

The beauty of the Roman coins, as compared with those of the Hindu princes, contributed to their diffusion throughout all parts of India, and was, perhaps, the principal cause of their preservation. The ordinary Hindu coins were without hesitation broken up to be made into jewellery, but the Roman coins must have been considered by many as jewels in themselves [16], and carefully preserved accordingly.

As the coins in question were discovered in the interior of the country (it is said in the bed of a river), it appears improbable that the persons who concealed them were themselves Roman merchants; but they may have been native agents of the Roman merchants, or persons extensively engaged in trade at the time the Romans maintained their intercourse with India.

Money and valuables were concealed on emergencies of various kinds, but especially on the breaking out of war between two neighbouring princes. Only one or two persons would be acquainted with the place of concealment, and, if it happened that they were killed in the war, or through the continuance of hostilities unable to return to the place, their secret died with them, and it was reserved for well-diggers or miners, for the action of rain, or changes in the course of rivers, to bring the hidden wealth to light."

The following coins are described by Bishop Caldwell:—

No. I.—Coin of the Emperor Augustus.

Obverse.—AVGVSTVS. DIVI. F. Head of Augustus, crowned with laurel.

Reverse.—IMP. XI. Diana Venetrix, a figure of the goddess Diana, represented as a huntress.

No. II.—Coin of Drusus senior, step-son of Augustus.

Obverse.—NERO. CLAVDIVS. DRVSVS. GERMANICVS. IMP. Head of Drusus crowned with laurel.

Reverse.—DE. GERMANIS. A triumphal arch decked with military trophies, on which stands an equestrian figure of Drusus.

No. III.—Coin of Caius, grandson and adopted heir of Augustus.

Obverse.—AVGVSTVS. DIVI. G.F. Head of Augustus, crowned with laurel.

Reverse.—C. CAESAR. AVGVSTI. F. An equestrian figure of Caius, the horse at full speed; infantry standards in the background.

---

[16] I have seen an aureus on the neck of a cooly woman, who was carrying a portmanteau up the Shevaroy Ghât. *Auct.*

No. IV.—Coin of Caius, referred to above, and his younger brother Lucius, grandsons and adopted heirs of Augustus.

Obverse.—CAESAR. AVGVSTVS. DIVI. F. PATER. PATRIAE. Head of Augustus, crowned with laurel.

Reverse.—Standing figures of Caius and Lucius, each holding a shield and spear, with sacerdotal instruments in the background. Under the figures, C. L. CAESARES ; over AVGVSTI. F. COS. DESIG. PRIN. JVVENT.

No. V.—Coin of Tiberius.

Obverse.—TI. CAESAR. DIVI. AVG. F. AVGVSTVS. Head of Tiberius.

Reverse.—DIVI. F. DIVVS. AVGVST. Head of Augustus, surmounted with a star.

No. VI.—Coin of Tiberius.

Obverse.—TI. CAESAR. DIVI. AVG. F. AVGVSTVS. Head of Tiberius.

Reverse.—PONTIF. MAXIM. A sitting figure of the emperor, holding in one hand a staff, in the other a leafy branch.

No. VII.—Coin of Caligula.

Obverse.—C. CAESAR. AVG. GERM. P.M. TR. POT. Head of Caligula, with laurel wreath.

Reverse.—GERMANICUS. CAES. P.C. CAES. AVG. GERM. Head of Germanicus, son of Drusus and Antonia, and father of the Emperor Caligula.

No. VIII.—Coin of Antonia, wife of Drusus, grandmother of the Emperor Caligula, and mother of the Emperor Claudius.

Obverse.—ANTONIA AVGVSTA. Head of Antonia.

Reverse.—SACERDOS. DIVI. AVGVSTI. Two torches.

No. IX.—Coin of Antonia.

Obverse.—ANTONIA. AVGVSTA. Head of Antonia, crowned with a cereal wreath.

Reverse.—CONSTANTIAE. AVGVSTI. A standing female figure, emblematic of Constancy, leaning on a staff and holding a cornucopia.

No. X.—Coin of Claudius.

Obverse.—TI. CLAVD. CAESAR. AVG. P.M. TR. P. IIII. Head of Claudius, crowned with laurel.

Reverse.—IMPER. RECEPT. A representation of the Prætorian camp at Rome, on the tribunal of which is a sitting figure of the emperor.

No. XI [17].—Coin of Claudius.

Obverse.—TI. CLAVD. CAESAR. AVG. P.M. TR. P. IIII. Head of Claudius, crowned with laurel.

Reverse.—PACI. AVGVSTAE. A figure of Victory with a caduceus, before whom a serpent is retreating.

---

[17] Another coin in the collection similar to this one, but of different mintage, has on the obverse TI. CLAVD. CAESAR. AVG. P.M. TR. P.X. IMP. P.P.

No. XII.—Coin of Claudius.

Obverse.—TI. CLAVD. CAESAR. AVG. P.M. TR. P. VI. IMP. XI. Head of Claudius, crowned with laurel.
Reverse.—CONSTANTIAE. AVGVSTI. A sitting female figure.

No. XIII[18].—Coin of Claudius.

Obverse.—TI. CLAVD. CAESAR. AVG. P.M. TR. P.X. IMP. P.P. Head of Claudius, crowned with laurel.
Reverse.—S.P.Q.R. P.P. OB. C.S. A wreath of oak leaves (the civic crown).

No. XIV[19].—Coin of Agrippina, wife of the Emperor Claudius.

Obverse.—AGRIPPINÆ. AVGVSTAE. Head of Agrippina.
Reverse.—TI. CLAVD. CAESAR. AVG. GERM. P.M. TRIB. POT. P.P. Head of Claudius, with the usual wreath.

No. XV.—Coin of Nero.

Obverse.—NERONI. CLAVDIO. DRVSO. GERM. COS. DESIGN. Youthful head of Nero.
Reverse.—EQESTER. ORDO. PRINCIPI. JVVENT. A shield.

No. XVI.—Coin of Nero.

Obverse.—NERO. CLAUD. CAES. DRVSVS. GERM. PRINC. JVVENT. Youthful head of Nero.
Reverse.—SACERD. COOPT. IN. OMNI. CONL. SVPRA. NVM. EX. S.C.[20] The lituus, tripod, and other sacerdotal instruments.

No. XVII.—Coin of Claudius, *struck after his death.*

Obverse.—DIVVS. CLAVDIVS. AVGVSTVS. Head of Claudius.
Reverse.—EX. S.C. A carpentum drawn by four horses.

No. XVIII.—Coin of Nero and his mother, Agrippina.

Obverse.—NERO. CLAVD. DIVI. F. CAESAR. AVG. GERM. IMP. TR. P. COS. Heads of Nero and Agrippina.
Reverse.—AGRIPPA. AVG. DIVI. CLAVD. NERONIS. CAES. MATER. A car drawn by four elephants, in which are seated two soldiers, one of whom has his helmet elevated on the point of his spear.

No. XIX.—Coin of Nero.

Obverse.—NERO. CAESAR. AVG. IMP. Head of Nero, without the usual laurel wreath.
Reverse.—A cereal wreath, within which EX. S.C.; round the margin PONTIF. MAX. TR. P.VI. COS. IIII. P.P.

---

[18] There are six coins in the collection similar to this, but varying from the XI to XVI year of Tribunitian power.
[19] There is another coin similar to this in the collection, but struck apparently from a different die.
[20] "Admitted as supernumerary priest into every college by decree of the Senate."

No. XX[21].—Coin of Nero.

Obverse.—NERO. CAESAR. AVG. IMP. Head of Nero without a wreath.

Reverse.—PONTIF. MAX. TR. P. VII. P.P. COS. IIII. P.P. Figure of a Roman soldier, holding in his hands some kind of orb, surrounded with a flat rim.

No. XXI.—Coin of Nero.

Obverse.—NERO. CAESAR. AVG. IMP. Head of Nero without a wreath.

Reverse.—PONTIF. MAX. TR. P. VII. COS. IIII. P.P. Across the coin EX. S.C. A female figure resting on a long-jointed staff or spear-shaft, holding in her right hand three darts.

No. XXII.—Coin of Nero.

Obverse.—NERO. CAESAR. AVG. IMP. Head of Nero, without a wreath.

Reverse.—PONTIF. MAX. TR. P. VIII. COS. IIII. P.P. Across the coin EX. SC. A standing figure of a soldier leaning on his spear.

"The next important discovery of gold coins," Dr. Bidie writes,[22] "took place in the Madura district in a piece of waste land near the village of Caliempootoor in the Iyempully taluk in the year 1856.[23] Two tank-diggers, while excavating brick-earth there, came upon an earthen pot, about the size of a mango, containing 63 coins of the Roman emperors. The pot was found about 1½ feet below the surface of the ground and near the bank of the river Shunmoogum Naddy, which is adjacent to the boundary of the Madura and Coimbatore districts. Before the authorities became aware of the discovery, 6 of the coins were made away with by the finders. The Government then directed that the whole of the remaining 57 should be purchased and sent to Madras, but only 28 were ultimately received, the remainder having been sold or lost in the Madura district. This is much to be regretted, as it is not improbable that, amongst those which were kept back, there may have been coins of dynasties not represented in the museum. The Madura coins form the chief portion of the Roman series in the museum." Concerning this series, Dr. Bidie writes further[24]: "The whole of the (gold) Roman coins in the museum belong to the *Imperial series* and extend from Drusus (B.C. 8) to Commodus, who ascended the throne 180 A.D. The following is a list of the emperors, etc., to whose reigns the coins belong:—

Drusus, senior (consul) ..	— 8 B.C.	Domitian ..	81— 96 A.D.
Tiberius ..	14— 37 A.D.	Nerva ..	96— 98 „
Caligula ..	37— 41 „	Trajan ..	98—117 „
Claudius ..	41— 54 „	Hadrian ..	117—138 „
Nero	54— 68 „	Commodus ..	180—193 „

[21] There is a coin similar to this in the collection, but struck, apparently, when Tribune for the tenth time, and from an improved die.

[22] Catalogue of Coins in the Madras Museum, 1874, p. 2.

[23] "About the same time three washerwomen of Karur, while searching for Fuller's earth, came upon a large chatty containing some hundreds, if not thousands, of *denarii*. There were five or six Madras measures of them. They were sold to Chetties for half their weight in rupees, and the finders have bought themselves land and built good houses with the proceeds. I cannot hear that a single *denarius* remained unmelted. My informant believes that most of them were like an Augustus I showed him."—The Rev. Henry Little, Madras Christian College Magazine, December 1883, p. 338.

[24] l.c., p. 5.

It will be observed that there are two breaks in the series, viz., from 68 to 81 A.D., and again from 138 to 180 A.D. On the whole, however, we have reason to be thankful for these rare and interesting records of the past, and it is quite within the range of possibility that the gaps may, in the course of time, be duly filled up by future finds of hidden treasure. As the collection stands even now, it looks so complete that one might almost suppose the coins had been carried to the East in the cabinet of some ancient coin collector, instead of having been introduced for purposes of commerce. It is to be regretted that there are no coins of the emperors who succeeded Commodus and reigned until the upper empire ceased and the anarchy of the thirty tyrants began."

In 1878 a find of Roman coins was made near Karur in the Coimbatore district, concerning which the Rev. Henry Little writes as follows[25] :—" One afternoon, last August (1882), while busy in my study, a native friend entered and placed on my table six small pieces of flat metal, almost round and a little larger than four-anna pieces, very black-looking, and much covered with earthy matter. To the inquiry what are these, an answer to the effect that they might be old Indian coins was returned, and then other matters were talked about. During this conversation one of the pieces of medal was rubbed quite mechanically a few times over the cloth on the table, and, when my eye next fell upon it, in silvery sheen and in somewhat antique Roman characters there appeared to my astonished gaze the letters MAX .... PONT. I at once saw that the black lumps in my hand were Roman coins, and when they had been cleaned by acid and 'the image and superscription' brought out there was no further room for doubt. I learnt that a Sowcar had about a hundred of these coins, and arrangements were made to obtain possession of them as expeditiously as possible. It seems they were dug up by a famine cooly in 1878 while engaged in deepening a water-course near Karur in the Coimbatore district, and that there were about 500 of them in an earthen pot. Two-thirds were melted to make bangles and what fell to me was the remainder.

"My Roman coins are silver *denarii*, the New Testament *penny*. For five centuries after the founding of Rome, that is up to the third century B.C., the Romans had copper money only. In 269 B.C. silver coins were struck, and during the ascendency of Julius Cæsar a gold coinage was introduced, the commonest piece being the *aureus*, equal to 25 *denarii*. The weight of the *denarius* varied. In the time of Augustus 84 were struck for a Roman pound, making each coin to be about 60 grains. Several of those in my possession are about 58 grains in weight, showing that the lapse of time has told very little upon them, and with respect to other matters the same remark applies. The letters of the inscriptions are clear and the 'image' of the emperors is very bold and distinct, suggesting the inference that soon after they left the mint these coins were buried, and so suffered little loss by passing frequently from hand to hand.

"Twenty-seven of the coins belong to the reign of Augustus, and ninety to that of Tiberius. Although all the former commemorate the same event, they are not all from one die. On the obverse of these coins is a laureate head of Augustus, facing to the right, and beginning from the right-hand side of the bust the inscription runs as follows :—

---

[25] Madras Christian College Magazine, October 1883, pp. 219-228.

CAESAR. AVGVSTVS. DIVI. F. PATER. PATRIAE. On the reverse side stand two draped figures, each grasping a shield and spear which are grounded between them. Above the shields are a *lituus* or divining rod and a *simpulum* or small vessel for pouring libations of wine to the gods, which from its small size gave rise to the proverb *excitare fluctus in simpulo*, i.e., 'much ado about nothing.' Below the figure, we read C. L. CAESARES., and following on from the right AVGVSTI. F. COS. DESIGN. PRINC. JVVENT."

"On the second coin we have a laureate head of Tiberius facing to the right with the following inscription:—TI. CAESAR. DIVI. AVG. F. AVGVSTVS. . . . . . On the reverse side of the coin we have a female figure seated on a chair of state. In her right hand is a spear, and the left holds a branch; the inscription is PONTIF. MAXIM., an abbreviation of Pontifex Maximus."

As regards the discovery of Roman copper coins in Southern India, Mr. Sewell says:[26] "A number of coins of all ages have been found at the 'Seven Pagodas', amongst others, Roman, Chinese and Persian. A Roman coin damaged, but believed to be of Theodosius (A.D. 393), formed part of Colonel Mackenzie's collection." The reading given by Prinsep[27] of the latter coin, which was found at the Seven Pagodas together with several others bearing the same device, but of smaller size, is:—

Obverse.— . . . . DOSIUS. P F. . . . . Head with star on the right.
Reverse.—GLORIA. ROMANORUM. Three figures standing, armed with spears.

After describing[28] the finds of Roman gold coins as affording testimony of the frequent intercourse of Roman traders with the Indian Ocean, Sir Walter Elliot goes on to say: "Still more decisive proof is supplied by the existence of great numbers of Roman coins occurring with Chinese and Arabian pieces along the Coromandel coast. The Roman specimens are chiefly oboli, much effaced, but among them I have found the epigraphs of Valentinian, Theodosius, and Eudocia. These are found, after every high wind, not in one or two places, but at frequent intervals, indicating an extensive commerce between China and the Red Sea, of which the Coromandel coast seems to have been the emporium. The Western traders must either have circumnavigated Ceylon or come through the Paumban passage, probably by the latter way, but in either case must have communicated freely with Ceylon." Further, Sir Walter Elliot says elsewhere[29] on the same subject: "Along the Coromandel coast, from Nellore as far south as Cuddalore and Pondicherry, a class of thin copper die-struck coins, which, although not directly connected with the Andhra type, may be appropriately considered next. They are found in considerable numbers in or near dunes and sand-knolls in the vicinity of the kupams or fishing hamlets that stud the shore, together with Roman oboli, perforated Chinese coins, bits of lead and other metal, beads, fragments of charcoal, &c.

---

[26] Op. cit., vol. i, p. 190.
[27] Journ. As. Soc. Beng. 1832, vol. i, p. 406, pl. x, fig. 45.
[28] Ind. Ant. 1873, vol. ii. p. 242.
Numismat Orient. Coins of Southern India, 1885, p. 35.

"These are collected by the wives and children of the fishermen after gales of wind or heavy rains, and purchased from them by the itinerant pedlars, called Labis and Merkayars, in exchange for useful necessaries, by whom they are sold to braziers and coppersmiths. The discovery of articles of this description in such localities indicates the existence of a considerable maritime trade in former times, probably during the first four or five centuries of the Christian era.

"The Roman coins are all of the smallest value, and are generally worn smooth, but on two or three the names of Valentinian and Eudocia have been read." It is much to be regretted that these coins are nearly always so worn that it is impossible to decipher their legend, and this is notably the case with the coins which are found, from time to time, in the Madura district. As regards this district, Mr. Sewell says: [30] "Mr. Scott, Pleader in the District Court of Madura, is in possession of a very fine collection of ancient coins, mostly found at Madura ..... The collection includes a large number of Roman copper coins (among which I noticed coins of Honorius and Arcadius), found in the bed of the river, as well as a Chinese coin from the same place. The discovery of so many *copper* coins of the Roman empire seems to argue the existence at Madura of a Roman colony at one period. If the coins were merely gold or silver, the discovery would not be so significant."

To the Rev. James E. Tracy I am indebted for the following list of Roman coins in his cabinet, which were collected in the Madura district.

GOLD.

Aureus of Domitian.

Obverse.—Laureate head of emperor r. GERMANIC. IMP. CAES. DOMITIANVS AVG.

Reverse.—Helmeted head of emperor r. P.M.TR. POT. III. IMP. V. COS. X. P.P.

Aureus of Theodosius.

Obverse.—Head of emperor, with the legend of his names and titles.

Reverse.—Standing figures of the two sons of the emperor, and the legend SALVS. REIPVBLICAE. In the exergum CONOB.

Found in the Tirumangalam taluk.

Aureus of Constans II ?

Found in the Tirumangalam taluk.

Copper coins of Theodosius, one of Honorius (?), and several other copper Roman coins with indistinct legends from Madura.

Two Roman copper coins have been recently sent to the Madras Museum from Keelakurai, on the Madura coast, where they were found by Mr. J. P. James, Port officer, together with a large number of Buddhist, Choḷa, Pândyan, and other coins, on which I shall report in detail elsewhere. Both coins are very much worn, and the legends on the obverse are entirely illegible. One bears on the obverse the head of some emperor, and on the reverse a cross within a circle; while the

---

[30] Op. cit., vol. i, pp. 285 and 291.

other bears on the obverse the head of an emperor (Decentius or Julianus II ?), and on the reverse VOT. XV. MULT. XX. in four lines within a laurel wreath fastened above with a circular ornament. As regards the question how the Roman coins were originally brought to India, I may with advantage quote extracts from the article by Captain Drury[31] to which I have already referred. "We will now," he says, "consider, in a brief and somewhat imperfect sketch, to what extent and in what manner the Roman trade first arose and was subsequently carried on with the countries of the East, and more especially with that part of India, to which we would more exclusively refer, the Malabar coast, and also what degree of information the Romans actually possessed of this part of the country, and what kind of commodities were chiefly sought for their luxury or use.

"Previous to their conquest of Egypt, the Romans derived the benefits of Eastern commerce indirectly from the merchants of that country, who, under the reign of Alexander and the Ptolemies, monopolised the entire trade of India and the adjacent countries. Besides this route, the articles of Indian produce and manufacture were imported into Europe by a longer and more tedious way than that of the Red Sea. Being brought in vessels up the Persian Gulf and Euphrates, they were conveyed thence across land to Palmyra, then the grand emporium of Eastern commerce, and which, in its central position, became an important place from its flourishing and prosperous trade. From Palmyra the goods were carried to the different ports of Syria, and thence distributed to the various countries bordering on the Mediterranean Sea. At last the Romans, having subjected Greece and Syria to their sway and overcome the Republic of Carthage, made a descent upon Egypt, which soon yielded to the force of their arms, and from this time that rich and celebrated country was transformed into a Roman province. This happened during the reign of Augustus, and about thirty years before the birth of Christ.

"From this time we may conclude that all direct intercourse of the Romans with the East commenced.[32]

"They followed up their victories with that characteristic energy for an increased trade which they ever displayed after the subjection of a

---

[31] Journ., As. Soc., Beng., 1851, vol. xx, pp. 376–380.

[32] Dr. G. Oppert writes (Madras Journal of Literature and Science, 1879, vol. xxiv, pp. 209-210): "The more the commerce increased between India and the Roman Empire, the greater progress was also made in the art of navigation. The Western trade was viewed in India with favorable eyes, and the occasional embassies which were sent from India to Roman emperors show this fact plainly. Thus we hear of Indian envoys with precious presents being sent to Augustus, Claudius, Antoninus Pius, and Julianus.

"With respect to the knowledge concerning India, it is certain that the author of the Periplus (Maris Erythræi) did not double Cape Comorin, but Plinius was acquainted with the Koromandel Coast, and Ptolemy's knowledge embraced Burmah and even China. This country was visited by a Greek merchant Alexandros, who stopped at Kanton. Markianos of Herakleа and Ammianus Marcellinus provide on these points still more accurate accounts. We may, perhaps, be allowed to call Naustathmos (Karaci), Theophila (Suradara) in Gujarat, Byzantium on the Malabar coast and other places Grecian colonies.

"As long as Rome was the sole capital of the empire, Indian goods went from Alexandria mainly to Rome; but when the empire became divided, Byzantium, or as it is now called Constantinopolis, participated in the receipt of the Eastern articles. Among the merchants who met in Alexandria, many Hindus were to be found, though the statue of the river-god Indus in that town was probably the gift of a Greek and not of a Hindu. The presence of Brahmans is even reported from Constantinople."

foreign people, and the glorious prospect of an undivided command of the Eastern trade added an unusual degree of vigour to their subsequent proceedings.

"Although the occupation of Egypt by the Romans offered them a far greater facility of communicating with India, yet their progress in this respect appears to have been slow and gradual, Augustus probably being more desirous of firmly establishing his authority in that country than extending his views to the conquest of remoter lands. No expedition to the countries bordering on the Red Sea appears to have been meditated till some seventy or eighty years after the Egyptian conquest. During all this time the trade had been carried on by Greek or Egyptian vessels. Without venturing far to sea, the commanders of these ships, starting from the port of Berenice (which still retains its ancient name), were in the habit of creeping slowly along the Arabian coast up the Persian Gulf, and never, perhaps, reaching farther than the mouths of the Indus, till at last a certain commander, more venturesome than his predecessors, boldly pushed across the ocean, and, favored by the monsoon, safely reached the port of Musiris on the Malabar coast.[33] This successful voyage was but the prelude to other more fortunate enterprises, and so rapid became the increase of communication that not long afterwards a fleet of one-hundred and twenty sail was annually wafted by the assistance of the monsoon from the Red Sea to the coast of Malabar, from which time a regular trade was established between the ports of Egypt and the Red Sea and those of the western coast of India.

"From the death of Augustus to the elevation of Trajan to the imperial throne, no important additions had been made to the limits of the empire with the exception of Britain. Trajan soon began to entertain the idea of carrying the Roman arms to the East, and, circumnavigating the coast of Arabia, vainly hoped at length to reach the shores of India; but the expedition was so far unsuccessful, and, the death of that emperor soon after taking place, the project was entirely abandoned by his successor Hadrian.

"The attempt of Trajan, who died 117 A.D., was never repeated by his successors, nor does there appear to have been any fresh acquisition made to the knowledge hitherto obtained of the western part of India until the reign of Justinian, when, owing to the increase of the silk trade, the rival power of the Persians sprang up. The empire was even then in its decline, and the traffic, and, consequently, the dominion over these seas being successfully disputed by a maritime people, the Romans were soon compelled to share, and finally to abandon, the profits of their commercial dealings with India, which had hitherto been crowned with such advantage and success.

"Even the information which the most celebrated writers of the first and second centuries had obtained of India was most inaccurate

---

[33] It is not exactly known where the present position of Musiris lies, or even of Barace, another port which was not far from it. Robertson adopting the opinion of Major Rennell is inclined to fix them both between the modern towns of Goa and Tellicherry, relying on a remark of Pliny that "they were not far distant from Cottonara, a country where pepper is produced in great abundance." In this case Barace might be Barcoor, as generally supposed, and Musiris in all probability Mangalore.

and imperfect, and Strabo, Ptolemy, Pliny, and others[34] equally acknowledge and regret the scanty materials which they possessed regarding the true position and places of the Indian continent; yet Cape Comorin was even then celebrated for its pearl-fisheries, and Ceylon, discovered under the reign of the Emperor Claudius, had already sent an embassy to Rome.

"It is most probable that the Romans never exerted themselves to penetrate to any great distance for the commodities they procured from the East, being contented to carry on their trade at those markets on the Malabar coast which were easiest of access and sufficient for the purposes required. One or more ports, such as Musiris or Barace, were most likely the chosen spots to which were gathered the necessary products of the Indian countries from whatever side they were brought, and from thence they were shipped to Egypt, and thence to the shores of Italy. Merchandise was also conveyed, and, perhaps, still more frequently than by sea, across the country, enriching several towns and cities on the route which became the emporia of such commercial goods as were despatched from the eastern to the western coast.

"Thus the modern town of Arambooly, called Arguropolis by the Greeks, was celebrated in those days for its extent and for the busy trade carried on there. Ptolemy also and Pliny mention Kotar or Nagercoil under the names of Cottiara and Cottora metropolis; while the Greek and Egyptian mariners being afraid of doubling Cape Comorin,[35] used to find a safe anchorage for their vessels in the little harbours of Covalum and Colachull to the northern part of that cape, and which were called in those days—the former Colis or Colias and the latter Cojaci.

"The chief articles of export from India during the time of the occupation of Egypt by the Romans were spices of various kinds, diamonds and other precious stones, ivory, pearls, silk, &c., the latter probably brought from China only. Cinnamon was perhaps more extensively imported from Arabia or the eastern coast of Africa, in

---

[34] "The principal classical works which speak of India include—

Diodorus Siculus	*circa*	8	A.D.
Strabo	*circa*	23	,,
Pliny	*circa*	77	,,
Periplus Maris Erythræi	*perhaps*	81– 96	,,
Ptolemy	*perhaps*	138–161	,,
Arrian	*perhaps*	150–160	,,
Pausanias	*perhaps*	166–180	,,
Bardesanes	*circa*	214	,,
Ælian	*circa*	225	,,

Dion Chrysostom and Plutarch (about 100 A.D.) also refer to India, and the Indian embassies are described by Strabo, Suetonius, Dion Cassius, and Pliny; but with exception, perhaps, of Pliny, the Roman historians seem to have had very little original information as to the far East." C. Reignier Condor, R.E. *Syrian Stone Lore*, 1886, p. 231.

[35] "It (Cape Comorin) is called Komaria Akron, Cape Komaria, by Ptolemy, and Komarei or simply Komar by the author of the Periplus. The latter says: "After Bakaré occurs the mountain called Pyrrhos (or the Red) towards the south, near another district of the country, called Paralia (where the pearl-fisheries are which belong to king Pandion) and a city of the name of Kolkhoi. In this tract the first place met with is called Balita, which has a good harbour and a village on its shore. Next to this is another place called Komar, where is the cape of the same name and a haven."—Bishop Caldwell's *History of Tinnevelly*, 1881, p. 19.

Mr. Scott suggests that the Pyrrhos of the author of the Periplus is probably Trichengode, "Teru sen kōdū," the holy red point or mountain.

allusion to which a modern writer has remarked that the seaport of Aden was in those days used by the Romans as an entrepôt for the merchandise passing from India to Egypt. That seaport was apparently the same place which Ptolemy named 'Arabiæ emporium,' and the author of the Periplus tells us that a little before his time it was destroyed by the Romans; but it is to be presumed that the Romans followed up their victory by occupation, for the position assigned in the Periplus to Arabia Felix together with the principle that it is nature which chiefly determines the site of a great maritime emporium proves that the place in question was no other than Aden, which in the fifth century was the Roman emporium of the Indian trade." Pepper was entirely supplied from the Malabar coast, and large quantities were shipped every season for the markets at Rome, where it was esteemed one of the greatest luxuries of the day. When Alaric was besieging Rome in the fifth century and condescended to accept a ransom for the city, he expressly stipulated for the deliverance 'of 3,000 lb. of pepper,' so much value was attached to that commodity. All sorts of precious stones were eagerly sought after by the wealthier inhabitants, though it is singular that the Romans set a higher value on pearls than they did on diamonds. The former were procured as at the present day near Ceylon and Cape Comorin, and the mines at Sumbhalapura, in Bengal, are probably the same which yielded their treasures for the Roman merchants some twenty centuries ago. Lastly, ivory, ebony, and a few commodities of minor importance completed the list of useful or luxurious articles which were transmitted from this country.

"From the above brief sketch of the communication which the Romans had with the western coast of India and the enumeration of the chief articles of commerce, which attracted their merchants hither for the purposes of trade, we have little occasion to be surprised at the discovery of such coins as have from time to time been found in this country. The great difficulty lies in determining by whom and how they were actually brought here, and how many centuries may have passed away since they were either lost or deposited in those spots whence they are now taken. The oldest coins in the present collection are those of Augustus and the latest those of Antoninus Pius, embracing a period of about one-hundred and forty years. We must, therefore, conclude that they were all brought here subsequent to, or during the reign of, the last-mentioned emperor, while the very remarkable state of preservation in which they exist would lead us to suppose that they had never been in extensive circulation or use previously. It can be no matter of surprise that no other memorials of those times are found upon this coast, such as buildings, &c., for the ancients obtained no footing in the country, but merely came and returned with their ships laden with merchandise.

"In the absence of all direct testimony as to the probable fact of these coins having been conveyed here by the Romo-Egyptian traders, there is another supposition, worthy of taking into consideration, whether they may not have been brought here by those Jewish refugees, who, emigrating from Palestine about the year 68 A.D., spread themselves over this part of the continent at that early period. That country was then a Roman province, and, consequently, Roman money was there in circulation. At that time ten thousand Jews with their families came and settled on the coast of Malabar, and dispersed themselves in various places, chiefly on the sea coast. Now supposing several emigrations of the kind to have succeeded each other and taken place during the third and fourth centuries (Palestine did not cease to be a Roman province until the beginning of the seventh century), it is not unlikely that these coins may have been brought by them, and either from suffering persecution or oppression at the hands of the natives, they may have buried these treasures for greater security or concealment; but besides the Jews, the Nestorian Christians may have been instrumental in conveying foreign coins to these countries. In 485 A.D., they obtained a footing in Persia, whence they spread into almost every country of the East; but I do not consider this theory entitled to so much consideration from the fact of the coins being found in greater numbers on or near to the sea coast, on which account it would assuredly be more plausible to support the idea of their having been brought by the Romans from Egypt, or the Jews from Palestine, presuming the latter people in their emigration came either by way of the Red Sea or the Persian Gulf."

CATALOGUE

OF

ROMAN COINS.

The [*] asterisk signifies that the coin was found in Southern India.

No.	Weight.[1]	Obverse.	Reverse.
		CAIUS OCTAVIUS CÆPEAS AUGUSTUS. 29 B.C.–14 A.D.	
		(a) SILVER.	
1*	55·8	. . . . . . DIVI. F. PATER. PATRIÆ. Head of Augustus r.	AVGVSTI. F. COS. . . In exergum CÆSARES. Two shields and spears supported by two figures.
2*	54·2	CÆSAR. AVGVSTVS. Head of Augustus r.	Inscription illegible. Two shields and spears supported by two figures.
		(b) COPPER.	
3	95·5	DIV. . . . . Head of Augustus l.	PROVIDE [NTIA]. In field S.C. A square altar divided into compartments.
4	141·7	AVGVSTVS. PATER. Head of Augustus l.	S. C. in field. Fasces ?
		(c) BRASS.	
5	206·5	[DI] VVS. CÆSAR. AVG. . . . . Head of Augustus l.	. . . . . AVGVSTA. In exergum S.C. Ceres seated l., holding ears of corn (?) in r. hand, lighted torch in l.

[1] The weight is given in grains.

No.	Weight.	Obverse.	Reverse.
		DRUSUS SENIOR,	
		CONSUL. 8 B.C.	
		GOLD.	
1*	113·37	NERO. CLAVD CÆS. DRVSVS. GERM. . . . . . . Unlaureate head of Drusus l.	[SACERD]. COOPT. IN. OMN. CONL. SUP. NUM. In the centre a caldron-like vessel on three legs, with a ladle-like implement above it; to r. the lituus or crooked staff of the Augur, with which he divided the face of the heavens.
2*	115·73	NERO. CLAVD. DRVSVS. GERM. PRINCP. JVVENT. Unlaureate head of Drusus l.	,,
3*	117·41	NERO. CLAVDIVS. DRVSVS. GERMANICUS. IMP. Laureate head of Drusus l.	Triumphal arch surmounted by two human figures seated and an equestrian r., holding a spear; horse prancing. Below the horse and over the crown of the arch DE (?).
4*	115·55	. . . . DRVSVS. GERMANICVS. IMP. Laureate head of Drusus l.	Trophy, consisting of a standard, two shields crossed, and arrows. Round the margin, between the rays of the trophy, DE. GERMANIS.
		ANTONIA,	
		WIFE OF DRUSUS.	
		GOLD.	
1*	114·8	[ANTONIA]. AVGVSTA. Head of Antonia, crowned with a cereal wreath.	CONS [TANTIAE]. AVGVSTI. A standing female figure, emblematic of Constancy, leaning on a staff and holding a cornucopia.

No.	Weight.	Obverse.	Reverse.
		TIBERIUS CLAUDIUS NERO.	
		14-37 A.D.	
		GOLD.	
1*	109·83	TI. CÆSAR. DIVI. AVG. F. AVGVSTVS. Laureate head of Tiberius r.	PONTIF. MAXIM. Vesta sitting on a square seat r.; a spear in r. hand, branch (?) in l.
2*	..	,,	,,
3*	116·28	CÆSAR. AVGVSTVS. DIVI. F. PATER. PATRIÆ. Laureate head of Tiberius r.	TI. CÆSAR. . . . . A triumphal quadriga; horses walking r.
4*	115·13	TI. CÆSAR. DIVI AVG. F. AVGVSTVS. Laureate head of Tiberius r.	DIVI. AVG. . . . . . DIVI. F. Laureate head r.
		SILVER.[1]	
5*	59·1	TI. CÆSAR. DIVI. AVG. F. AVGVST. . . Laureate head of Tiberius r.	PONTIF. MAXIM. Female figure seated r., holding spear in r. hand, branch in l.
6*	57·1	,,	,,
		CAIUS CÆSAR CALIGULA.	
		37-41 A.D.	
		GOLD.	
1*	117·11	C. CÆSAR. AVG. GERM. P.M. TR. POT. Laureate head of Caligula r.	GERMANICVS. CÆS. P.C. CÆS. AUG. GERM. Unlaureate head of Germanicus r.

[1] A coin of this type has been quite recently found at Bezwáda by Mr. A. Rea of the Archæological Survey.

No.	Weight.	Obverse.	Reverse.
		TIBERIUS CLAUDIUS DRUSUS GERMANICUS. 41–54 A.D. GOLD.	
1*	115·43	TI. CLAVD. CÆSAR. AVG. P.M. TR. P.X. IMP. P.P. Laureate head of Claudius r.	Oak wreath in field, encircling the inscription S. P. Q. R. P. P. OB. C. S.
2*	115·32	TI. CLAVD. CÆSAR. AVG. P. M. TR. P. VI. IMP. XI. Laureate head of Claudius r.	DE. BRITANN . . . On the frieze of a triumphal arch, surmounted by an equestrian figure l. and trophies of arms at each corner.
3*	117·32	TI. CLAVD. CÆSAR. AVG. P.M. TR. P.X. IMP. P.P. Laureate head of Claudius r.	PACI. AV [GVSTÆ]. Winged naked figure, holding in r. hand ?, in l. caduceus held over head of an erect snake.
4*	..	,,	,,
5*	116·5	TI. CLAVD. CÆSAR. AVG. GERM. P.M. TR. . . . . Laureate head of Claudius r.	NERO. CLAUD. CÆS. DRVSVS. GERM. PRINC. JVVENT. Unlaureate head of Drusus, senior, l.
6*	115·72	DIVVS. CLAVDIVS. AVGVSTVS. Laureate head of Claudius l.	Quadriga, drawn by horses r. EX. S. C. in exergum.
		TIBERIUS CLAUDIUS NERO DRUSUS. 54–68 A.D. GOLD.	
1*	115·13	NERO. CÆSAR. AVG. IMP. Head of Nero r.	PONTIF. MAX. TR. P. VII. COS. VIII. P.P. Draped figure of Ceres l. EX. S. C. in field.

TIBERIUS CLAUDIUS NERO DRUSUS—*continued.*

54-68 A.D.—*continued.*

GOLD—*continued.*

No.	Weight.	Obverse.	Reverse.
2*	114·8	NERO. CÆSAR. AVG. . . . . . Head of Nero r.	The same as 1.
3*	117·11	NERO. CÆSAR. AVG. IMP. Head of Nero r.	PONTIF. MAX. TR. . . . . .In the field a wreath, enclosing the legend EX. S. C.
4*	117·6	,,	PONTIF. MAX. TR. P. VI. COS. IIII. P.P. In the field a wreath enclosing the legend EX. S. C.
5*	116·62	,,	PONTIF. MAX. TR. P. II. P.P. In the field a wreath enclosing the legend EX. S. C.
6*	112·86	,,	PONTIF. MAX. TR. P. VIIII. COS. IIII. P.P. Full length figure l, with clothes descending to the knees; helmet on head, l. foot resting on a pedestal, l. knee bent and supporting a globe (?) held in the hands. EX. S. C. in the field.
7*	117·96	,,	,,
8*	115·97	,,	,,
9*	117·1	,,	PONTIF. MAX. . . . . In the field EX. S.C. A full length figure l., clothed, helmet on head, and having winged sandals; r. knee raised and bent, foot resting on pedestal; r. hand holding quiver, l. hand grasping spear.

No.	Weight.	Obverse.	Reverse.
		FLAVIUS DOMITIANUS CÆSAR. 81–96 A.D. GOLD.	
1*	113·83	IMP. CÆS. DOMITIANVS. AVG. P.M. Laureate head of Domitian r.	JVPPITER. CONSERVATOR. Eagle on perch, with extended wings.
2*	110·75	,,	DOMIT. AVGVSTA. IMP. DOMIT. Head of Domitian; back hair in plaits and tied in long-looped knots; shoulders draped.
3*	114·02	IMP. CÆS. DOMIT. AVG. GERM. P.M .... Laureate head of Domitian r.	IMP. . . . Seated nude figure of Jupiter.
4*	111·91	IMP. CÆS. DOMITIANVS. AUG. P.M. Laureate head of Domitian r.	TR. POT. II. COS. VIII. DES. X. P.P. Standing figure of Domitian r., draped as Mars, with shield on l. arm, and throwing javelin with r. hand.
5*	115·11	IMP. CÆS. DOMIT. AVG. GERM. P.M. TR. P.V. Laureate head of Domitian r.	IMP. XI. COS. XII. . . P.P. The emperor standing l., robed as Jupiter.
6*	106·97	DOMITIANVS. AVGVSTVS. GERMANICVS. Laureate head of Domitian r.	COS. XIII. LVD. SÆC. FECIT. Salic priest standing l., with rod in r. hand and sacred shield on l. arm.
		COPPER.	
7	163	IMP. CÆS. DOMIT. AVG. GERM. COS. XII. CENS. PER. P. P. Laureate head of Domitian r.	ANNONA ....S. C. in exergum. Ceres seated r.; a figure standing in front of her; in background stem of a galley.

FLAVIUS DOMITIANUS CÆSAR—*continued.*

81-96 A.D.—*continued.*

COPPER—*continued.*

No.	Weight.	Obverse.	Reverse.
8	159·5	. . . . GERM. COS. XII. CENS. PER. P.P. Laureate head of Domitian r.	[FIDEI]. PVBLICÆ. In the field S.C. A female standing; in l. hand a basket of fruit (?), in r. two ears of corn and a poppy.
9	166·6	. . . . VESP. F. DOMITIAN . . . COS. VII. Laureate head of Domitian r.	Inscription illegible. S. C. in the field. Minerva standing with spear in r. hand, circular shield on l. arm.

MARCUS COCCEIUS NERVA.

96–98 A.D.

GOLD.

No.	Weight.	Obverse.	Reverse.
1*	111·52	IMP. NERVA. CÆS. AVG. P.M. TR. POT. Laureate head of Nerva r.	COS. III. PATER. PATRIÆ. A small vessel, a torch, a vase-like vessel, and the lituus.
2*	115·36	IMP. NERVA. CÆS. AVG. P.M. TR. P. COS. II. P. P. Laureate head of Nerva r.	CONCORDIA EXERCITVVM. Two hands joined and holding a military ensign crowned with an eagle. The foot of the ensign rests on the prow of a vessel.

MARCUS ULPIUS TRAJANUS CRINITUS.

98–117 A.D.

GOLD.

No.	Weight.	Obverse.	Reverse.
1*	108·31	IMP. TRAIANO. AVG. GER. DAC. P.M. TR. P. Laureate head of Trajan r.	COS. V. P.P. S.P.Q.R. OPTIMO. PRINC. A full length figure l., draped; holding a palm leaf (?) in r. hand and spear in l.

No.	Weight.	Obverse.	Reverse.
		PUBLIUS ÆLIUS HADRIANUS.	
		117–138 A.D.	
		GOLD.	
1*	113·2	IMP. CÆSAR. TRAIAN. HADRIANVS. AVG. Laureate head of Hadrian r.	COS. III. A draped figure l., holding? in r. hand.
		TITUS AURELIUS FULVIUS BOIONIUS ARRIUS ANTONINUS.	
		138–161 A.D.	
		(*a*) SILVER.	
1	45·3	ANTONINVS. PIVS. AVG. Laureate head of Antoninus r.	PONTIF. TR. P. VIII. COS. III. Britannia (?) seated l.
		(*b*) BRASS.	
2	163·5	[ANT] ONINVS. AVG. PIVS. Head of Antoninus r., diademed	R. POTX. CO ...... In the field S C. Standing figure l., holding spear in r. hand, ? in l.
		(*c*) COPPER.	
3	398·4	IMP. CÆS. T. ÆL. HADR. ANTONINVS. AVG. Head of Antoninus r., diademed.	Inscription illegible. Figure seated.
4	41·9	IMP . . . IVS. AVG . . . . Head of Antoninus r., with radiate crown.	[VIC] TORIA. Standing figure of Victory l.
		MARCUS ANNIUS VERUS CATILIUS SEVERUS.	
		161–180 A.D.	
		SILVER.	
1	37·9	IMP. C. M. AVR . . ALEXAND. AVG. Laureate head of Marcus Aurelius r.	VIRTVS. Armed figure r., holding spear in r. hand, shield in l.

No.	Weight.	Obverse.	Reverse.
		MARCUS ANNIUS VERUS CATILIUS SEVERUS—*continued.*	
		161–180 A.D.—*continued.*	
		SILVER—*continued.*	
2	39·6	. . . . AVRELIVS . . . . Unlaureate head of Marcus Aurelius r.	. . . COS . . . . Standing figure l., holding cornucopia in l. hand, branch (?) in r.
		ANNIA FAUSTINA,	
		WIFE OF MARCUS AURELIUS.	
		COPPER.	
1	137·5	[F] AVSTINA. AVG. . . . . . . Head of Faustina r; her hair tied in a knot behind.	. . . . . REG . . . . s.c. in the field. Female figure (Juno ?) standing l., holding ? in r. hand, spear in l.
2	149·9	FAVSTINA. AVGVSTA. Head of Faustina r; hair dressed as before.	HILARITAS. Female figure standing l., holding cornucopia in l., hand ?, in r. ?
		MARCUS ÆLIUS AURELIUS COMMODUS ANTONINUS.	
		180–193 A.D.	
		GOLD.	
1*	111·62	L. ÆL. AVREL. COMM. AVG. P.P. . . . . . Laureate head of Commodus bearded, r.	AV. III. . . . . . II. Figure of Minerva (?) l., holding spear in r. hand and a small figure in l.

No.	Weight.	Obverse.	Reverse.
		MARCUS ÆLIUS AURELIUS COMMODUS ANTONINUS—*continued.*	
		180–193 A.D.—*continued.*	
		GOLD—*continued.*	
2*	..	L. AEL. AVREL. COMM. AVG. . . P. FEL. Laureate head of emperor r.	HERCVLI. ROMANO. AVG. Commodus as Hercules, standing naked l. having a club on his left arm, and a lion's skin pendent from the arm; his right hand is resting on a trophy of arms, which stands at the right of the field.
		COPPER.	
3	357	L. AVREL. COMMODVS. TR. P.V The youthful head of Commodus r.	JOVI. VICTO [RI] . . . S.C. in the field. Jupiter, bare to the waist, seated on a throne; hasta pura in l. hand, victoriola in r.
4	157·6	Inscription illegible. Laureate head of Commodus r.	Inscription illegible. S. C. in the field; COS. V. P. P. in exergum. Jupiter seated, holding in l. hand hasta pura, in r.?
5	133·2	. . . . MODVS . . . AVG. PIVS Laureate head of Commodus r.	[P] M. T.R. P. VIII . . . . . . VI. COS. IIII. . . . . S. C. in the field. Female figure standing facing, holding sword in l. hand, ? in r.
6	207·6	COMMODVS . . . . . . Laureate head of Commodus r.	VOTA. DECENN. SUSCE. [PTA]. . . . . S.C. in the field. The emperor robed as Pontifex, standing l. and pouring out a libation on to a tripod altar, on which a fire is burning.

No.	Weight.	Obverse.	Reverse.
		MARCUS ÆLIUS AURELIUS COMMODUS ANTONINUS—*continued.*	
		180–193 A.D.—*continued.*	
		COPPER—*continued.*	
7	145	COMM. ANT. P. . . . . Laureate head of Commodus r.	APOL. In the field COS. VI. S. C. Apollo standing with legs crossed; r. hand extended over his head; l. arm resting against a column.
		BRUTTIA CRISPINA,	
		WIFE OF COMMODUS.	
		COPPER.	
1	150	CRISPINA. AVGVSTA. Head of Crispina r.; her hair braided and tied in a knot; shoulders draped.	CONCORDIA. In the field S.C. A female figure seated l., with cornucopia on l. arm; r. arm extended and holding patera.
		JULIA DOMNA,	
		WIFE OF SEPTIMUS SEVERUS.	
		SILVER.	
1	42·7	IVLIA. AVGVSTA. Head of empress r., her hair in broad bands at the sides; shoulders draped.	PIETAS. AVG. . . Female figure standing before an altar, on which she is pouring a libation from a patera in r. hand.
		FULVIA PLAUTILLA,	
		WIFE OF CARACALLA.	
		COPPER.	
1	95·3	PLAVTILLA. AVGVSTA.[1] Head of Plautilla r., her hair braided; shoulders draped.	Undecipherable.

[1] "Her Latin coins are exceedingly rare. One among General Ramsay's coins was the only one I ever saw at sale, and a wretched thing it was, not worth having. It was bought for Mons. Herpin of Paris, whose cabinet was afterwards sold at Sotheby's, 3rd August 1857, and the same coin again sold. Her best coins, though very rare, are Greek." Hobler, *Records of Roman History*, 1860, vol. ii, p. 654.

No.	Weight.	Obverse.	Reverse.
		MARCUS AURELIUS ALEXANDER SEVERUS. 222–235 A.D. COPPER.	
1	124·2	IMP. CÆS. M. AVR. SEV. ALEXANDER. AVG. Head of Severus r., with radiate crown.	PROVIDENTIA. DEORUM. In the field S. C. A robed female figure standing full front with legs crossed; l. arm resting on a column, above which rises a cornucopia; on the ground at her feet a globe, to which she points with r. hand.
2	277·6	IMP. ALEXANDER. PIVS. AVG. Laureate head of Severus r.	PROVIDENTIA. AVG. In the field S. C. Robed female figure, holding ears of corn in r. hand over a corn modius; ? in l. hand.
		MARCUS ANTONIUS GORDIANUS PIUS. 238–244 A.D. COPPER.	
1	198·9	IMP. GORDIANVS ... AVG. Laureate head of Gordianus r.	P. M. TR. P. III. COS. ..... In exergum S. C. The emperor in his robes, seated; r. hand extended holds a globe; in l. hand a short staff.
		CAIUS MESSIUS QUINTUS TRAJANUS DECIUS. 249–251 A.D. SILVER.	
1	61·4	IMP. M.Q. TRAJANUS. DECIUS. AVG. Head of Trajan with radiate crown r.	PANNONIÆ. Two female figures robed and veiled, holding military standards.

No.	Weight.	Obverse.	Reverse.
		LUCIUS CLAUDIUS DOMITIUS AURELIANUS. 270–275 A.D. COPPER.	
1	46·4	IMP. AVRELIANVS. Head of Aurelianus, wearing radiate crown r.	.... DVX .... Figure seated on a shield, with a tree behind.
		MARCUS AURELIUS PROBUS. 276–282 A.D. COPPER.	
1	45·6	IMP. PROBVS. P. F. AVG. .. Head of Aurelius, wearing radiate crown l.	Illegible.
		FLAVIUS GALERIUS VALERIUS CONSTANTINUS. 323–337 A.D. COPPER.	
1	49·8	CONSTANTINVS. AVG. Head of Constantine r., with crested helmet; bust in armour.	Inscription illegible. A warrior holding shield on his lap with × marked on it.
2	63·9	IMP. CONSTANTINVS. AVG. Laureate head of Constantine r.[1]	SOLI. [INVICTO]. COMITI. In field S.C.; in exergum P.L.N. Apollo standing, looking l.; r. hand raised.

[1] This coin was struck in London.

No.	Weight.	Obverse.	Reverse.
		FLAVIUS GALERIUS VALERIUS CONSTANTINUS —*continued.*	
		323–337 A.D.—*continued.*	
		COPPER—*continued.*	
3	32·4	CONSTANTINOPOLIS. Female head l., wearing crested helmet.	T.R.P. in exergum. Winged Victory standing with spear in r. hand, l. hand resting on a shield.
4*	25·7	Inscription illegible. Head of Constantine r., diademed.	GLORIA. EXERCITVS. Two soldiers with shield and spear on either side of an ensign.
		FLAVIUS JULIUS CONSTANTIUS.	
		350–361 A.D.	
		COPPER.	
1	43·7	D. N. CONSTANTIUS. P. F. AUG. Head of Constantius r., diademed.	FEL. TEMP. REPARATIO. In exergum E. C. P. (?). Armed soldier spearing a warrior who has fallen to the ground.
		UNCERTAIN EMPERORS.	
		COPPER.	
1*	..	Head of emperor r.	A cross within a circle.
2*	..	Head of emperor r.	Inscription VOT. XV. MULT. XX. in four lines, within a laurel wreath, fastened above with a circular ornament.

TABLE SHEWING SOME OF THE INSCRIPTIONS ON THE ROMAN COINS IN THE MADRAS MUSEUM.

Inscription.	Remarks.
ANNONA	On a copper coin of Domitian, struck on the occasion of one of the periodical distributions of coin. Type borrowed from the coinage of Nero.
APOLLO	On a copper coin of Commodus. The figure of Apollo was probably copied from the Lycian Apollo.
CONCORDIA	On a copper coin of Crispina. The inscription and device point to the concord between Commodus and his wife.
CONCORDIA EXERCITVVM ..	On a gold coin of Nerva, signifying the fidelity plighted to the emperor by the army.
CONSTANTINOPOLIS	On a copper coin of Constantinus Magnus. The city of Byzantium was dedicated to, and named after, Constantine, 330 A.D.
DE. BRITANN	On one of the *aurei* of Claudius, struck in commemoration of the conquest of Great Britain. Another *aureus* (not in the museum collection) bears the legend OB. BRITANNOS. DEVICTOS.
DE. GERMANIS	On a gold coin of Drusus, Senior. The inscription alludes to his victories over German tribes.
FEL. TEMP. REPARATIO	On a copper coin of Constantius II.
FIDEI. PUBLICÆ	On a copper coin of Domitian.
GLORIA. EXERCITVS	On a copper coin of Constaninus Magnus.
HILARITAS	On a copper coin of Faustina Junior.
JOVI. VICTORI	On a copper coin of Commodus, struck after the victories over the Marcomanni and other German triedes.
JVPITER. CONSERVATOR.. ..	On a gold coin of Domitian and a sign of the emperor's gratitude to Jupiter for success in his campaigns.
LUD[OS]. SÆC[VLOS]. FEC[IT] ..	On a gold coin of Domitian, referring to the sæcular games held at Rome.

Inscription.	Remarks.
PACI. AVGVST	On a gold coin of Claudius.
PANNONIÆ	On a silver coin of Trajan Decius, referring to the tribes of Pannonia, by which Trajan was saluted imperator after quelling an insurrection. The plural number is used, as there were two divisions, Pannonia prima and secunda.
PIETAS. AUGVST	On a copper coin of Julia Domna.
PROVIDENTIA	On a copper coin of Augustus.
PROVIDENTIA. AVG.	On a copper coin of Severus Alexander. The inscription and device (Ceres) refer to the forethought of Augustus in providing a proper supply of corn to the citizens.
PROVIDENTIA. DEORUM	On a copper coin of Severus Alexander.
SOLI. INVICTO. COMITI	On a copper coin of Constantinus Magnus struck in London.
VICTORIA	On a copper coin of Antoninus Pius.
VIRTVS	On a copper coin of Marcus Aurelius.
VOTA. DECENN. SVSCEPTA ..	On a copper coin of Commodus in allusion to the performance of the decennial vows.

SOME TYPES OF TITLES, ETC., ON THE ROMAN COINS IN THE MADRAS MUSEUM.

Title, etc.	Remarks.
CENS. PER.	"Censor perpetuus." On a copper coin of Domitian.
DACICO.	On a gold coin of Trajan, who assumed the title Dacicus after his successful campaign in Dacia.
DIVVS.	The title given to deified Emperors.
DIVI. F.	"Divi Filius."
D. N.	"Dominus noster." On a copper coin of Constantius II.
EX. S. C.	"Ex senatûs consulto."
OPTIMO. PRINCIPI.	On a gold coin of Trajan.
PATER PATRIÆ	....
P. M. TR. POT. X. IMP. P. P. ..	"Pontifex Maximus, Tribunitiâ potestate X, Imperator, Pater Patriæ."
PONTIF. MAX. TR. P. VII. COS. VIII. P. P.	"Pontifex Maximus, Tribunitiâ potestate VII, Consul VIII, Pater Patriæ."
PRINC. JVVENT.	"Princeps Juventutis." On gold coins of Drusus Senior and Claudius. The title "Prince of Youth" was, at an early period of the Empire, conferred on the Cæsar, or heir apparent to the throne.
SACERD. COOPT. IN. OMN. CONL. SVP. NVM.	"Sacerdos cooptatus in omni conlegiâ supra numerum." On a gold coin of Drusus Senior.
S. C.	"Senatûs consulto."
S P. Q. R. P. P. OB. C. S. ..	"Senatus, Populusque Romanus, Pater Patriæ, ob cives servatos." On a gold coin of Claudius.

ADDENDUM.

It is only since the final proof sheets have been revised that my attention has been called to a notice by Captain R. H. C. Tufnell, in the Madras Journal of Literature and Science, on the small Roman coins found in the neighbourhood of Madura, which he attributes to a local mint. "What more natural," he says, "than that, as trade increased and eastern luxuries became more and more popular with the fair dames of Rome, small settlements of agents should be established to collect on the spot the produce of the country and convey it to the ships of their employers on their periodical visits to the ports of call. True no traces of those fine Roman buildings one sees and admires so much in Europe have been discovered, but could one expect to find, in a small community of mercantile agents settled for a short period in the heart of a foreign and uncivilized nation, any evidence of their existence that would last as many centuries as have rolled by since Roman merchants traded in the East, unless it be such coins as I describe, struck specially for the purposes of trade with a pauper population? Looking then to the facts that all the coins of this series are well worn as though they had been in regular circulation, that they are of a type differing from those usual to the Imperial mints,—that they are of so small a value as to be what one would expect to find in use when dealing with a people as poor as the early Hindus,—that they are found almost exclusively in one locality,—that they are *constantly* being found and not occurring in a glut at intermittent periods,—surely all these arguments point to the possible, if not indeed the probable, truth of the theory that they were of local mintage."

I have also recently had an opportunity of examining Mr. Tracy's coin collection, and have to add to the coins mentioned on page 23 a coin of Anastasius, found in the Tirumangalum taluq, and bearing on the obverse the inscription D. N. ANASTASIVS. P. P. AVG. and a figure of the emperor wearing a tiara and oriental ornaments, and on the reverse, the inscription VICTORIA. AVG. G. G. S. and a winged figure of victory.

II.—INDO-PORTUGUESE COINS.

INDO-PORTUGUESE COINS.

THE history of the coinage for the Portuguese possessions in India, from the foundation of the Goa mint in 1510 by Afouso Dalboquerque down to the present time, has been fully dealt with by Mr. J. Gerson Da Cunha in his admirable "Contributions to the Study of Indo-Portuguese Numismatics,[1]" to which I would refer the reader who is interested in the subject, and to which I am indebted for the description of the coins.

The present catalogue contains only a description of the coins, which are contained in the collection of the Madras Museum, and, to any one familiar with the history of the Indo-Portuguese coinage, it will be at once evident that the collection is very deficient in the coins struck prior to the latter half of the last century, and my efforts to improve it in this respect have proved fruitless; but this is not to be wondered at, for Mr. Da Cunha says: "The subject of the Portuguese coinage in India is involved in much obscurity. Money was first minted at Goa in 1510 A.D., only 370 years ago; but its history is more vague and undefined than that of either the Greek or Roman coinage. The issue of coins by the viceroys, and often by the officers of the mint, without any intervention on the part of the viceroys or governors-general, was conducted in the most unsystematic, not to say capricious, fashion. The coins not seldom bore impresses, effigies, and legends which had no connection whatever with the reigning monarchs of the period when they were issued. Some of them were still minted long after a new currency with crowned or profile busts of kings was introduced. Again, some of these latter coins were struck years after the kings whose busts they bore had ceased to live. These whimsical variations both in types and in the standard of money are in themselves enough to cause no little confusion in the study of Indo-Portuguese numismatics. But these difficulties are increased tenfold by an absolute want of examples of the early periods of the Portuguese rule in India, their place being but inefficiently supplied by some written reports and private memoirs. The coins of the XVIth, XVIIth, and XVIIIth centuries are not only scarce, but even the written documents relating to them are rare or deficient."

[1] Bombay: Printed at the Education Society's Press, Byculla, 1880.

ABBREVIATIONS.

Au. = Gold.		Ae. = Copper.	
Ar. = Silver.		Br. = Brass.	
Tg. = Tutenag.			

CATALOGUE

OF

PORTUGUESE COINS.

No.	Date.	Metal.	Obverse.	Reverse.
			KING D. JOAO V.	
			1706–1750.	
			RUPEE. 1748.	
1	1748	Ar.	Bust of the king r. with the legend JOANNES. V.R.P. The date 1748 in the exergum.	The coat-of-arms of Portugal.
			KING D. JOSÉ I.	
			1750–1777.	
			MEIO PARDAO. 1753.	
2	1753	Ar.	Bust of the king r. with the legend 10 ZEPH. IR.P. The date 1753 in the exergum.	The coat-of-arms of Portugal.
			MEIA TANGA. 17*xx*.	
2·1		Ar.	Bust of the king r. The date 17*xx* in the exergum.	A crown with 30 (the value of the coin in reis) below. [Da Cunha, pl. VII, 7.]
			S. THOMÉ. 1766.	
3	1766	Au.	The coat of arms of Portugal.	The cross of St. Thomas in the field, having at its upper angles 2—x, and the date 1766 in the lower ones.
			5 REIS. 1768.	
4	1768	Ae.	The coat of arms of Portugal.	Cross of the Order of Christ, having in the angles the date 1768. [Da Cunha, pl. VII, 11.]

No.	Date.	Metal.	Obverse.	Reverse.
			12 Reis. 1769.	
5	1769	Tg.	The coat-of-arms of Portugal between the letters G—A.	The numeral XII with the date 1769 below it, all within a wreath. [Da Cunha, pl. VII, 10.]
			6 Reis. 1769.	
6	1769	Tg.	,,	The same except the numeral VI.
			4 Reis. 1769.	
7	1769	Tg.	,,	The same except the numeral IV.
			Tanga. 1774.	
8	1774	Ae.	The coat-of-arms of Portugal.	*Tanga* in the field, surrounded by a laurel wreath, and having on the top astar. [Da Cunha, pl. VII, 8.]
			Meio Tanga. 1774.	
9	1774	Ae.	The coat-of-arms of Portugal.	G. between two stars in the field, having 30 R. above, and the date 1774 below: all encircled by a laurel crown. [Da Cunha, pl. VII, 9.]
			20 Reis. 1774.	
10	1774	Ae.	,,	The same except 20 R.
11	1774	Ae.	,,	,,
			10 Reis. 1774.	
12	1774	Ae.	,,	The same except 10 R.
			Pardao. 1776.	
13	1776	Ar.	Bust of the king r: 1776 behind: PARDAO in front.	The coat-of-arms of Portugal.

No.	Date.	Metal.	Obverse.	Reverse.
			RUPEE. 1777.	
14	1777	Ar.	Bust of the king r : 1777 behind : RVPIA in front.	The coat-of-arms of Portugal. [Da Cunha, pl. VII, 4.]
			D. MARIA I. 1777–1799.	
			MEIO PARDAO. 1782.	
15	1782	Ar.	The laureate busts of the Queen and her husband (D. Pedro III). r: GOA behind: 150 R in front: 1782 in exergum.	The coat-of-arms of Portugal.
			RUPEE. 1786.	
16	1786	Ar.	The laureate busts of the Queen and her husbund : GOA behind : RVPIA in front: 1786 in exergum.	The coat-of-arms of Portugal.
			PARDAO. 1786.	
17	1786	Ar.	The laureate busts of the Queen and her husband : GOA behind PARDAO in front : 1786 in exergum.	The coat-of-arms of Portugal.
			S. THOMÉ. 1792.	
18	1792	Au.	The coat-of-arms of Portugal.	The cross of St. Thomas, having at its upper angles 12—x, and at its lower angles the date 1792.
			RUPEE. 1793.	
19	1793	Ar.	Bust of the Queen with widow's cap : GOA behind : RVPIA in front : 1793 in exergum.	The coat-of-arms of Portugal.

No.	Date.	Metal.	Obverse.	Reverse.
			D. JOAO VI.	
			REGENT FROM 1799–1818.	
			KING FROM 1818–1826.	
			RUPEE. 1813.	
20	1813	Ar.	Bust of the regent laureate r.	The coat-of-arms of Portugal.
			PARDAO. 1818.	
21	1818	Ar.	Bust of the King laureate r: GOA behind: PARDAO in front: 1818 in exergum.	The coat-of-arms of Portugal.
			PARDAO. 1820.	
22	1820	Ar.	Bust of the King laureate r: GOA behind: PARDAO in front: 1820 in exergum.	The coat-of-arms of the United Kingdom (*i.e.*, the arms of Portugal with the sphere of Brazil).
			D. PEDRO IV.	
			1826–1828.	
			TANGA.	
23		Br.	The coat-of-arms of Portugal.	Within a laurel crown AP. (Asia Portuguese), and T. below it. [Da Cunha, pl. VIII, 9.]
24		Br.	,,	,,
			MEIO TANGA.	
25		Br.	The coat-of-arms of Portugal.	The same design with the addition of ½ between the letters AP. and T.
26		Br.	,,	,,

No.	Date.	Metal.	Obverse.	Reverse.
			RUPEE. 1828.	
27		Ar.	Bust of the king r: GOA. behind: RVPIA in front: 1828 in exergum.	Coat-of-arms of the United kingdom.
			D. MARIA II.[1] 1834–1853.	
			RUPEE. 1833.	
28	1833.	Ar.	Bust of Pedro IV. laureate r: GOA behind: RVPIA in front: 1833, in exergum.	Coat-of-arms of the United kingdom.
			PARDAO. 1833.	
29	1833.	Ar.	Bust of Pedro IV. laureate r: GOA behind: PARDAO in front: 1833, in exergum.	Coat-of arms of the United kingdom.
			PARDAO. 1839.	
30	1839.	Ar.	Bust of the queen l. with the legend PARDAO. DE. GOA. The date 1839 in the exergum.	The coat-of-arms of Portugal surrounded by a laurel wreath.
			RUPEE. 1840.	
31	1840.	*Ar.	Bust of the queen l. with the legend RVPIA. DE. GOA. The date 1840 in the exergum.	The coat-of-arms of Portugal surrounded by a laurel wreath.

1. "This distinguished prince (D. Pedro IV) abdicated the crown on behalf of his daughter, D. Maria, on the 2nd of May 1826, which abdication was ratified on the 2nd of March 1828. He then declared himself regent of the kingdom on the 3rd of March 1832."
J. Gerson Da. Cunha, *Indo-Portuguese Numismatics*, Bombay, 1880.

No.	Date.	Metal.	Obverse.	Reverse.
			TANGA. 1840.	
32	1840.	Ae.	The coat-of-arms of Portugal between two laurel branches: 1840 in exergum.	60 R. inside a laurel crown. [Da Cunha, pl. IX, I.]
33	1840.	Ae.	"	"
			MEIA TANGA. 1840.	
34	1840.	Ae.	"	The same except 30 R.
35	1840.	Ae.	"	"
			15 REIS. 1843.	
36	1843.	Ae.	The coat-of-arms of Portugal within two flowery embellishments: 1843 in exergum.	15 R—D. within a beaded circle.
			RUPEE. 1845.	
37	1845	Ar.	Bust of the queen diademed l. with the legend MARIA II. PORTUG. ET. ALGARB. REGINA: 1845 in exergum.	RUPIA. encircled by a laurel wreath. [Da Cunha, pl. IX-2].
			PARDAO. 1845.	
38	1845	Ar.	"	PARDAO. encircled by a laurel wreath.
			10 REIS. 1845.	
39	1845	Ae.	The coat-of-arms of Portugal: 1845 in exergum.	10 R.
40	1845	Ae.	"	"
			7½ REIS. 1845.	
41	1845	Ae.	"	7½ R.

No.	Date.	Metal.	Obverse.	Reverse.
			6 REIS. 1845.	
42	1845	Ae.	The coat-of-arms of Portugal: 1845 in exergum.	6 R.
			4½ REIS. 1845.	
43	1845	Ae.	,,	4½ R.
			PARDAO. 1846.	
44	1846	Ar.	Bust of the queen diademed l. with the legend MARIA II. PORTUG. ET ALGARB. REGINA: 1846 in exergum.	PARDAO. encircled by a laurel wreath.
			MEIO PARDAO. 1846.	
45	1846	Ar.	,,	MEIO P. encircled by a laurel wreath.
			6 REIS. 1848.	
46	1848	Ae.	The coat-of-arms of Portugal: 1848 in exergum.	6 R.
			3 REIS. 1848.	
47	1848	Ae.	,,	3 R.
			RUPEE. 1850.	
48	1850	Ar.	Bust of the queen diademed l. with the legend MARIA II. PORTUG. ET ALGARB. REGINA: 1850 in exergum.	The coat-of-arms of Portugal: RUPIA DE GOA in exergum.
49	1850	Ar.	,,	,,
			PARDAO. 1851.	
50	1851	Ar.	The same, except the date 1851.	The coat-of-arms of Portugal: PARDAO DE GOA in exergum.

No.	Date.	Metal.	Obverse.	Reverse.
			100 Reis. 1853.	
51	1853	Ar.	Bust of the queen diademed l. with the legend MARIA II. PORTUG. ET ALGARB. REGINA: 1853 in exergum.	100 REIS. encircled by a laurel wreath.

D. PEDRO V.

1853—1865.

No.	Date.	Metal.	Obverse.	Reverse.
			Meio Tanga. 1861.	
52	1854	Ae.	The coat-of-arms of Portugal within two laurel branches: 1854 in exergum.	30 R. inside a laurel crown.
53	1854	Ae.	,,	,,
			Rupee. 1856.	
54	1856	Ar.	Head of the young king r. with the legend PETRUS V. PORTUG. ET ALGARB. REX: 1856 in exergum.	RUPIA. GOA. within a laurel crown. [Da Cunha, pl. ix. 6.]
			Rupee. 1857.	
55	1857	Ar.	The same, except the date 1857.	,,
			Pardao. 1857.	
56	1857	Ar.	,,	PARDAU. GOA. within laure crown.
			Meio Pardao. 1857.	
57	1857	Ar.	,,	MEIO. P. within a laurel crown.

No.	Date.	Metal.	Obverse.	Reverse.
			PARDAO. 1860.	
58	1860	Ar.	Head of the young king r. with the legend PETRUS V. PORTUG. ET ALGARB. REX: 1860 in exergum.	PARDAU. GOA. within a laurel crown.
			D. LUIZ 1.	
			1861.—	
			PARDAO. 1868.	
59	1868	Ar.	Bust of the young king l. with the legend LUDOVICUS I. PORTUG. ET ALGARB. REX: 1868 in exergum.	PARDAU. GOA. within a laurel crown.
			RUPEE. 1869.	
60	1869	Ar.	The same, except the date 1869 in exergum.	RUPIA GOA. within a laurel crown. [Da Cunha, pl. ix, 8.]
			TANGA. 1871.	
61	1871	Ae.	The coat-of-arms of Portugal with the legend INDIA PORTUG 1871 in exergum.	TANGA 60 REIS. within a laurel crown. [Da Cunha, pl. ix, 9.]
62	1871	Ae.	,,	,,
			MEIO TANGA. 1871.	
63	1871	Ae.	,,	½ TANGA 30 REIS. within a laurel crown.
64	1871	Ae.	,,	,,
			QUARTER TANGA. 1871.	
65	1871	Ae.	,,	¼ TANNA 15 REIS. within a laurel crown.

No.	Date.	Metal.	Obverse.	Reverse.
66	1871	Ae.	The coat-of-arms of Portugal with the legend INDIA PORTUG 1871 in exergum.	¼ TANNA 15 REIS. within a laurel crown.
			10 REIS. 1871.	
67	1871	Ae.	,,	10 REIS. within a laurel crown.
68	1871	Ae.	,,	,,
			5 REIS. 1871.	
69	1871	Ae.	,,	5 REIS. within a laurel crown.
			3 REIS. 1871.	
70	1871	Ae.	,,	3 REIS. within a laurel crown.
			RUPIA. 1881.	
71	1881	Ar.	Bust of the king r. with the legend LUDOVICUS I. PORTUG. ET. ALGARB. REX : 1881 in exergum.	The coat-of-arms of Portugal with laurel branches, and the legend INDIA PORTUGUEZA UMA RUPIA. [Da Cunha, pl. ix, 11.]
			MEIA RUPIA. 1881.	
72	1881	Ar.	,,	The same except MEIA RUPIA.
73	1881	Ar.	,,	,,
			QUARTO DE RUPIA. 1881.	
74	1881	Ar.	,,	The same except QUARTO DE RUPIA.
			OCTAVO DE RUPIA. 1881.	
75	1881	Ar.	,,	The same except OCTAVO DE RUPIA.

No.	Date.	Metal	Obverse.	Reverse.
			QUARTO DE TANGA. 1881.	
76	1881	Ae.	Bust of the king r. with the legend LUDOVICUS I. PORTUG. ET. ALGARB. REX : 1881 in exergum.	The royal crown with the legend INDIA PORTUGUEZA QUARTO DE TANGA. [Da Cunha, pl. IX, 10.]
77	1881	Ae.	,,	,,
			RUPIA. 1882.	
78	1882	Ar.	Bust of the king l. with the legend LUDOVICUS I. PORTUG. ET ALGARB. REX : 1882 in exergum.	The coat-of-arms of Portugal with laurel branches, and the legend INDIA PORTUGUEZA UMA RUPIA.

III.—CEYLON COINS.

CEYLON COINS.

THE coinage of the island of Ceylon, both ancient and modern, has been already fully dealt with in the Numismata Orientalia [1] by Mr. T. W. Rhys Davids, who gives the following list of the kings of Ceylon from 1153–1296 A.D., those whose coins are extant being indicated by a star :—

1. Parákrama Báhu, 1153.*
2. Vijaya Báhu 11, 1186, nephew of the last.
3. Nissanka Malla,* 1187, a prince of Kalinga.
4. Wikrama Báhu 11, 1196, brother of Nissanka Malla.
5. Coḍaganga,* 1196. Nephew of nissanka Nalla.
6. Líláwatí (queen),* 1197, widow of Parákrama Báhu.
7. Sáhasa Malla,* 1200, brother (?) of Nissanka Malla.
8. Kalyánawati (queen), 1202, widow of Nissanka Malla.
9. Dharmáoka,* 1208.
10. Lílawatí (restored), 1209.
11. Pánḍi Parákrama Báhu 1211, Malabar usurper.
12. Mágha 1214, a Kálingan prince.
13. Dambadeniya Wijaya Báhu, 1235, founder of a new dynasty.
14. Dambadeniya Parákrama, 1259, son of the last king.
15. Bosat Wijaya Báhu, 1294, son of the last king.
16. Bhunaweka Báhu,* 1296, brother of the last king.

Of the coins of Nissanka Malla and Coḍanga the Madras Museum contains no specimens, nor does it contain specimens of the copper half *massa* of Parákrama Báhu. The coinage of that monarch is, however, well represented in the museum collection by specimens of the gold Lankeswara, copper lion coin, of which a specimen was recently found at Kilakarai on the coast of the Madura district, copper *massa*, and a copper coin similar in every respect to the gold Lankeswara, found at Kilakarai, and to the existence of which type no reference is made by Mr. Rhys Davids. I have also seen a specimen of the latter coin in the collection of the Rev. J. Tracy.

Following the same course as that adopted by Mr. Rhys Davids, I have placed the gold *Lakshmi*, *Tamraki* and *Iraka* coins with the Ceylon coins, though, as that authority says, "their classification is, at present, quite uncertain, and it is doubtful whether some of them belong to Ceylon at all." As regards the *Iraka* coin, which is named from the word *Iraka* (?) on the reverse, Mr. Rhys Davids suggests that the word may possibly be *Haraka* or *Daraka*. Of this coin, Captain Tufnell says [2] :—"It bears the word 'Iraha,' a Prakrit form of the Sanskrit word 'Rakshasa' (demon), above which is what may be the lotus, or possibly the conch shell of Vishnu, and it is not improbable that the Cholas of the 12th and 13th centuries were followers of that deity." Further, Sir Walter Elliot says [3]:—"Gold fanams with the Ceylon

[1] On the Ancient Coins and Measures of Ceylon. International Numismata Orientalia, 1877.

[2] Madras Journal of Literature and Science.

[3] Numismata Orientalia, 1885. Coins of Southern India, p. 133.

type on the obverse, and an indistinct Nágari reverse, are occasionally met with. I received from Tanjore two gold pieces, weighing about 8 grains...... The reverse has three old Nágari letters, which may be read *iraka?* or *daraka?*, throwing no light on their origin.... I was inclined, when I first obtained them, to assign them to the Cholas; as they are not infrequent in the island (Ceylon) their origin is but doubtful."

I have omitted from the present catalogue, though the Madras museum contains specimens, the large and small *sétu* bull coins, which are included by Mr. Rhys Davids in his work. These coins, which bear on the obverse the standing figure of a Rája with a weapon (?) in his right hand, and a trisúla and sceptre in front, and on the reverse the sacred bull Nandí with the emblems of the sun and moon above, and the legend *Sétu* below, doubtless belong to Southern India, and are attributed by Sir Walter Elliot [4] to the Zamindárs of Ramnád, and Sivaganga, the office of Sétupati or guardian of Adam's bridge being one which, "though claiming a high antiquity, appears to have been conferred or restored on the Zamindár by Muttu Krishnappa Náyak, the father of Tirumala Náyak, of Madura."[5]

I have also omitted the copper coins of the Chola dynasty of the same type (called by Sir. W. Elliot the Ceylon type) as the Lankeṣwara coin of Parákrama Báhu, bearing on the obverse the standing figure of a Rája, and on the reverse the same figure in a sitting posture with the legend *Rája Rája*. (Pl. I, 1). These coins, Mr. Rhys Davids says, are the coins from which he believes the whole of the Ceylon series to be derived, and they must have been introduced into Ceylon during the invasion of the island by the Cholas, prior to the time of Parákrama Báhu.

The first settlement of Europeans, the Portuguese, in Ceylon took place in 1517, in which year Albergaria obtained permission from the King of Kotta, whose territory closely adjoined Colombo, to build a factory on the latter spot for purposes of trade.

Concerning the arrival of the Portuguese off Colombo Davy says: [6] "The natives, who first saw them, went to Cotta and informed the king that a new people was arrived, white and beautifully made, who wore iron coats and iron caps, and drank blood and ate stones; who gave a gold coin for a fish or even a lime; and who had a kind of instrument that could produce thunder and lightning; and balls which, put into these instruments, would fly many miles, break ramparts, and destroy forts."

"The appearance," says Tennent,[7] "of the Portuguese in Ceylon at this critical period, saved not only to check the career of the Moors, but to extinguish the independence of the native princes; and looking to the facility with which the former had previously superseded the Malabars, and were fast acquiring an ascendancy over the Cinghalese chiefs, it is not an unreasonable conjecture that, but for this timely appearance of a christian power in the island, Ceylon, instead of a

---

[4] Op. cit., p. 134.

[5] Sir W. Elliot, op. cit., p. 134.

[6] Account of the Interior of Ceylon and of its Inhabitants, with Travels in that Island, 1821.

[7] Ceylon, vol. I, p. 633, 1860.

PLATE I.

CEYLON COINS.

possession of the British crown, might, at the present day, be a Mahometan kingdom, under the rule of some Arabian adventurer." The occupation by the Portuguese was, however, the cause of constant dissension with the natives, and eventually an alliance was formed between the native princes and the Dutch to expel the Portuguese, the conditions of the treaty being made by Rajah Singha, who afterwards became sole king of the interior, on board one of the Dutch ships off Batticoloa.

In his work on Ceylon[8] Bertolocci says:—" Whatever was the currency of Ceylon during the government of the Portuguese, no vestige now remains of it; and an investigation of that subject could throw no light upon its present condition." On this point Mr. Rhys Davids says:—" No coins are known to have been struck by the Portuguese in or for Ceylon. Knox says that of three sorts of coin in use one was coined by the Portugals; the king's arms on one side and the image of a friar on the other, and by the Chingulays called tangom massa. The value of one is nine-pence English; poddi tangom, or the small tangom, is half as much; but these were probably struck in Portugal, and not for use in Ceylon."

The last stronghold of the Portuguese in Ceylon, Jaffna, was given up in 1658, and the Dutch occupation continued till 1796, in which year the island was ceded to the English. So far back as 1763 an embassy had been despatched by the Governor of Madras to propose a treaty to Kirti Sri, the king of Kandy, but no immediate result followed. Twenty years later Trincomallee was occupied by a British force under Sir Hector Munro, but the fort was surprised by a French fleet, and the British garrison transported to Madras. In 1795 an expedition, commanded by Colonel Stuart, landed at Trincomallee, which capitulated in three weeks. Later in the same year Calpentyn was occupied, and early in 1796 Negombo and Colombo were taken possession of, and a convention was signed, by which Point de Galle, Matura, and the remaining fortified places were ceded to Great Britain.

During the Dutch occupation large numbers of the coins of the Dutch East India Company, many bearing the monogram, V.O.C. found their way to the island, but these I shall deal with on a future occasion. As regards the European coins, which were struck specially for Ceylon, I cannot do better than quote in detail the observations of Mr. Rhys Davids, who says:—" The Dutch struck only a very few silver rix dollars, which are very rare, if not entirely extinct, and which I have never seen. A thick copper *Stuiver* having on the obverse the monogram, V.O.C., the O and C written over the sides of the V, and in the open part of the V the letter C, perhaps for Colombo or Ceylon, is occasionally met with. On the reverse is the legend 1 *stuiver*, the numeral 1 being above the word *stuiver* (which occupies the centre of the field coin), and having four dots on each side of it. Below is the date, the dates in my collection being 1784, 1785, 1786, 1789, 1791, 1793, 1795. It is possible, however, that this C is only a mint mark, and that these coins, whose rough execution shows them to have been struck in the Dutch East Indies (the monogram, V.O.C., stands for the initial letters of Vereinigte Ostindische Compagnie, *i.e.* Limited East

---

[8] View of the Agricultural, Commercial, and Financial Interests of Ceylon, 1817.

India Company) were not, after all, struck in Ceylon. There are similar coins with two apparently Tamil letters below the words stuiver, and with T and G in the place of C. If these letters stand for Trinkomalei and Galle, then one would expect Cinghalese letters, but they look like the Tamil letters I. L. for Ilankei, the Tamil form of Lanká, that is, Ceylon.

"The English have issued four types of coins besides the present one. Type 1, which is thick and coarsely executed, has on the obverse an elephant, below which is the date; on the reverse the words CEYLON GOVERNMENT round a circle, within which is the value of the coin. Of this type, there are three thick silver pieces (very rare) of the value of 96, 48, and 24 stuivers (4 of which = 1 fanam), weighing 280, 140, and 70 grains, respectively. The 48 stuiver piece is equal to the rix dollar, and the three thick copper pieces of this type are, respectively, worth $\frac{1}{12}$, $\frac{1}{24}$, and $\frac{1}{48}$, of its value. These copper coins weigh 50 stuivers to the pound, and are now difficult to procure.

"Of this type, specimens of the following years, without letters, are in my collection, and those of the years marked (B.M.), are added from the British museum collection:—

Silver,	96	Stuivers,	1808 (B.M.), 1809 (B.M).
,,	48	,,	1803 (B.M.), 1804 (B.M.), 1808, 1809 (B.M.).
,,	24	,,	1803, 1804 (B.M.), 1808 (B.M.)
Copper,	4	,,	1803 (B.M.), 1804, 1805 (B.M.), 1811 (B.M.). 1814, 1815.
,,	2	,,	1801, 1802, 1803, 1805 (B.M.), 1811, 1812 (B.M.), 1813 (B.M.), 1814, 1815, 1816.
,,	1	,,	1801, 1802, 1803 (B.M.), 1809, 1811 (B.M.), 1812, 1813, 1814, 1815, 1817.

"Of Type 2 one issue was made, in copper, in 1802, of stuivers, half stuivers, and quarter stuivers; they are thin, like modern coins, and well executed, weighing 36 stuivers to 1 lb., obverse and reverse as on the last type. The British museum has specimens of this type, dated 1804, but it is not certain whether they were ever in circulation.

"Of type 3 also one issue was made, in 1815, of two-stuiver, stuiver, and half stuiver pieces in copper and one issue of rix dollars in silver in 1821. Obverse of the copper, head of George III to right, with legend GEORGIUS. III. D.G. BRITANNIARUM. REX.: of the silver, head of Geo. IV. to left, with legend GEORGIUS. IV. D.G. BRITANNIARUM. REX. F.D. Reverse of the copper, an elephant to left; above the legend, *Ceylon two stivers*, one *stiver*, or *one-half stiver*, with the date below. The silver the same, but the legend is *Ceylon one rix dollar*, and round the elephant a wreath of flowers. The coins of this type are still occasionally met with in the bazárs, but the half stuiver is very difficult to get. Both this and the last issue were struck in England.

"Lastly, fanam pieces of two kinds were struck in silver. The first, which is very rare, and was issued about 1820, has simply round a small circle with a dot in its centre FANAM on one side and TOKEN on the other of a silver coin less than $\frac{3}{4}$ of an inch in diameter, and without date. The work-people, who built Baddegama church, the oldest English church in Ceylon, are said to have been paid in this coin, which is roughly executed. The other, which is half an inch in diameter, has on the obverse the bust of Victoria surrounded by the legend VICTORIA. D.G. BRITANNIAR. REGINA. F.D. and on the reverse the figures 1½ and the date 1842, surmounted by a crown and surrounded by a wreath. This little coin, seldom met with in Ceylon, is beautifully executed, and was struck in England; whilst the *fanam tokens* were struck in Ceylon.

"There is, in the British Museum, one silver specimen of another type, but whether this is a proof of an unpublished coin, or a specimen of a coin in actual circulation, I have been unable to ascertain. It has on the obverse the words TWO RIX DOLLARS in a square tablet surmounted by a crown; above it, Ceylon; below it on a scroll, DIEU ET MON DROIT, and below that again the word CURRENCY; on the reverse an elephant to the left, and below it the date 1812."

As regards the little coin mentioned above, with the figures 1½ and the date 1842, Captain Tufnell says:[9] "The description so exactly corresponds with that of the 1½*d*. of the 'Maunday' money, that I cannot but think that the specimens alluded to belong to that series, or to an issue of this silver piece, still to a certain extent in circulation in Malta as a fraction of 3*d*, which sum appears to be the most usual charge for all small commodities and services in Valetta."

Of the European coins struck in Ceylon, only a few typical specimens are here catalogued, more extensive notice being reserved for the future.

---

[9] Madras Journ. Lit. and Science, 1888, p. 187.

CATALOGUE

OF

CEYLON COINS.

No.	Metal.	Obverse.	Reverse.
		PARÁKRAMA BÁHU.	
		1153–1186 A.D.	
		LANKEṢWARA GOLD COIN.	
1	Au.	Standing figure r; dhoti in folds on each side of, and between the legs; conical hat on head; in the r. hand a weapon, and to l. of this a sceptre (?); in l. hand a lotus flower. The figure stands on a snake with a small hole in the centre. To l. below l. arm are five dots, and a lotus flower.	The same figure as on the obverse seated, and holding lotus flower in l hand; a grating below l leg. on the l. side of the figure inscription. *Ṣrí. Lankeṣwara.* [Pl. I, 2, 3.]
2	Au.	,,	,,
		LANKEṢWARA COPPER COIN.	
3	Ae.	,,	,,
		COPPER MASSA.	
4	Ae.	Standing figure holding weapon in r. hand; below to r. lotus flower and five dots.	Seated figure and inscription. *Ṣrí. Parákrama Báhu.* [Pl. I, 4.]
5	Ae	,,	,,

No.	Metal.	Obverse.	Reverse.
		COPPER LION COIN.	
6	Ae.	Standing figure holding weapon in r. hand, and lotus flower in l. A lion sitting r. with mouth open, and exposing the teeth in the upper jaw.	Seated figure and inscription. *Ṣri. Parákrama Báhu.* [Pl. I, 5.]
7	Ae.	,,	,,
		VIJAYA BÁHU. 1186–1187 A.D.	
8	Ae.	Standing figure holding weapon in r. hand below to r lotus flower and dots.	Seated figure and inscription. *Ṣri. Vijaya Báhu.* [Pl. I, 6.]
9	Ae.	,,	,,
		LÍLÁVATÍ. 1197–1200 A.D.	
10	Ae.	,,	Seated figure and inscription. *Ṣri. Rája Lílávati.* [Pl. I, 7.]
		SÁHASA MALLA. 1200–1202 A.D.	
11	Ae.	Standing figure holding weapon in r. below to, r; and a lotus flower and dots.	Seated figure, and inscription. *Ṣri. Mat. Sáhasa. Malla.* [Pl. I, 8.]
12	Ae.	,,	,,
		DHARMÁSOKA. 1208–1209 A.D.	
13	Ae.	Standing figure holding weapon in r. hand; below to r lotus flower and dots.	Seated figure and inscription. *Ṣri. Dharmmáṣoka Deva.* [Pl. I, 9.]

No.	Metal.	Obverse.	Reverse.
		BHUVANAIKA BÁHU. 1296 A.D.	
14	Ae.	Standing figure holding weapon in r. hand; below to r. lotus flower and dots.	Seated figure and inscription. *Şrî Bhuvanaika Báhu.* [Pl. I, 10.]
		GOLD LAKSHMÍ COIN.	
15	Au.	Standing figure, with ornament above r. arm, and trident below l. arm.	Inscription *Lakshmî* with symbol of lotus (?) above. [Pl. I, 11.]
		GOLD TAMRAKÍ COIN.	
15·1	Au.	,,	Inscription *Tamrakî* with symbol of lotus (?) above.
		GOLD IRAKA COIN.	
16	Au.	Standing figure with weapon in r. hand, and lotus flower in l; trident below l. arm.	Inscription *Iraka* (?) with symbol of lotus flower (?) and a stroke and dot above. [Pl. I, 12.]
17	Au.	,,	,,
18	Au.	,,	The same inscription, with a circle and two dots above. [Pl. I, 13.]
		SILVER: HOOK MONEY.[1]	
19	Ar.	A bar of silver bent into a hook, with a mark stamped upon it.	
		SILVER: LANKA MONEY.	
20	Ar.	A bar of silver bent so as to be slipped into the belt, with an Arabic inscription on both sides.	

[1] For note on this money *see* Rhys Davids' Numismat. Orient., 1877, pp. 33-35.

No.	Metal.	Obverse.	Reverse.
		EUROPEAN COINAGE.	
		DUTCH 1790.	
21	Ae.	Monogram, V.O.C. with the letter T. in open part of the V.	I ST. 1790.
		DUTCH 1795.	
22	Ae.	Monogram V.O.C., with the letter C. in open part of the V.	I STUIVER, 1795.
		BRITISH.	
23	Ae.	Inscription CEYLON GOVERNMENT round a circle, within which is the number 12.	Elephant l. with date 1801 below.
24	Ae.	Inscription CEYLON GOVERNMENT round a circle, within which is the number 48.	Elephant l. with date 1802 below.
25	Ae.	,,	,,
26	Ae.	,, but 96.	,,
27	Ae.	,, but 192.	,,
28	Ar.	Inscription CEYLON GOVERNMENT round a circle, within which is the value of the coin 24 ST.	Elephant l. with date 1805 below.
29	Ar.	,, but 48 ST.	,, but date 1808.
30	Ar.	Same as No. 28.	,, but date 1809.
31	Ae.	Inscription CEYLON GOVERNMENT round a circle, within which is the number 24.	Elephant l. with date 1815 below.
32	Ae.	,,	,,
33	Ae.	Bust of king George III. r. inscription GEORGIUS III. D. G. BRITANNIARUM REX.	Elephant l. with inscription CEYLON TWO STIVERS above, and date 1815 below.
34	Ae.	,,	,,
35	Ae.	,,	,, but ONE STIVER.
36	Ae.	,,	,, but HALF STIVER.

No.	Metal.	Obverse.	Reverse.
		EUROPEAN COINAGE—*continued.*	
		SILVER FANAM TOKEN.	
37	Ar.	FANAM round a circle with a dot in centre.	TOKEN round a circle with a dot in centre.
38	Ar.	"	"
		SILVER RIX DOLLAR.	
39	Ar.	Bust of king George IV. l. inscription GEORGIUS IV D. G. BRITANNIAR. REX.	Elephant l. with inscription CEYLON ONE RIX DOLLAR above, floral wreath and date 1821 below.
40	Ae.	Bust of queen Victoria l. inscription VICTORIA QUEEN in ornamental border.	Inscription CEYLON FIVE CENTS 1870 round a circle, within which is a palm tree, and the value of the coin—5 cents—in Tamil and Cinghalese.
41	Ae.	"	"
42	Ae.	"	Inscription CEYLON ONE CENT 1870 round a circle, within which is a palm tree, and the value of the coin—1 cent—in Tamil and Cinghalese.
43	Ae.	"	"
44	Ae.	"	Inscription CEYLON HALF CENT 1870 round a circle, within which is a palm tree, and the value of the coin—½ cent—in Tamil and Cinghalese.
45	Ae.	"	Inscription CEYLON QUARTER CENT 1870 round a circle, within which is a palm tree, and the value of the coin—¼ cent—in Tamil and Cinghalese.

GOVERNMENT CENTRAL MUSEUM,
MADRAS.

COINS.

CATALOGUE No. 3.

SULTÁNS OF DEHLÍ.

BY

EDGAR THURSTON,

SUPERINTENDENT, MADRAS GOVERNMENT MUSEUM.

MADRAS:
PRINTED BY THE SUPERINTENDENT, GOVERNMENT PRESS.

1889.

PREFACE.

In the present Catalogue of Coins of the Sultáns of Dehli, which are contained in the collection of the Madras Museum, the references allude to (I) Thomas' Chronicles of the Pathan Kings of Dehli; (II) the British Museum Catalogue of the Coins of the Sultáns of Dehli, 1884; (III) the articles, with two exceptions by Mr. C. J. Rodgers, published in the Journal and Proceedings of the Asiatic Society of Bengal, and in the Indian Antiquary.

I shall be glad to receive specimens of coins which are wanting in the collection, either as donations, by purchase, or exchange.

EDGAR THURSTON,
Superintendent.

Government Central Museum,
Madras,
August 1889.

COINS OF THE SULTÁNS OF DEHLÍ.

No.	Thomas.	British Museum.	Rodgers.
	MUHAMMAD IBN SÁM. A.H. 589–602.		
1	No. 3.	No. 1.	
2-4	„ 6.	„ 10-11.	
5-6	„ 8.		
7-8	„ 9.		
9-10	„ 10.	„ 12–16.	
11	„ 11.	„ 17-19.	
12	„ 13.		
13-14			J.A.S.B. 1880, No. 6, p. 81.
15-16			„ „ „ 7, p. 82.
17			Ar. antiq. No. 28, p. 433.
	ISSUES OF TÁJ-AD-DÍN YILDIZ.		
18	No. 20 (?)	No. 7 (?)	
19-20	„ 24.	„ 24–26.	
21	P. 27. Foot-note. Binomial coin.		
22			J.A.S.B. 1880, No. 15, p. 209.
23			„ „ „ 16, p. „
24			„ „ „ 17, p. 210.
25			„ „ „ 18, p. „
	KANAUJ ISSUES.		
26-27	No. 16.		
28			Ar. antiq. No. 2, p. 435.
29			„ „ „ 3, p. „
30	„ 19.		

No.	Thomas.	British Museum.	Rodgers.
	SHAMS-AD-DÍN ALTAMSH.		
	A.H. 607–633.		
31			J.A.S.B. 1880, No. 7, p. 209.
32	No. XXIX VAR.		
33-34	,, 42.	No. 40-41.	
35-36	,, 48.	,, 48–50.	
37	,, 50.		
38	,, 52.		
39	Do. but half size.		
40-41	No. 53.	,, 54.	
42	,, 55.	,, 58.	
43-44	,, 57.		
45	,, 58.		
46			
47-48		,, 55.	J.A.S.B. 1880, No. 8, p. 209.
	RUKN-AD-DÍN FÍRÓZ SHÁH I.		
	A.H. 633-634.		
49	No. 89.	No. 61.	
	RIZÍYAH.		
	A.H. 634–637.		
50	No. 91.	No. 63-64.	
51-52			J.A.S.B. 1880, No. 8, p. 82.
53			,, 1881, No. 4, p. 208.
	MU'IZZ-AD-DÍN BAHRAM SHÁH.		
	A. H. 637–639.		
54	No. 92.	No. 67.	
55	,, 94.	,, 70–72.	
56	,, 95.		

No.	Thomas.	British Museum.	Rodgers.
		'ALÁ-AD-DÍN MASÚD SHÁH. A.H. 639-644.	
57-58	No. 97.	No. 73.	
59-60	„ 99.	„ 78-80.	
61	„ 100.		
62	„ 101.		
		NAṢÍR-AD-DÍN MAHMÚD SHÁH I. A.H. 644-664.	
63-67	No. 106.	No. 86-95.	
68			J.A.S.B. 1886, No. 11, p. 188.
69			„ „ „ 15, p. 189.
70-71	„ 107.	„ 96-98.	
72-73	„ 108.		
		GHIYÁS-AD-DÍN BALBAN. A. H. 664-686.	
74	No. 111.	compare No. 100.	
75-77	„ 112.	„ 103-104.	
78-79	„ 113.	„ 115-118.	
80-81	„ 114.	„ 119-120.	
82	„ 115.	„ 121-122.	
		MU'IZZ-AD-DÍN KAI-KUBAD. A.H. 686-689.	
83		No. 123.	
84	No. 116.	„ 126-127.	
85-86	„ 117.	„ 129-130.	
87-88	„ 118.	„ 131-133.	

No.	Thomas.	British Museum.	Rodgers.
		JALÁL-AD-DÍN FÍROZ II.	
		A.H. 689–695.	
89-90	No. 121.	No. 139–145.	
91–93	,, 122.	,, 146–148.	
94-95	,, 123.	,, 149–151.	
96-97	,, 124.	,, 152-152*a*.	
		RUKN-AD-DÍN IBRÁHÍM SHAH I.	
		A.H. 695.	
98-99	No. 127.	No. 154-155.	
		'ALÁ-AD-DÍN MUHAMMAD SHÁH I.	
		A.H. 695–715.	
100		No. 157.	
101–104	No. 130.	,, 158.	
105–112	,, 132.	compare No. 164–181.	
113	,, 134.		
114	,, 135.	,, 196–201.	
115-116	,, 136.	,, 182–191.	
117-118	,, 137.	,, 202-203.	
		KUṬB-AD-DÍN MUBÁRAK SHÁH I.	
		A.H. 716–720.	
119	No. 142.	No. 206-207.	
120	,, 145.		
121			J.A.S.B. 1880, No. 7, p. 210.
122-123	,, 147.	,, 214.	
124-125	,, 148.	,, 216.	
126	,, 149.	,, 217-218.	
127	,, 150.	,, 221-222.	
128	,, 151.	,, 225–227.	
129	,, 152.	,, 230–232.	
130-131	,, 154.	,, 233-234.	
132-133			J.A.S.B. 1880, No. 14, p. 211.
134			,, 1875, No. 3, p. 126. (Delmerick).

No.	Thomas.	British Museum.	Rodgers.
NASÍR-AD-DÍN KHUSRÚ SHÁH. A.H. 720.			
135		No. 235.	J.A.S.B. 1886, No. 18, p. 189.
136	No. 156.	,, 236.	
GHIYÁS-AD-DÍN TAGHLAK SHÁH I. A.H. 720–725.			
137-138		No. 238.	
139	No. 158.	,, 241.	
140	,, 159.		
141–143	,, 161.	,, 245-247.	
144-145	,, 163.		
146	,, 164.	,, 249–254.	
147	,, 165.	,, 258-259.	
148-149			P.A.S.B. 1879, No. 9, p. 179.
MUHAMMAD II-IBN TAGHLAK. A.H. 725–752.			
150	No. 171.	No. 260-262.	
151	compare ,, 172.		
152	,, ,,		
153	,, 174.		
154	,, 173.	,, 264.	
155	,, 175-175*a*.		
156	,, 176.		
157	,, 177.		
158	compare ,, 179.	compare ,, 265.	
159		,, 273.	

No.	Thomas.	British Museum.	Rodgers.
	MUHAMMAD II-IBN TAGHLAK—*continued.*		
	A.H. 725–752.		
160-161	No. 184.	No. 274.	
162	compare No. 188.		
163	„ 189.	„ 280.	
164-165	„ 190.	„ 278-279.	
166-167	„ 193.	„ 288.	
168-169	„ 194.	„ 295-296.	
	FORCED CURRENCY.		
170-17	No. 195.	No. 300–303.	
172-173		„ 305 *a*.	
174			J.A.S.B. 1883, No. 34, p. 62.
175		„ 305 *d*.	
176	„ „		
177	„ 196.	„ 306.	
178-179	„ 197.	„ 309-310.	
180-181	„ 198.	„ 311-312.	
182-183	„ 200.	„ 316.	
184-185	„ 202.	„ 319.	
186-187	„ 203.	„ 320-321.	
188	„ 205.	„ 323.	
189-190	„ 208.	„ 325-326.	
	COINS STRUCK IN THE NAME OF THE 'ABBÁSÍ KHALÍFAHS OF EGYPT.		
191	No. 212.	No. 328.	
192	„ 213.		
193		„ 336–338.	
194-196	„ 218.		

No.	Thomas.	British Museum.	Rodgers.
		MAHMÚD SHÁH. IBN MUHAMMAD IBN TAGHLAK. (*Pretender.*) A.H. 752.	
197		No. 342.	
		FÍRÓZ SHÁH III. A.H. 752-790.	
198	No. 223.	No. 343.	
199	,, 224.	compare ,, 345-347.	
200-202	,, 225.	,, 344.	
203-204	,, 226.		
205-206	,, 228.	,, 349.	
207	compare ,, ,,	compare ,, ,,	
208-210	,, 229.	,, 369-370.	
211	,, 230.	compare ,, 361.	
212	,, 231.		
213-214	,, 233.	,, 374-378.	
215	,, 235.	,, 366-368.	
216	,, 236.		
		POSTHUMOUS	
217	No. 238.	No. 364-365.	
218	,, 239.	,, 379.	
		WITH FATḤ KHÁN.	
219	No. 241.		
220	,, 242.	No. 384-385.	
221-222	compare ,, ,,	compare ,, ,, ,,	
223	,, 244.		

No.	Thomas.	British Museum.	Rodgers.
		WITH ẒAFAR.	
224	No. 245.		
225-226	,, 247.	No. 387.	
227	,, 248.	,, 389-390.	
228	,, 249.	,, 391-392.	
		GHIYÁS-AD-DÍN TAGHLAK SHÁH II. A.H. 790-791.	
229	No. 254.	No. 396-397.	
		ABÚ-BAKR SHÁH. A.H. 791-792.	
230	No. 255.	No. 399-400.	
231–233	,, 260.	,, 406-407.	
		MUHAMMAD SHÁH III-IBN FÍRÓZ. A.H. 792–798.	
234	No. 262.		
235-236	,, 265.	No. 411-412.	
237-238	,, 267.	,, 418.	
239-240	,, 268.		
		POSTHUMOUS.	
241	No. 271.		
		SIKANDAR SHÁH I. A.H. 795.	
242	No. 274.	No. 427-428.	

No.	Thomas.	British Museum.	Rodgers.
		MAHMÚD SHÁH II. A.H. 795–815.	
243	No. 276.	No. 431.	
244-245	,, 278.		
246-247	,, 280.	,, 436–441.	
		NASRAT SHÁH. (*Interregnum*). A.H. 797. *ff.*	
248	No. 283.		
		MUBÁRAK SHÁH II. A.H. 824–837.	
249	No. 288.	No. 446.	
250-251	,, 289.	,, 448.	
		MUHAMMAD SHÁH IV-IBN FARÍD. A.H. 837–847.	
252	No. 293.	No. 456–458.	
253–255	,, 295.	,, 460–464.	
		'ALIM SHÁH. A.H. 847–855.	
256	No. 301.		

No.	Thomas.	British Museum.	Rodgers.
		BUHLÓL LÓDI. A.H. 855–894.	
257-258	No. 311.	No. 473.	
259	" 312.	" 491-492.	
260-261	" 313.	" 483.	
262-263	" 315.	" 479.	
		SIKANDAR II-LÓDI. A.H. 894–923.	
264-265	No. 316.	No. 495.	
266-267	" 317.	" 516-517.	
		IBRÁHÍM LÓDI. A.H. 923–937.	
268	No. 330.	No. 518.	
		SHÉR SHÁH. A.H. 946–952.	
269			J.A.S.B. 1880, pl. XVIII *a*, 1.
270			Ind. Ant.,[1] 1888, No. 1, p. 65.
271			" " " " 2, p. 65.
272			" " " " 3, p. 66.
273			" " " " 4, p. 66.
274			" " " " 5, p. 66.
275			" " " " 6, p. 66.
276			" " " " 7, p. 66.
277			" " " " 8, p. 66.
278			" " " " 9, p. 66.
279			" " " " 10, p. 66.
280			" " " " 11, p. 66.
281			" " " " 12, p. 66.
282			" " " " 13, p. 66.
283			" " " " 14, p. 66.

[1] The Rupees of the Suri Dynasty.

No.	Thomas.	British Museum.	Rodgers.
		SHÉR SHÁH—*continued.*	
		A.H. 946–952—*continued.*	
284			Ind. Ant., 1888, No. 16, p. 67.
285			„ „ „ „ 17, p. 67.
286			„ „ „ „ 18, p. 67.
287			Unedited.
288	Foot-note, p. 399.	No. 551.	
289	No. 354.	„ 547.	
290	„ 355.	compare „ 560–564.	
291	„ 357.	„ 569.	
292	(Narnól) „ 358.		
293	„ „	„ 570–572.	
294	„ „	„ 568*a*.	
295	(Alwar) „ „		
296	(Sambhol)„ „		
		ISLÁM SHÁH.	
		A.H. 952–960.	
297			Ind. Ant., 1888, No. 19, p. 67.
298			„ „ „ „ 20, p. 67.
299			„ „ „ „ 21, p. 67.
300			„ „ „ „ 22, p. 67.
301			„ „ „ „ 23, p. 67.
302			„ „ „ „ 24, p. 67.
303			„ „ „ „ 25, p. 67.
304			„ „ „ „ 26, p. 67.
305			„ „ „ „ 27, p. 67.
306			„ „ „ „ 28, p. 67.
307			„ „ „ „ 29, p. 67.
308–310	No. 363	No. 621-622.	
311		„ 624.	
		MUHAMMAD 'ADÍL SHÁH.	
		A.H. 960–964.	
312			Ind. Ant., 1888, No. 30, p. 67.
313-314	No. 366.	No. 634-635.	

GOVERNMENT CENTRAL MUSEUM,
MADRAS.

HISTORY OF THE COINAGE OF THE TERRITORIES OF THE EAST INDIA COMPANY IN THE INDIAN PENINSULA:

AND

CATALOGUE OF THE COINS IN THE MADRAS MUSEUM.

With Twenty Plates.

BY

EDGAR THURSTON,
SUPERINTENDENT, GOVERNMENT CENTRAL MUSEUM, MADRAS.

MADRAS:
PRINTED BY THE SUPERINTENDENT, GOVERNMENT PRESS.

1890.

PREFACE.

In the preparation of the present work, which gives a general sketch of the early development of the East India Company and of its coinage, to which I have added a catalogue of those coins which are contained in the collection of the Madras Museum, I have received great assistance from Bruce's "Annals of the Honorable East India Company," Neumann's "Beschreibung der bekanntester kupfermünzen," and Weyl's "Verzeichniss von Münzen und Denkmünzen der Jules Fonrobertschen sammlung."

To the British Museum I am greatly indebted for casts of many coins which are not in the Madras Museum collection.

When recently in Europe I was able to procure from the coin-dealers many coins which are either rare, or, so far as I know, not to be obtained at all, in India at the present day. I then, too, became aware, for the first time, that Atkins' "Coins and Tokens of the Possessions and Colonies of the British Empire" was in the press, and to this book, which has since been issued, I acknowledge my indebtedness.

No attempt has been made by me to give a complete record of the various proof and pattern pieces, though some are referred to and described.

In 1887 I was engaged in going carefully over the records of the Madras Mint, from which such information was extracted as I thought to be of value and interest. The opportunity of examining, in like manner, the records of the other Indian mints did not offer itself; but it is to be hoped that this somewhat ungrateful task will eventually be carried out by numismatists in the other Presidencies.

The plates were lithographed by Kell and Son from drawings made by a Native draftsman. The coins figured on plates i to xvi are in the Madras Museum collection, which is wanting in those figured on plates xvii to xx.

EDGAR THURSTON.

January 1890.

I.—HISTORY OF THE COINAGE.

HISTORY OF THE COINAGE OF THE TERRITORIES OF THE EAST INDIA COMPANY IN THE INDIAN PENINSULA:

AND

CATALOGUE OF THE COINS IN THE MADRAS MUSEUM.

IN the year 1599 an Association of Merchant Adventurers was 1599.
formed to embark what Bruce says,[1] "was then considered a large stock on a voyage to the East Indies. The contract of these adventurers is valuable, from its being the first authentic deed which occurs in the annals of an East India trade; it is entitled 'The names of suche p'sons as have written with their owne handes, to venter in the p'tended voiage to the Easte-Indias (the which it maie please the Lorde to prosper) and the somes that they will adventure; the xxij September 1599.' The fund subscribed amounted to £30,133 6*s.* 8*d.*, which was divided into one hundred and one shares or adventures, the subscriptions of individuals varying from £100 to £3,000."

At "an assemblie of the committies or ye directors of the viage the xxvth of Septembr 1599" it was resolved that a petition shal be exhibited to ye LL. of her maes most honorable privy counsell in the name of the adventuror shewing ther honors that divers merchaunts induced by the successe of the viage pformed by the Duche nation [who] and beinge informed that the duchemen prepare for a newe viage and to that ende have bought divers ships heere in England, were stirred vp wth noe lesse affection to advaunce the trade of ther native cuntrey then the duche merchaunts were to benefite ther comon wealthe, and vppon that affection have resolved to make a viage to the Est Indias yf her maie wil be pleased to add to ther entention the better to pforme the enterprise, these severall petitions or Requests following, viz.:—

"To graunt to the adventures a priviledge in succession and to incorporate them in a companie for that the trade of the Indias being so farre remote from hence cannot be traded but in a joint and a vynted stock.

"That the shipping of the adventurors being prepared for ther viages be not staied vppon anie pretence of [anie] service for yt the stay of one moneth loseth the oportunetie of a whole yeres viage.

---

[1] *Annals of the Honorable East India Company from* 1600–1707-8, by John Bruce, Esq., M.P., F.R.S., Keeper of His Majesty's State Papers, and Histiographer to the Honorable East India Company. London, 1810; vol. i, p. 111.

"That it may be lawfull for the adventurors anie Stat notwth-standing to sende out forrein coyne, and yf ther shal be a want of forrein coyne to furnishe this present viage that ther may be quyned in her maes mynt so muche forrein quyne as shal be brought in by the adventurors or by ther meanes."

1600-1. On the last day of the year 1600, being the 43rd year of the reign of Queen Elizabeth, the first Royal Charter was issued for erecting an East India Company. By this Charter the Queen (upon the Petition of the Earl of Cumberland, and Two hundred and fifteen other Persons, among whom were several Knights and Aldermen of London, praying the Queen's licence to adventure and set forth one or more Voyages, by way of Traffic and Merchandise, to the East Indies, in the Countries and Parts of Asia and Africa, and to the islands thereabouts; divers of which Countries and Islands had been long since discovered, though not frequented in Trade and Merchandise) incorporated the said Earl and other persons, by the name of "The Governor and Company of Merchants of London trading into the East Indies."

On the 8th of October 1600, the following ships were taken up for the first voyage, and assigned over to five of the Committee of seventeen Directors, to whom the management of the business was entrusted, in trust for the Adventurers:—

	Men.	Tons.
The Malice Scourge	200	600
The Hector	100	300
The Ascension	80	260
The Susan	80	240
A pinnace	40	100

At a General Meeting of the Adventurers held in the same month (October 1600) it was resolved that the management of the concern should be conducted, in future, by twenty-four Committees or Directors, instead of seventeen. These twenty-four Directors were elected on the 30th October 1600, and Alderman Thomas Smith was chosen the first Governor.

The arrangements for the first voyage being nearly complete, the Society of Adventurers resolved "that the goodes shipped by the Companie, and the caskes, shall be marked with this genrall marke, as in the mergent, and that an iron be prepared, whch shall make the saide marke." This trade mark was subsequently reproduced on the copper coinage of the Company.

Concerning the earliest coinage of the Company Ruding says:[1] "By virtue of a Commission, dated January 11 in the same year (1600 or 1601), money was made of a kind unknown to the British mint either before or since her (Elizabeth's) time, for it was by law exportable, and intended for the use of the East India Company. It bore on one side the Queen's Arms, and on the other a portcullis; and was called either India money, from the purpose for which it was struck, or portcullis money, from the device impressed upon it. The weight of it was regulated according to the respective weights of the Spanish piastre, or piece of eight reas, and the half, the quarter, and half-quarter of the same (pl. xvii,

[1] *Annals of the Coinage of Great Britain and its Dependencies.* Third ed., 1840, vol. i, p. 353.

1–4), though they are now usually called the crown, half-crown, shilling, and sixpence. Some coinage of this sort was necessary, for the Queen, when she first incorporated the East India Company, would not permit them to transport the King of Spain's silver coins to the East Indies, though she was frequently solicited by the merchants. The reason which they assigned to induce her to grant this permission determined her to strike coins for the particular purpose of circulation in Asia. They represented to her Majesty that her silver coin and stamp were not known in the East Indies, which they supposed would induce her to grant them a licence to send thither what silver they pleased. The Queen and her Privy Council replied that, for the very reason alleged, it was her fixed and unalterable resolution not to permit them to send the coin of the King of Spain, or of any foreign prince, to India; and that no silver should be exported by her merchants but only such as should be coined with her effigies and picture on the one side, and the portcullis on the other, of the just weight and fineness of the Spanish pieces of eight and pieces of four rials.[1]

"Her prudent reason for this was that her name and effigies might hereafter be respected by the Asiatics, and she be known as great a prince as the King of Spain.

"Of this money, however, they were not to be permitted to export what quantity they thought fit, but only so much as the Queen and her Privy Council should approve of; for her Majesty declared that she held it as a special and chief prerogative of her crown and dignity to put the portcullis upon all the silver the Company should send to the East Indies; and that she would have her merchants, as to the quantity to be exported, subordinate to her will, and not her will to be ruled at the merchants' pleasure."[2]

The Crown or Piece of Eight Reals (pl. xvii, 1) bears on the obverse the English shield crowned in the centre, with the initials E.R. crowned at the sides, and the legend O: ELIZABETH: D: G: ANG: FRA: ET: HIB: REGINA; on the reverse a portcullis crowned, and the legend O: POSVI: DEVM: ADIVTOREM: MEVM. with chains. The Half Crown or Piece of Four Reals (pl. xvii, 2) and Shilling or Piece of Two Reals (pl. xvii, 3) are similar to the crown, except that they have HIBER: on the obverse; while the

[1] Notwithstanding this determination the pieces have her arms and not her portrait on the obverse.

[2] "*Violet's Appeal to Cæsar*, page 25, where he has given the figure of the piece of the eight reas, which he calls the true figure of the silver coin that Queen Elizabeth allowed the East India merchants to send to those Indies. He has also given the representation of three square weights (marked respectively India VIII testernes, India IIII testernes, and India II), as being the standard poises of the abovesaid coin remaining in his Majesty's mint, within the Tower of London, and in the custody of Sir William Parkhurst, Warden of his Majesty's said mint. See also *Folkes*, p. 61, and *Leake*, p. 255. Malynes says, that of these pieces were coined in the Tower of London for a trial (in January 1600) some six thousand pounds, which could not be made current in the East Indies, because the Spanish pieces of eight royals had been before that time counterfeited by other nations, which made the East Indians to doubt of our coin, although without cause. [*Lex Mercatoria*, pt. 1, chap. 35, p. 135]" Ruding, op. cit., p. 354, foot-note.

sixpence or Real (pl. xvii, 4) is similar to the half-crown and shilling, except that the legend on the obverse ends with REGIN or REGI.

1602. The first expedition of the Adventurers reached Acheen on the 5th of June 1602, and returned to the Downs on the 11th of September 1603, having on the homeward voyage taken in cargo at Bantam in the Island of Java, where the privileges of trade were acquired from the king, and a factory or house of trade was started.

1604. The following is a copy of a Commission of James I, dated 23rd of February 1604, authorising the East India Company to export the value of £12,000 in foreign coin:—

"James by the grace of God, etc. To all men to whom theise p'esentes shall come greetynge. Whereas our late deare sister Elizabeth by her l'res patents under the greate seale of England bearing date at Westm' the one and thirtith day of December in the three and fortith year of her raigne did uppon peticion made unto her by her deare and lovinge cosen George earle of Cumb'-land and divers other her welbeloved subjects for her royall assent and licence to be graunted unto them that they at their owne adventure costs and charges as well for the honor of this realme of England as for the increase of navigation and advancement of trade of merchandise within the same mighte adventure and sett fourthe certayne voyages with a convenient nomber of shippes and pynnaces by waie of traffique and merchandize into the East Indies in the countries and parts of Asia and Africa did incorporate the saide petitioners into a bodie politique by the name of the governour and companie of the marchaunts of London tradinge into the East Indies to have houlde and enjoy the sole benefit of the trade and trafficque of the saide Easte Indies for the space of fifteene years from the birth of our Lord God then last paste before the date of the said l'res patents. And whereas by the saide l'res patents licence is graunted to the saide governour and companie of marchaunts of London tradinge into the East Indies to t'ans-porte oute of this realme into the saide Indies in everie of their voyages duringe saide tearme of fifteene yeares all such forrein coyne of silver Spanishe or other forreyn silver or bullion of silver as they shall duringe the saide tearme bringe or cause to be broughte into this realme of England from the parts beyond the seas either in the same kynde sorte stampe or fashion which it shall have when they brynge it in or anie other forme stampe or fashion to be coyned in the mynte within the Tower of London soe as the whole quantyties of coyne or monies by them to be transported in anie their saide voyages duringe the saide terme doe not exceede the value of thirtie thousande pounds in any one voiage and so as the som'e of six thousand poundes at the leaste parcell of the same som'e or value of thirtie thousande poundes soe to bee trans-ported as aforesaide be first coyned within the saide Tower of London before the same shal bee transported in anie the saide voyages as by the saide l'res patents more at large appeareth. Nowe forasmuch as the saide governour and company of the saide marchants since the saide l'res patents to them granted have made one voyage in the saide East Indies and retourned their shippes from thence laden with sondry kinds of marchandize and have alsoe prepared and are readie to set forth another voiage into the saide East Indies and they the saide governor and company being desirous and endevouring by all good meanes to manage and carry their saide trade as neere as they can rather by the t'ansportac'on of the native com'odities of our kingdomes and by the bartering and exchange of them for forren com'odities then by using the benefit granted them by the said l'res patents for the carying out of so much tresure in every of their voiages doe content themselves in this p'esent voyage with the lib'ty of t'ansportac'on of twelve thousand pounds in forrein coyne without t'ansportac'on of anie other coyne bulloyn or silver and to that end have made humble peticyon unto us that they may t'ansport the saide value of twelve thousand pounds of forreyn coine without coyning the same or anie part thereof in our mynt within our Tower of London the rather for that they found by experience in their last voiage that they could not without great difficulty and some losse to the said marchants in the value of their monies newe coyned for that voiage make trade for their marchandize in the said East Indies because the said mony being stamped with the ymage and sup'sricpc'on of our said deare sister was strange and unknowne to the people of those parts and the monies now to [be] coyned in our said mint being to be coined with a new stamp of our owne ymage and sup'scripc'on will nott only draw them into the like hindrance in their trade when they shall come into the saide Indies but will cause their shipps which are nowe allmoste ready to depart in their voiage to stay and to be detained here to their further damage and hindrance untill new stamps for the coyning of the said monies in our mynt shall be graven and made for that purpose. Wee therefore favouring the saide marchants and being desirous to give them all furtherance and expedic'on in their p'esent intended voiage of our esp'iall grace ce'ten knowledge and mere moc'on have granted and by theis p'esents for our heires and successors doe grant unto the said governor and company of marchants tradyng into the East Indies that it shall and may bee lawfull for them their factors and assignes in thys p'esent intended voiage which is prepared or in p'eparing for the secónd voiage into the said East Indies to t'ansport out of this our realme of England all such forreyn coyne or silver either Spanish or other forrein silver as they have prepared p'cured or gotten or shall prepare p'cr'se or gett being already broughte or to be broughte from the parts beyond the seas before the dep'ting of their shipps out of the river of Thames so as the wholl quantity of the coyne and monies by them to be t'ansported in this their p'esent intended voiage being the second voiage toward the said Indies does not exceed the saide value of twelve thousand pounds the same to be t'ansported in the same kinde sort stamp or fashion as the said moneys is or shal be p'cured gotten or broughte into this realme of England and that withoute anie newe coyning or alte'ing of the said monies or anie part thereof from the stampe which it beareth. Anie statute restraint p'hibic'on in that behalf to the cont'ary in any wise notwithstanding. In witness whereof, etc. Witness ourself at Westim' the xxiijth day of February."

A quarter Real of James I, bearing on the obverse a thistle and portcullis with chains, and on the reverse an anchor-cross, is referred by Weyl to the Madras Presidency.[1]

1612. In 1612 trade was opened with Surat by Mr. Kerridge, who was well received by the merchants and inhabitants, but opposed by the Portuguese. The Company's ships were attacked by the Portuguese at Swally on the 29th of November 1612, and repulsed. In the following month a Firman was obtained from the Emperor of Delhi, allowing the English to establish a factory at Surat, where Captain Best left ten persons with a stock of £4,000 to purchase goods or provide an investment for him. The agreement with the Governor of Surat for allowing to the English liberty of trade at that port, in addition to other stipulations, contained one to the effect that the English should be allowed to settle factories at the cities of Amadevar (Ahmedhabad), Cambaya, and Goga, as well as at Surat.

1614. On the 14th of January 1614, in compliance with the wishes of the Company, King James I granted a commission to Sir Thomas Roe "to be Ambassador to the Great Mogul, or King of India." The Governor of Surat was dismissed, and a treaty concluded with the Mogul, in which it was stipulated, *inter alia*, that the English should have liberty of trade, and be allowed to settle factories in any port of the Mogul empire, specifying Bengal, Scindy, and Surat.

1615. Meanwhile the Company was making considerable progress with its commercial speculations on the Malabar coast, and Captain Keelinge, on his arrival at Cranganore in March 1615, obtained liberty of trade and permission to settle a factory; and it was agreed by treaty that the English and the Zamorin should join their forces, and expel the Portuguese from Cochin, which, when conquered, should be ceded to the English, they paying one half of the expenses of the expedition, and the Zamorin the other half.

1616. In the following year (1616) a Dutch ship was wrecked near Surat, and ten merchants were left there as the managers of a projected trade, the remainder of the officers and crew proceeding overland to the factory at Masulipatam.[2]

1625. In 1625 the English President and Council at Batavia submitted to the Court to direct their attention to the trade on the Coromandel coast, and dispatched a vessel to Masulipatam. Further, having obtained from the Naig, or Chief of the district, a piece of ground, the English erected a factory at Armagon, which it was intended to make a subordinate agency to Masulipatam.

1628. On account of the oppressions which the English factors at Masulipatam experienced at the hands of the native Governor of that port, it was resolved in 1628 to abandon the factory at that

---

[1] Cuartino (¼ Real, o.J.) Distelkopf, Fallgilter, an den Seiten mit Ketten versehen. *Rf.* Ankerkreutz mit ·.· in den Winkeln. Weyl.

[2] Note from "Hobson-Jobson" by Colonel Henry Yule and Arthur Coke Burnell, 1886. "1789. Masulipatam, which last word, by the way, ought to be written, Machlipatan (Fish-town) because of a whale that happened to be stranded there 150 years ago." Note on *Seir Mutagherin*, iii, 370.

place, leaving behind only one of the factors to recover the debts. The representation of the Agents at Bantam to the President and Council at Surat of the necessity of being supplied with Coromandel cloths, to furnish that station and the Southern markets with the means of increasing their investments in pepper and spices, had determined the Presidency to re-establish the factory
at Masulipatam, and to strengthen Armagon; and the necessary 1632.
authority to do so was obtained in November 1632.

A Firman was obtained on the 2nd of February 1633 for 1633.
liberty of trade to the English in the Province of Bengal, without any other restriction, than that the English ships were to resort only to the port of Pipley. This event marks the date at which the English first obtained the right to enter the Ganges, and those countries which, subsequently, opened up a most lucrative trade.

In 1639 Mr. Day, one of the Council at Masulipatam, was sent 1639.
to explore the country in the neighbourhood of the Portuguese station at St. Thomé, and reported that Madraspatan[1] was a situation, at which, in his opinion, the best coast goods could be procured. The land was purchased from the Raja of Chandragiri and, without waiting for orders from the Court, Mr. Day commenced building, at the expense of the Company, a fortification to which the name of Fort St. George was given. The continuation of this work was ordered later by the President and Council of Surat, and the new station, to which the factory of Masulipatam was transferred, made subordinate to Bantam.

The early gold coin of Madras was the *pagoda*, a word which, Moor says[2] "is a word altogether unknown beyond the corrupting influence of European colloquial example, whether used descriptively of a coin or a temple; the former being generally called by Hindus *Pun*.

"As to the word pagoda, applied either to a coin or a temple, to the latter especially it ought to be dropped as inaccurate and barbarous, and not at all used by the natives out of the reach of European tradition. I find an attempt to derive the word from *Mahomedan* authority, imagining that anti-idolatrous people to have called the temples of the *Hindus* by the debasing but accurate appellation of *bút-gáda*: from *bút*, an idol, and *gáda*, a temple. Bartholomeo says the coin, being impressed with the goddess Bhagavada, is, therefore, so called: pagoda being a corruption or abbreviation. But, admitting Bhagavada to be a name of Dévi, and to be borne by some *puns*, it would apply to such only; whereas we give it to all gold coins of about the value of seven or eight shillings, be the impression what it may. And, indeed, I have lately seen a silver coin, worth about four shillings, with the word *pagoda*, or half *pagoda*, in English, with

---

1 Note from Yule and Burnell, op. cit. "1672...... following upon Madraspatan, otherwise called *Chinnepatan*, where the English have a fort called St. George, chiefly garrisoned by *Toepasses* and *Mistices*; from this place they annually send forth their ships, as also from Suratte." *Baldævs*, Germ. ed., 152.

1726. "The Town or Place, anciently called *Chinapatnam*, now called Madraspatnam and Fort St. George." *Letters Patent*, in *Charters of East India Company*, 368-9.

2 Hindu Pantheon. Ed. 1864, pp. 310-11.

some oriental characters stamped on it, and a representation of a Hindu temple. This coin I imagine to be intended for Madras, and cannot but lament that so miserable a specimen of our taste and talents should be suffered to go forth. To say that the execution is worthy of the design is to stigmatise both with deserved reprobation." Writing about the Pagoda, Dr. Bidie remarks[1] "The common Tamil name for the pagoda is Varáha, an appellation due to the circumstance that some of the older types had on the obverse the figure of a *Varáha* or *Boar*, the symbol of the Chalukyas and kings of Vijayanagar, or the image of Vishnu in the Varáha *avatár*. The Hindustani name of the pagoda is *Hun*, a word probably derived from *Honnu*, the Canarese designation of the half pagoda. That the Mahomedans should have adopted this corruption of the Canarese term for the coin is explained by the fact that, when they invaded the Carnatic, they first saw the pagoda or half pagoda in the hands of a Canarese-speaking people. According to Sir Walter Elliot the term *varáha* is never used in ancient Tamil records in connection with money, but the word *pon*, which was a piece equal to the modern half pagoda, the pagoda itself being the double *pon*, which ultimately became the *varáha*."

Speaking of the Chandragiri Pagoda Marsden says:[2] "*Chandragiri* or Chandergherry, which gives name to these huns, is a town in the Karnatik, formerly the capital of what was called by our early travellers the kingdom of *Narsingha*, in consequence of its having been rendered a place of great strength by *Narsingha Rájá* of *Vijayanagara*. After the conquest of the latter city by the Mahometan States of the peninsula, in the sixteenth century, a descendent of *Narsingha* transferred the seat of Hindu government to *Chandra-giri*, from whence the last of the race was expelled in 1646. It was from one of these rájás that the English East India Company purchased, in the year 1620, the spot of ground on which stood the old fort and factory of Madras, now inclosed within the works of Fort St. George, together with the privilege of coining money, under the stipulation that the English should not fail to preserve on their coinage the representation of that deity, who was the favourite object of his worship. . . . . The female figure on the obverse appears to be that of *Lakshmi*. There are other specimens precisely resembling this as to the reverse, which have three erect figures (a male accompanied by two females) on the obverse, whose costume denotes them to be mortal rather than divine personages. These are vulgarly termed three-*swámi*[3] pagodas, and

---

[1] Journ. As. Soc., Beng., 1883, p. 35.
[2] Numismata Orientalia, 1825, pt. ii, p. 739, pl. xlviii, fig. mlxxvi.
[3] Notes from Yule and Burnell, op. cit.

"Swamy, Sammy, s. This word is a corruption of the Skt. suamin, 'Lord.' It is especially used in South India, and in two senses: (a) a Hindu idol; especially as Sammy, in the dialect of the British soldier. This comes from the usual Tamil pronunciation sâmi; (b) the Skt. word is used by Hindus as a term of respectful address.

"Swamy-pagoda, s. A coin formerly current at Madras; probably so called from the figure of an idol on it. Milburn gives Swamy-pagodas = 110 Star Pagodas. A '*three*-swâmi pagoda' was a name given to a gold coin bearing on the obverse the effigy of Chenna Keswam Swâmi (a title of Krishna) and on the reverse Lakshmi and Rukmini."

weigh 2 dwt. $4\frac{1}{2}$ grs. M. Tavernier's Plate Nos. 5 and 6 are imperfect representations of them under the name of the rájá of Carnatica's pagoda." According to Dr. Bidie[1] the standing figures on this pagoda are intended to represent Venkatesvara and his two wives. In connection with this coin Sir Walter Elliot writes[2]:—"The type of the first class (having the standing figure of Vishnu, with or without his two wives, on the obverse, and a granulated reverse) appears to have been derived from the favour in which the Vaishnava tenets were held by the later Vijayanagar princes of Chandragiri, the chiefs of Venkatagiri, and at the sacred shrine of Tripati. It thus came to be adopted by the European factories, and by the Nawábs of the Carnatic. Conspicuous examples of these are found in the *Star Pagoda* (*vide* pl. xi, 3) of the English East India Company at Madras, and in the *Porto Novo Pagoda* (*vide* pl. xi, 2) believed to have been first coined by the Portuguese at Porto Novo or Feringhipet, and at Arcot under the Nivayat Nawábs of the Carnatic. The huns of Sa'adut Ulla Khán of this type, who succeeded Nawáb Dáwad Khán, and died in 1731, are recognised by the Persian letters (*illah*) on the granulated reverse, which is replaced on those of his relative Safdar 'Ali Khán by the letter (*ain*). On his murder in 1741, the office of Nawáb was conferred by the Nizam on another family, that of Anwar-ud-dín-Khán, but his son Muhammad 'Ali received his investiture direct from Delhi, with the high-sounding title of Walaják Nawáb-ul-hind in 1766. In 1858 I received some information regarding his coinage with extracts of the mint accounts from the Dewán of the late Nawáb. By these it appears Walaják struck coins at other places besides Arcot, viz., Porto Novo, Trichinopoly, and Tiruvamur, and among the coins named are the *Walájahi*, *Kuruki*, *'Umdat-ul-Mulki*, *Star*, and *Feringhipet*.[3] Some of these I have not seen. The *Kuruki* is not uncommon. It has the three standing figures strongly marked, and a plain granulated surface. It and the *Star*, so called from the star impressed on the granulated surface, were probably coined at Tiruvamur, beyond the precints of the English factory, at which place the mint was said to be still standing in 1858. According to the Imperial Gazetteer the Madras mint was built

---

[1] L. c., p. 50.

[2] Numismat. Orient. Coins of Southern India, 1885, pp. 143-4.

[3] The mint records of Hijri 1186 = A.D. 1772 show that the gold coinage was —

Walajáhi	*pagodas*	$1,370\frac{17}{32}$
Kuruki	,, ...	$22,654\frac{11}{32}$
'Umdat-ul-Mulki	,, ...	$995\frac{31}{32}$
Star	,, ...	$3,81,052\frac{23}{32}$
Feringhipet	,, ...	$15,098\frac{7}{32}$
	Total ...	$4,21,171\frac{1}{8}$

The silver coinage for the same year was —

Arcot	*rupees*	7,230	12	9
Tirumavur	,, ...	2	3	0
Old Pondicherry	,, ...	0	10	6
	Total ...	7,233	10	15

within the walls of Fort St. George in 1723. But the factory must have exercised the right of coining at a much earlier period, for the Madras Public Records state that consignments of bullion despatched to Fort St. George on the appointment of Sir George Winter as Governor in 1661 were coined into pagodas in the Fort mint, of what denomination, however, is not stated.[1] Also that in 1688 a proclamation was issued forbidding the introduction into the factory of a counterfeit pagoda, fabricated at the Dutch mint of Pulicat[2] "of the same stamp, but not three-quarters the value of ours, which has raised great doubts and scandals upon our coin, to the depreciating it two or three per cent. below Pulicat pagodas, even in our city, by the Merchants and Shroffs to the great prejudice and discredit of our pagodas, and loss of our mint custom: it is therefore agreed and ordered that Proclamation be made in several parts of the town and city, prohibiting all persons whatever from advancing anything upon the Pulicat pagoda by exchange; and whosoever shall offend herein, to pay twenty pagodas for the first fault, and double for the second, and a twelve months' imprisonment for the third. Also that all persons be forbidden to send gold from hence to be coined at Pulicat mint, upon forfeiture thereof upon due proofs; and that the Justices of the Peace do appoint the publishing and affixing these orders in English, Portuguese, and Gentoo at several public places of the city." Still later, during the siege of Fort St. George in 1702, among other conditions of surrender, Nawáb Dáwad Khán demands the surrender of the mint."

In addition to the Three-Swámi and Porto Novo or Scott Pagodas, the old Star pagoda of Madras, or, as it is also called Company varáha or *Puli* varáha, was struck in the early days of the Company, but I am unable to find any reference which indicates its earliest date of circulation. It bears on one side a figure intended apparently for Vishnu with a star above the head, and on the other side a granulated surface with a 5-rayed star (pl. xi, 3). In this coin all public and private accounts were kept, and all dues and salaries paid for a number of years.[3] A brass coin of the same type is contained in the collection of the Madras Museum, to which I can find no reference in the Records, and it is possibly only a fraudulent imitation.

The double and single star pagodas represented on plate xi, figs. 4 & 5 are a more modern development of the old Star Pagoda, and concerning them Dr. Bidie writes:[4] "It is of this

---

[1] Wheeler, *Madras in the Olden Time*, vol. i, p. 32.

[2] As regards Pulicat Pagodas Tavernier says: "Figs. 3 and 4 is the Gold Money which the *Hollanders* coin at *Palicate*, which is a Fort they possess upon the coast of *Coromandel*. Those pieces are also call'd Pagods, and are of the same weight with the others; but for the goodness, I think they are better by two or three in the hundred, than those of the Kings and *Rajas* of the Country, or which the *English* make. I made this observation, being at the Diamond-Mines, and in other parts of the *Indies* where there is any great trade. For the first thing they ask you is, whether you have any Pagods of *Pelicate*; and, if you have, you speed much better in your business." Voyages through Turkey, Persia, and the Indies. London, 1678, pt. ii, p. 6.

[3] See Dr. G. Bidie, *Pagoda or Varáha Coins*. Journ. As. Soc., Beng., vol. 52, 1883, p. 51.

[4] L. c., pp. 51-2.

form that Moor in his 'Hindu Pantheon' says:—"this coin I imagine to be intended for the use of Madras, and cannot but lament that so miserable a specimen of our taste and talents should be suffered to go forth." In designing it the artist seems to have deemed it necessary to give some reason for the name *pagoda*, by putting on the reverse the figure of the gopuram of a Hindu temple, and he then surrounded this with stars to indicate that it was a star pagoda. Again on the obverse, to keep it in harmony with the old forms, he has introduced the figure of a Hindu god, which is apparently intended for Vishnu. There is no date on the coin, but it appears to have been first brought into circulation early in the present century.

Obverse.—The gopuram of a temple surrounded with stars, and the inscription in English "TWO PAGODAS."

Reverse.—Vishnu surrounded with dots, and the inscription "two pagodas" in Tamil and Telugu.

"Counterfeit specimens of this pagoda are very often seen in jewelry, but may usually be easily detected, as in the genuine huns the milling on the edge is oblique like a section of a rope, whereas in the forged ones the milling is like that on modern English coins. The coin as a whole is certainly a hideous production, but curious as perhaps the first departure from a native towards a European type."

There is in the Madras Museum a necklet made up entirely of single pagodas of the last type, but bearing the word DEITY above the gopuram instead of PAGODA, and having a straight milling instead of an oblique milling on the edge. I am unable to find any reference to similar coins, and they must, I think, be regarded as ornamental imitations.

In the year 1642 the first regular despatch was received by the Company from Bengal, Mr. Day recommending therein that the Court should establish a station at Ballasore, and declaring that it would be unwise either to neglect or desert the speculation of a trade in Bengal. Four years later the Agent and Council of Fort St. George were raised to the rank of a Presidency. 1642.

By the eleventh article of the Treaty of Marriage between King Charles II and the Infanta Catherine of Portugal, dated 23rd June 1661, the Crown of Portugal ceded and granted to the Crown of England the Island and Harbour of Bombay, in full sovereignty; and it was understood that this grant would enable the two Crowns to maintain their respective dominions in the East Indies against any future aggressions and encroachments on their subjects and trade by the Dutch Company. On the 27th of March 1668 the King, by Letters Patent, transferred the Island of Bombay from the Crown to the East India Company, granting the Port and Island of Bombay to the London East India Company in perpetuity, "with all the rights, profits and territories thereof, in as full manner as the King himself possessed them, by virtue of the Treaty with the King of Portugal, by which the Island was ceded to his Majesty, to be held by the Company of the King, in free and common soccage, as of the manor of East 1661.

Greenwich, on payment of the annual rent of £10 in gold on the 30th September in each year."

As regards the coinage of the Company during the reign of Charles II, Ruding says:[1] "The English merchants trading to the East Indies did in this reign strike silver money in India for the use of their factory at Bombaim, formerly a settlement of the Portuguese, but yielded up to his Majesty upon his marriage with the Infanta of Portugal in 1662. I have not been able to discover the time when the licence to coin this money was granted to the Company, but the earliest of the coins that are known bear date of 1678.

"The earliest coins for the use of the East India Company were either struck by our monarchs, or coined by their authority. Of the former kind were the portcullis pieces of Elizabeth in 1600-1.

"In the reign of Charles II the Company began, by authority from the Crown, to strike silver coins for the use of the factory at Bombay. They were fanams and rupees, all of which bore either the name, or some reference to the sovereign."

Writing further concerning the early coinage of the Company, Ruding says:[2] "Soon after the East India Company obtained territorial possessions in India, it began the exercise of that privilege, which in all countries, and in the East especially, has been considered the right and proof of sovereignty—the coining of money. The circumstances of the Company's coinage were, however, as anomalous as those of the Company itself, which, although to a certain extent possessed of territory, was for a long time obliged to conciliate the native princes, under whom mediately or immediately it held dominion, by professing to acknowledge their supremacy, whilst it still continued necessarily included amongst the subjects of Great Britain. It therefore adopted the policy of seeking the sanction of the Crown to its establishment of local mints; and at the same time it fabricated in these mints coins not in its own name in general, nor with English legends and devices, but in imitation of the established currency of the country, with inscriptions in the Persian or other native language, and in the name of the Emperor of Delhi, or some other Indian prince. The coinage of money on its own account appears to have commenced at Bombay, which island was held in more independence, at first, than any other landed possession. Accordingly in 1671 the Court of Directors gave instructions to their servants at Bombay to establish a mint upon the island, and a few years afterwards the measure was sanctioned by the Crown. A clause in the Charter granted in the 26th year of the reign of Charles II, dated the 5th of October 1677, empowers the East India Company to stamp and coin money at Bombay, to be current wherever the Company's privilege of trade in the East Indies extended, to be called by the name of

[1] Op. cit., vol. ii, p. 18, and foot-note, p. 112.
[2] Op. cit., vol. ii, p. 418.

rupees, pices, and budgrooks,[1] and to bear any such seal, impression, and inscription, as the Company should think proper, so that such moneys so stamped and coined should not be called or known by any other name or names of money current in the realm of England or any other part of the British dominions, the East Indies excepted."

Writing during the reign of Charles II concerning the money coined by the English in the Indies, Tavernier says:[2] "Figure 1 and 2 is the money which the *English* coin in their Fort *St. George*, or else at *Madrespatan*, upon the coast of *Coromandel*. They call them Pagods, as those of the Kings and *Rajas* of the country are called. They are of the same weight, the same goodness, and pass for the same value. Formerly the English never coined any silver or copper money; for in some parts that border upon the *Indians*, where they have factories, as at *Surat*, *Masulipatam*, or at *Bantam*, they find it more profitable to carry gold from *England* than silver; gold lying in less room, and not being so troublesome; besides, that by carrying gold they more easily escape the paying those customs which the Kings impose upon gold and silver. But since the present King of *England* (Charles II) married the Princess of Portugal, who had in part of her portion the famous Port of *Bombeye*, where the *English* are very hard at work to build a strong fort, they coin both silver, copper, and tinn. But the money will not go at *Surat*, nor in any part of the Great *Mogul's* Dominions, or in any of the territories of the *Indian* Kings; only it passes among the English in their fort, and some two or three leagues up in the country, and in the villages along the Coast; the country people that bring them their wares being glad to take that money; otherwise they would see but very little stirring, in regard the country is very poor, and the people have nothing to sell but *Aqua vitæ*, made of coco-wine and rice."

With regard to the tin money referred to in the last paragraph, I cannot do better than quote the remarks of Mr. T. G. DaCunha, who says:[3] "Tin coin was current in Portuguese districts round about Bombay, and the English of Bombay issued—it may be for the sake of uniformity—theirs of the same material. The specimens of the latter coinage which have hitherto reached us appear to have been struck between 1708 and 1773, subsequent to the

---

[1] Notes on Budgrook from Yule and Burnell, op. cit.

"Budgrook, s. Port. bazarucco. A coin of low denomination, and of varying value and metal (copper, tin, lead, and tutenague) formerly current at Goa and elsewhere on the Western coast, as well as at some other places on the Indian seas. It was also adopted from the Portuguese in the earliest English coinage at Bombay. In the earliest Goa coinage, that of Albuquerque (1510) the *leal* or *bazarucco* was equal to 2 reis, of which *reis* there went 420 to the gold cruzado."

1638. "They have (at Gombroon) a certain copper coin which they call *Besorg*, whereof 6 make a *Peys*, and 10 *Peys* make a *Chay* (*Shāhī*) which is worth about 5*d*. English."— *V. and Tr. of J. A., Mandelslo into the East Indies*, E.T. 1669, p. 8.

[2] Voyages through Turkey into Persia and the East Indies. Ed., London, 1678, p. 5.

[3] Contributions to the Study of Indo-Portuguese Numismatics. 1880, pp. 24–27.

Mutiny of the Bombay troops under Keigwin, the fusion of the old and new East India Companies into the United East India Company, and the creation of the three Presidencies ruled by Governors in Council, those of Calcutta, Madras and Bombay, each of them absolute within its own limits, until the appointment of a Governor-General for all India in 1773. It is true that, during the time of the Commonwealth, pewter was employed in coining farthings, and some *pattern* farthings of tin were also prepared in the reign of Charles I, and the early part of that of Charles II, which were made current in 1684, and continued to be coined until 1692, when this currency ceased. Those dates are, however, too early to account for the existence of the Bombay tin coinage, which appears to be an imitation, from reasons to be mentioned hereafter, of a similar Portuguese mintage . . . . . .
It was not only by the adoption of this material for their coinage, but even by the imitation of types and symbols, which were originally Portuguese, that the rising power of the English of Bombay gave a tacit proof of their appreciation of the inventive power of their allies and neighbours, the Portuguese, whose star was now declining, but were still masters of all the districts round about Bombay up to the year 1740. The Portuguese of Chaul had struck a copper *bazarucco*, bearing a sheaf of arrows and a bow on the obverse, and the Coat-of-Arms of the Kingdom on the reverse. This coin was issued some time prior to 1577, and must have been current in the environs of Bombay. This device is found engraven on one of the ruined gates of that once famous city. The gate was built in 1577, as testified to by an inscription, a fac-simile of which, with a lithograph representing the gate itself, is inserted in my work on that city.[1] The gate is surmounted by the well-known D. Manuel's terrestrial globe, three arrows in a sheaf, the Coat-of-Arms of the Kingdom of Portugal, and the Cross of the Order of Christ above them all. Here the globe denotes the power, the broad belt which encircles it being intended to represent the conquests and discoveries of the Portuguese throughout the world, and the three arrows tied together peace, which the Portuguese had enjoyed before the building of this part of the fortifications uninterruptedly for thirty long years, which was an unusual occurrence in those troublous times.

Now the three arrows tied together were engraven or represented not only on lithic, but even on numismatic monuments of the Portuguese in India. The English of Bombay copied this emblem on their copper pieces, bearing on one side a crown and on the other three arrows tied together, flanked by the letters *G* and *R* in italic for Georgius and Rex, with the legend *Auspicio Regis et Senatus Angliæ* below. To the Portuguese, who appear to have imitated this device from a Spanish coin current in Portugal between 1557 and 1641, called *real de prata*, or 'silver real,' it was an emblem of peace, to the English of Bombay probably a mere ornament, if not a meaningless type."

[1] History and Antiquities of Chaul and Bassein. Bombay, 1876, p. 81.

The following types of Anglo-Indian money were issued during the reign of Charles II[1]:—

1. Silver Rupee A.D. 1667.
Obverse.—Within a beaded circle MON. BOMBAY. ANGLIC. REGIMS. A°7° ; around A. DEO. PAX. & INCREMENTVM.
Reverse.—A shield with the arms of the Company within a beaded circle ; around IND. ORI. HON. SOC. ANG. (pl. xviii, 1).

2. Silver Rupee A.D. 1677.
Obverse.—In centre THE RVPEE. OF BOMBAIM with rosettes ; around BY. AVTHORITY. OF CHARLES. THE. SECOND. 1677.
Reverse.—In centre the Royal arms of England in a shield, and a crown above the shield ; around KING. OF GREAT. BRITAIN. FRANCE. AND IRELAND.

Coins of the same type were struck, with both plain and milled edge in 1678 (pl. xviii, 2).

3. Silver Rupee. Without date.
Obverse.—A shield of arms between two wreaths.
Reverse.—In centre PAX DEO within a beaded circle ; around MONETA BOMBAIENSIS.
(pl. xviii, 5).

4. A half Rupee with device and legends similar to No. 3.

5. A pattern Rupee, in the British Museum, bearing on the obverse a shield of arms similar to No. 3, and on the reverse C.R. 1673.

6. Copper Pice with device and legends similar to No. 1 and, as Atkins suggests, probably from the same die. The character of the letters on the obverse varies somewhat in different coins of this type, the legend being blundered in various ways, and reading, *e.g.*, ONET. ONBAY. NGIEG. GIM. A coin of the same type is referred to by both Thomas and Atkins, in which the legend reads MOET. BOMBAY. ANGLIC. REG. A°9° (pl. xviii, 3).

7. A copper Cash of the year 1678, bearing on the obverse an orb and cross inscribed 78, and on the reverse some undecipherable native characters, to the interpretation of which I have not been able to find any clue.

8. A Farthing of the year 1674, in the British Museum, bearing on the obverse CAROLVS A CAROLO, and on the reverse REX BRITANNIA, re-struck with the die for the silver rupee No. 2.

9. A lead coin in the British Museum of the year 1678 ?, mentioned by Thomas as having types and legends as in the silver rupees.

10. A pewter (*Zinn*) coin of the year 1675 referred to by Weyl as being of the value of 2 Cash, and having on the observe device and legends similar to the rupee No. 3, and on the reverse 2·75 (pl. xix, 4).

---

[1] *Vide* Weyl, Neumann, Atkins, and an article by Mr. Edward Thomas, F.R.S., in the *Indian Antiquary*, 1882.

11. Silver Coins, bearing on the obverse two C's interlinked, and on the reverse the figure of a deity (Vishnu ?).

Two different sizes of the silver coin of Charles II with the linked C's and figure of a deity, called by Atkins[1] the double and single Fanam, and of the type represented on pl. xi, 11-12, are still met with in the bazaars of Southern India. Of this type coins of three sizes, called respectively the double Fanam, Fanam, and half Fanam, are mentioned by Weyl, who calls the deity on the obverse "der Gott Swami." Another type (pl. xv, 8) of which the Madras Museum possesses specimens, and which I saw for the first time in the British Museum, differing from the preceding in the character of the devices, which are encircled by a ring of dots, was also struck. As regards the source from which the Fanams were issued, they are attributed by Weyl to the Madras Presidency, and Captain Tufnell writes[2]:— "It has usually been attributed to the Bombay Mint, though for the following reasons I am inclined to think it more probable that it is an issue of Madras, coined during Charles' reign. In the first place the *type* of coin connects it with the design imposed by the Vijeyanagar king on the Madras Mint; secondly, it differs entirely from all the known issues struck at the time in Bombay; thirdly, it fits in with the Hindu system of the South; and, lastly, it is occasionally met with in this Presidency, while, from inquiries I have made from collectors in Bombay, I find that it is rarely, if ever, found there."

1686. In consequence of fruitless negotiation for many years to obtain permission from the Native Powers to coin the country money, the Court in 1686 applied to the King for authority to institute a mint for this purpose, and his Majesty (James II) granted a new Charter, dated the 12th April 1686, by which all the former Charters were renewed and confirmed, and power was given the Company to "coin in their forts any species of money usually coined by the Princes of those countries, so that it be made agreeable to the standards of those Princes in weight and fineness, and so that they do not coin any *European* money; and it is declared that all such money so to be coined by them shall be current in any city, town, port, or place, within the limits of the Company's Charters, but not elsewhere." Thus authorised, the Court directed the President and Council of Fort St. George to take particular care that the coins, in stamps, inscriptions, and fineness, should resemble those issued by the Mogul at Rajahmahl, particularly the rupees, it being of inferior moment to offend that sovereign, in this respect, from the war which had been resolved on against his dominions. Application was, at the same time, to be made to the King of Golcondah[3] for

---

[1] Atkins' Coins of British Possessions and Colonies, 1889.

[2] Madras Journal of Literature and Science, 1888, p. 191.

[3] Extracts from a letter from the Company to Fort St. George, dated London, 24th December 1675: "As to the Piscash for the King of Golcondah, if it be not already done, we do hope with it you may obteyn our liberty to coyne silver Rupees and copper Pice at the Fort, which would be a great accommodation in our trade. But in this and all other Piscashes be as sparing as you can."

"Inconvenience having resulted from valuing the Pagoda at 8 shillings and the Rupee at 2s. 6d., order that in future in account the Pagoda be valued at 9 shillings, and the Rupee at 2s. 3d., but the soldiers to receive as many Fanams per Pagoda as of old."

a *Phirmaund*, giving his authority to the Company to coin rupees, and other money in the mint at Madras, and that this money might be current in his dominions; and in all future treaties with the Country Powers, an article was to be introduced, stipulating that the Company's coin should be allowed to be current in their territories. The Presidency of Surat were, further, directed to use such stamps, dies, and tools, as were common in the country, and to issue a coinage, which might facilitate equally the administration of the Company's affairs in Bombay, and their commercial transactions at the ports, where corresponding coins were current. Instructions were also given, relative to the mint at Madras, that this Presidency should make use of the country stamps and dies, under the King's authority, and coin small copper money, proportions of which were to be circulated at Bencoolen.

A silver Rupee of James II was struck in 1687, which bears the 1687.
following legends and devices :—

Obverse.—

Centre.— PAX DEO.

Margin.— BOMBAIENSIS MONETA. 1687.

Reverse.—

Centre.—Shield, with the arms of the East India Company (pl. xviii, 4).

During the season 1688-9 the Court received information that 1688-9.
a treaty had been made with the Moghul, and that Sir John Child had negotiated a Provisional Convention with Muchtar Khan, the Governor of Surat, by which the Company were allowed to coin money at Surat, in the Moghul's mint-house; but the Court preferred acting on the authority given them by their recent Charter, of having a mint at Bombay, as this would impress the Natives with the importance of the place; and they hoped that, in time, they would be able to supply the Bengal market with rupees coined at Bombay, or, at any rate, exchange their Bombay rupees for those coined at Surat, which would pass current in Bengal, or in any part of the Moghul's dominions. The Court, on this occasion, submitted the question to the consideration of the General, whether the coinage at Bombay ought not to include gold mohurs, as the Company had the Moghul's *Phirmaund*, and the King's Charter, to exercise this branch of delegated sovereignty.

Under the arrangements which were suggested about this time for making Bombay the seat of the Regency, Sir John Child was ordered to be specially attentive to the out-factories on the Malabar coast; the station at Retorah, in the Queen of Attinga's country, was ordered to be fortified, and the factory of Tellicherry strengthened. At the latter place were subsequently minted the silver coins, represented on pl. ii, 1-2 & pl. iii, 2-3, specimens of which in the Madras Museum bear the dates [17] 99 (?) and 1805 respectively. As regards the former of these coins Captain Tufnell says: [1] "I had always looked upon this 99 as being an abbreviated form of the date 1799, but ...... I have seen a small *gold* coin exactly corresponding to the one here described, but with the date 1801 in

[1] Madras Journal of Literature and Science, 1888, p. 192.

the exergue, the '99' still appearing at the top." The gold coin of the type here referred to is contained in the collection of the Madras Museum (pl. iii, 4).

1688-9. At this period (1688-9), when the affairs of the Company were generally unsettled, Fort St. George and Madras, which had recently been made a Corporation by Charter, were in a state of tranquillity, the mint was prosperous, and the Company's rupees were in considerable request, though, on account of their intrinsic value, they were melted down by the country people, under the idea of deriving profit from the sale of bullion.

1691. In 1691 the Court ordered the factories at Conimere and Cuddalore to be withdrawn, as a purchase had been made, from the Ram Raja, of a new settlement at Tegnapatam or Fort St. David. The gold coin known as the Porto Novo, Scott, Purunki, &c., pagoda, [pl. xi, 2] appears, says Dr. Bidie,[1] "to have been first struck by the Dutch, and to have had an extensive circulation. Subsequently it was copied by agents of the East India Company, as is evident from the following extract from a letter from the Madras Council to the Deputy Governor of Fort Saint David (near Cuddalore), under date the 21st July 1691.[2] "We doubt the Dutch will make a clamour at your coining their pagodas, and decry them all they can; however, make the experiment, but be sure to equal them in all respects both in fineness and weight and stamp, and we shall give them all the reputation we can here and to the southward, and, could you effect it, currently it would be of great service to the Honourable Company in their trade in those parts, but if you fail you must make another stamp."[3]

1693-5. A copper Cash is referred to by Weyl, and attributed to William and Mary, bearing on the obverse the monogram C.C. E. and on the reverse the date . . 95 (1695 ?); and copper *Faluce* or 20 cash are mentioned by Atkins, bearing on the obverse an orb and cross with the letters C.C. E. within a radiate border, and on the reverse the dates 1693 and 1695, respectively, with a wavy line above and below.

1698. In 1698 the Company acquired a grant from Azim, grandson of Aurungzeeb of Chutanultee Govindpore, and Calcutta,[4] and the fortifications at the latter place were increased, and called Fort William. Four years later the English East India Company and London East India Company, between which there had been great rivalry during the last few years, came to terms under the

---

[1] L. c., p. 51, pl. iii, fig. 21.

[2] *Vide* Garstin's Manual of South Arcot, p. 33.

[3] For further information as to the Porto Novo pagoda, see p. 13.

[4] Notes on Calcutta from Yule and Burnell, op. cit.

1698. "This avaricious disposition the English plied with presents, which in 1698 obtained his permission to purchase from the Zemindar . . . . . the towns of Sootanutty, Calcutta, and Goomopore, with their districts extending about 3 miles along the eastern bank of the river."—*Orme*, repr. iii, 71.

1702. "The next morning we pass'd by the *English* factory belonging to the old Company, which they call Golgotha, and is a handsome building, to which they were adding Stately Warehouses."—*Voyage to the East Indies by Le Sieur Luillier*, E.T. 1715, p. 259.

1726. "The ships which sail thither (to Hugli) first pass by the English Lodge in Collecatte, 9 miles (Dutch miles) lower down than ours, and after that the French one called *Chandarnagor*." *Valentijn*, v, 162.

title of "The United Company of Merchants of England trading to the East Indies," whose monogram, V.E I.C., is reproduced on many of the copper coins of the last, and early part of the present, century. The London Company agreed to transfer to the English Company, *inter alia*, their rights to all their several forts and factories, within the limits of their Charter, in the East Indies, viz., the factories depending on the Presidency of Bombay; or Surat, Swally, Broach, Ahmedhabad, Agra, and Lucknow; on the Malabar coast, the forts and factories of Carwar, Tellicherry, Anjengo, and Calicut; the factories on the coast of Coromandel, Gingee and Orixa, depending on the Presidency of Fort St. George; on Fort St. George and the City of Madras, Fort St. David, Cuddalore, Porto Novo, Pettipolee, Masulipatam, Madapollam, and Vizagapatam; the factories dependent on the Presidency of Fort William, or Fort William, Ballasore, Chutanultee, Cossimbuzar, Dacca, Hughly, Malda, Rajahmahl, and Patna.

From the Records of the year 1705 it appears that £12,000 in 1705.
bullion was sent out, to be coined into rupees at Fort St. George, and transmitted to Bengal to clear off all demands, and that President Pitt and his Council were censured for having allowed the demands of certain native merchants to be paid, with interest, without having previously ascertained the frauds, which had been committed by them in making up their accounts, and for having allowed Mr. Tillard to draw on the Court for the amount, at the rate of ten shillings and sixpence, instead of the current rate of nine shillings the pagoda.

In his Report in 1707 Sir Nicholas Waite, General, Bombay, 1707.
stated that the Arrack Farms had been placed in the hands of Agents, who were to manage them, because, when put up to sale, no person offered to take them; that the same method had been adopted with the tobacco farms, by which a gain had been made, this season of 22,328 Xeraphins. Concerning this species of money (Xeraphin), which is frequently mentioned in the early transactions of the Company, I cannot do better than quote the following extracts from "Hobson-Jobson":—

"Xeraphine, Xerafim, &c. The word in this form represents a silver coin, formerly current at Goa and several other Eastern ports, in value somewhat less than 1s. 6d. It varied in Portuguese currency from 300 to 360 *reis*. But in this case as in so many others the term is a corruption applied to a degenerated value. The original is the Arabic *ashrafi*, (or *sharīfi*, 'noble,') which was applied properly to the gold dīnār, but was also in India, and still is occasionally by natives, applied to the gold mohr.

1498. "And (the King of Calicut) said that they should tell the Captain that if he wished to go he must give him 600 Xarifes, and that soon, and that this was the custom of that country, and of those who came thither." *Reteiro de V. da G.*, 79.

1523. "Antonio de Saldanha . . . . agreed with the said King Turuxa (Turun Sháh) . . . that the said King . . . . should pay to the King our Lord 10,000 Xarafins more yearly . . . . in all 25,000 Xarafins.

Tombo da India, Subsidios, 79.

1598. "The chief and most common money (at Goa) is called Pardanne Xeraphin. It is of silver, but of small value. They strike it at Goa, and it is marked on one side with the image of St. Sebastian, on the other with 3 or 4 arrows in a sheaf. It is worth 3 testoons or 300 Reys of Portugal, more or less." *Linschoten* (from French ed., 71).

1610. "Imprimis of Seraffins *Ecberi*, which be ten *Rupias* a piece, there are sixtie Leckes." *Hawkins* in *Purchas* i, 217.

c1610. "Les piéces d'or sont cherafins à vingt-cinq sols piece." *Pyrard de Laval* ii, 40.

c1675. "Coins . . . . . of Rajapore. Imaginary coins. The Pagod is 3½ Rupees, 48 Juttals is one Pagod, 10 and ½ Larees is 1 Pagod. Zeraphins 2½, 1 Old Dollar.

"Coins and weights in Goa . . . The *Cruzado* of gold, 12 Zeraphins. The *Zeraphin* 5 Tangoes. The Tango, 5 *Vinteens*. The *Vinteen*, 15 Basrooks, whereof 75 make a *Tango*, and 60 Rees make a *Tango*." *Fryer*, 206.

1727. "Their Soldiers' Pay (at Goa) is very small and ill paid. They have but six Xerapheens per month, and two suits of Calico, stript or chequered, in a year . . . . . and a Xerapheen is worth about sixteen Pence half Peny *Ster*." *A. Ham.* i, 249.

In 1707 the Bengal Council sent to Madras a specimen of the new Emperor, Bahádur Shah's rupee, and desired that all rupées coined at the Fort for Bengal might be made to resemble it, as such coin only would be received or pass in Bengal, whereas at the Fort those rupees could not be circulated for fear, as President Pitt expressed it, of giving offence to Khan Buksh, the apparent King.

During the reign Queen Anne (1702–1714) copper coins were struck, bearing on the obverse the monogram $^{C.C.}_{E.}$ and on the reverse the date. The coins of this type, referred to by Weyl, bear the dates 1702, 1705, and 1709. Copper *Dudu* or *Faluce* (Atkins) were also issued, bearing on the obverse an orb and cross inscribed with the letters $^{C.C.}_{E.}$ within a radiate border, and on the reverse the date, with a wavy line above and below, within a dotted circle. Coins of this type, referred to by Atkins, bear the dates 1702, 1703, 1705, 1706 and 1709. A copper Pice, bearing on the obverse the English crown, and on the reverse the motto [AVSP] I [CIO] REGIS E ASIT AN NGLI, is also attributed by Weyl to the reign of Queen Anne.

1716-17. The Company's presuming to coin money drew down upon them, in the reign of William III. the high displeasure of the reigning Great Moghul, the Emperor Aurungzeeb, whom they had to appease by an explanation. Elphinstone in his "History of India," Vol. II, pp. 555, 556 mentions that A.D. 1693 Khazi Khan was sent to Bombay on this and various alleged delinquencies of the Company, "and that they explained their coining money in their own king's name (which was another complaint against them) by stating that they had to purchase investments at places, where the Moghul's money did not pass."

Marsden in his 2nd Vol. of Numismata Orientalia, p. 663, in his series of the coins of the Moghul Emperors of Hindustan, states:—"It was in this year of Farakhsirs's reign (fifth year, A.D. 1716-17) that the English East India Company obtained from him (through the agency of Mr. John Surman, factor, and Mr. Hamilton, Surgeon, with Khojal Serhad, an Armenian, as linguist) the memorable Firman or Edict exempting them from the payment of customs, authorising them to coin money of the Empire in the Island of Bombay, as had been usual at Chinnapatnam or Madras, and granting them the exercise of many other important privileges." In a note Marsden adds "it is dated the fourth day of the second month (1129), and in the fifth year of the reign (16th January 1716-17)."

A translation of it will be found in Frazer's "History of Nadir Shah," p. 45, and the details of many circumstances respecting it in Scott's "History of Aurangzeeb's successors," p. 139.

Auber in his "Rise and Progress of British Power in India," vol. I. p. 21, gives many particulars of this grant, which, however, Jaffier Khan, the Moghul Governor of India, manifested an indisposition to obey; and, in a despatch from the members of the Embassy, dated Coimbuzar, 15th August 1717, they say "we went ourselves to him, and showed him the Fhermand, and demanded the free use of the mint as before advised." Jaffier put them off, as they say "with a few sweetening words," and by a despatch of the directors, dated 16th February 1721, we find that up to that time the matter still remained as it had been; for then write the directors: "By all this we hope you will lay hold of the present opportunity to get the grants confirmed. First that of the mint." The "present" opportunity was probably the accession of a new emperor (Muhammad Shah), and in 1725 they had obtained the boon; for, in a despatch of the Directors, dated 5th December 1725, they say: "For the reasons by you given we permit you to rebuild your Silver Mint."

In 1717 the Company obtained the island of Diu, 37 townships in Bengal, which gave it the command of the river for 10 mile, S. of Calcutta, and had certain villages restored to it near Madras, which had formerly been given by the Arcot ruler, and resumed. The earliest coins of the Company in the Madras Museum which bear a date are a thick copper coin bearing on one side the monogram of the Company, and on the other the date 1722, and a smaller thin coin likewise bearing the monogram, and the date 1733. Coins of the latter type were also issued by the Dutch East India Company, bearing their monogram, V.O.C. (*Vereinigte Ostindische Compagnie*), to which a letter was frequently added, representing the initial letter of the mint town, e.g., P (Pulicat) and N (Negapatam).

The following copper or lead (*Zinn*) coins are attributed to the reign of George I (1714–1727):—

1. Lead. Double and single Pice—

Obverse.—The English Crown with G.R. above, and BOMB below.

Reverse.—The motto AVSPICIO REGIS ET SENATVS ANGLIÆ.

[pl. xvi, 8].

As regards lead coins of this type (of which the later issues bear the dates) struck during the reigns of the Georges, the writer of an article in the Numismatic Chronicle remarks [1]: "Ruding . . . gives engravings of a large lead piece from Bombay, which has no date, but, from the letters G.R. on it, he assigns it with probability to George I. I have a similar coin with the date 1741, weight

[1] Vol. xviii, p. 76.

1 oz. 6 grs., and another with date 1771, weight 15 dwts. 15 grs. and I have seen two pieces of similar type and metal half their size. The coins of 1741 came to me from Dublin: that of 1771 was found a few years since at Kinsali in repairing a house. These three specimens in lead, being of the reigns of George I, II, and III, from their succession, would seem to indicate some established and continuous purpose. It is unlikely that anything honorary would be struck in so worthless and easily injured metal as lead; yet, as they all bear the authoritative inscription "Auspicio Regis et Senatus Angliæ," we may presume, in the absence of any information, that they were current coin."

2. Copper Pice. Without date—

Obverse.—The English Crown with G.R. above, and BOMB below.

Reverse.—The motto AVSPICIO REGIS ET SENATVS ANGLIÆ.

3. Copper Pice. 1714—

Obverse.—The Company's bale mark, and date 1714.

Reverse.—A lion right, within a dotted circle.

Coins of this type, of three sizes, are contained in the collection of the British Museum (pl. xix, 5, 6, 7).

4. Silver three, double, and single Fanams, presumably struck for the Madras territories:—

Obverse.—Orb and cross inscribed, with the letters C.C. / E. within a dotted circle.

Reverse.—An undecipherable Indian inscription within a dotted circle.

[pl. xix, 1, 2].

5. Copper coins with device and legends similar to No. 4.

[pl. xix, 3].

"In 1725," says Sir Walter Elliot,[1] "the attention of the factory was attracted to the coinage of the rupee. It appears that the profits gained at the Madras mint on the coinage of silver had encouraged the issue at the native mints at Arcot, St. Thomé, and Covelong, of rupees inferior in standard, but of the same nominal value, so as to divert the flow of bullion from the Company's mint to their own. This led to stringent regulations prohibiting the export of bullion from the Factory, and to a reduction of the mint charges." On this subject Mr. Wheeler says[2]: "The first important matter which received the attention of Governor Macrae was that of the coinage of rupees at the Madras mint. It seems that the Native chiefs had awakened to the profit derived by the Madras Government from the coinage of rupees; and accordingly they had not only set up mints of their own, but, about this time, they contrived to make more rupees out of the same quantity of silver, than were made by the Company. For instance out of every hundred ounces of silver, the mints at St. Thomé and Arcot turned out to the merchant Rupees 266, annas 14; whilst the mint in Fort St. George only turned out Rupees 257, annas 7. Thus the merchant obtained nine rupees seven annas more for his hundred ounces of silver at St. Thomé and Arcot than he could

[1] Op. cit., p. 145.   [2] Op. cit., vol. ii., pp. 387—92.

obtain at Fort St. George. In other words the Madras rupee was 2 per cent. dearer than the rupee of Arcot or of St. Thomé. The consequence was that the merchants preferred coining their silver at the latter mints; and the Company found its custom decreasing. Accordingly Governor Macrae directed Messrs. Pitt, Benyon and Emmerson to enquire into the whole matter ..... It will be seen by the following resolution that Governor Macrae endeavoured to put matters to rights; 1st—by prohibiting the export of silver from the Company's bounds, and thus compelling the merchants to coin their silver at Fort St. George; 2nd—by lowering the Company's custom ½ per cent. and the mint charges ½ per cent., or altogether 10 rupees per thousand. Henceforth then the custom and charges at Madras would be 30 rupees per thousand; whilst the custom and charges at St. Thomé, Arcot, and Covelong would be nominally 21 rupees per thousand, but actually 31 rupees 11 annas per thousand. The original entry will serve to render the subject more intelligible.

"Monday, 8th March 1725. Messrs. Pitt, Benyon and Emmerson deliver in a report of the coinage, together with an account of the charges and customs collected at our mint, and those in the country; as likewise an account of the produce of a hundred ounces of silver of the fineness of the rupee in our and St. Thomé mints.

"This matter being fully debated, it was upon the whole agreed that no silver except rupees shall be permitted to be exported to any part of the coast of Coromandel under penalty of confiscation, half to the informer and half to the Company; and the Secretary do give notice hereof at all the public places in the town.

"As by the calculates and reports abovementioned, it appears that our rupee is two per cent. dearer to the merchants than the St. Thomé and Arcot rupee, it was further argued that we ought to find out some method to lessen the charge of coinage, that so we may bring it nearer to a par with the country coin; and it appearing that the Brahmins actually indisburse 11¼ rupees per thousand, and that they must have something besides for their trouble, it was plain their custom could not be reduced above a ½ per cent., which not being sufficient, it was agreed to strike off a half per cent. likewise from the custom paid the Company; which it is hoped will be approved by the Honorable Court of Directors for the following reasons:—

"First, that the present charge of coinage being 4 per cent. in our mint, and but 21 per thousand in the St. Thomé mint, nobody will bring any silver to us, but on the contrary carry it away thither; but that when our custom is reduced to three per cent., the difference will be so much less that probably we may have the greatest part of the coinage return to us, especially since our rupee is in greater esteem in the country than theirs.

"Secondly, that we shall receive orders from Europe in two years; and if our Honorable Masters shall disapprove hereof, which we cannot believe they will, it may be laid on again.

"Thirdly, that at present the revenue is sunk to almost nothing, so that should no more silver be coined here than has been for sometime past, the difference will be very inconsiderable; whereas should we hereby regain the coinage it will be very apparently advantageous to the Company.

"Lastly, that the Company will save ½ per cent. in the coinage of their own silver; which, as we coin one-third generally of what goes down to the Bay, will very near if not over compensate for the reduction of the custom on other silver.

These being the causes why it is thought necessary to lessen the charge of the coinage, it was recommended to the President to talk with the mint Brahmins, and bring them to an agreement for lowering the charge agreeable to the above resolve, which he accordingly promised."

To the time of George II, who reigned from 1727 to 1760, the following copper and lead coins must be referred:—

1. Copper double Pice.
Obverse.—The English crown, with G.R. above, and BOMB below.
Reverse.—The motto AVSPICIO REGIS ET SENATVS ANGLIÆ and the date (pl. xix, 8.)

2. Copper Pice—
Obverse.—The English Crown, with G.R. above, and BOMB and the date below.
Reverse.—The Bale mark of the Company.

3. Copper half Pice with device and legends similar to No. 2.

4. Copper quarter Pice of a similar type, but without the date, are referred to by Atkins.

5. Copper Pice (*Weyl*)—
Obverse.—The Company's shield.
Reverse.—The date 1742 (pl. xx, 1, 2.)

6. Copper Pice. (*Weyl*)—
Obverse.—The Company's shield.
Reverse.—MON. BOMB 1745 (?).

7. Copper Pice, bearing the Company's shield on both obverse and reverse.

8. Copper Cash.
Obverse.—The Bale mark of the Company.
Reverse.—The date (pl. i, 2, 4.)
The earliest date on coins of this type in the Madras Museum is 1733.

9. Copper *Dudu* or *Faluce* (Atkins)—
Obverse.—Orb and cross inscribed with the letters C.C. E. within a radiate border.
Reverse.—The date, with a wavy line above and below, within a beaded circle. [pl. i, 6, 7, 8].

10. Copper half Faluce of the same type as No. 9.

11. Lead double Pice.

Obverse.—The English crown, with G.R. above, and BOMB below.

Reverse.—The motto AVSPICIO REGIS ET SENATVS ANGLIÆ, and the date. [pl. xvi, 8.]

12. Lead Pice of the same type as No. 11.

The following extract from the notice of a Meeting held on Saturday, 5th September 1730, throws light on the origin of the "M. Pagoda." "At that Meeting the President observing to the Board what is recommended in the last general letter concerning the badness of pagodas, desires this affair may now be taken into consideration, and that the Assay Master may be sent for to assist with his advice. Mr. Weston was accordingly called in, and acquaints us that the pagodas grow daily worse; and that some he tried in May last were no better than eighty-three and a half touch; whereas they ought to be of the value of the Negapatam pagodas, which is eighty-five and three-quarters. The Board taking into consideration the danger the Company's estate is in, and that commerce must inevitably suffer if this uncertain money circulates longer unsuspected; and that, though we defer taking proper measures to prevent this abuse at present, at last there will be an absolute necessity to do it (may be, when it will give a much greater shock to trade); and likewise no time can be so proper as when the Company's cash is so low as now by the large draught sent to the Bay by the "Cadogan." We therefore come to the following resolution, in order to secure the Company's estate, which we hope will be sufficient to open the eyes of everybody else, who must otherwise be undone by their credulity. 1730.

"That a new pagoda be coined of equal weight and fineness with the Negapatam pagoda, and with the same stamp, only distinguished with the letter M on each side the image; which shall be current in all branches of the Company's business, and that no other sort shall be paid or received, except in the Northern investments, where the old Madras pagoda is only current. But as this resolution cannot be put in practice till we have a supply of gold from China and elsewhere to make a circulation, we declare that this order of the Board shall not be in full force till the First of May ensuing; when we are in hopes the Eastern ships will be returned, and the merchants have sufficient time to coin the gold they purchase into the abovesaid specie; which were we to insist upon before a supply arrives, they must be obliged to melt down the present coins, and be considerable losers in giving it a new stamp."

"From these extracts," says Sir Walter Elliot,[1] "compared, with the information of the Dewán, it appears that these Vaishnava *húns* were struck at the same time by the English, the Portuguese, and perhaps the Dutch, as well as by the Nawábs of Arcot, and though bearing the same name, were not confined to the same mints. Thus the *Star*, *Kuruki* and *Porto Novo* were struck equally at the factory and the Nawáb's mints, the latter being

[1] Op. cit., p. 145.

situate, according to the Factory records, at Arcot, St. Thomé and Covelong, but according to the Dewán at Arcot, Tiruvamur, and Porto Novo. By St. Thomé and Covelong are probably meant the obscure village of Tiruvamur. The *Porto Novo húns* I apprehend to have been first produced by the Europeans at that place, whence it came to be also designated as Feringhipet. When the influence of the Portuguese on the Coromandel coast was circumscribed by the Dutch and the Muhammadans, the mint appears to have passed into the hands of the Nawáb, who continued to issue *húns* under the name of *Porto Novo*, *Feringhipet*, *Negapatam* (where had also been a Portuguese Factory), and afterwards of *Scot pagodas*. Buchanan found in 1800 that at Pálghát "the accounts were kept in *Feringy* or *Porto Novo pagodas* or varahuns; *pudameni* [1] commonly called vir ráya fanams, and *cash*," and that there was a profit in bringing *Porto Novo pagodas* from Dhárapuram in Coimbatore to Pálghát, and carrying back *vir ráya* fanams."

1742. The following letter from Mr. Sidney Foxall, dated Fort St. George, 16th August 1742, furnishes us with a description of the process employed in the coinage of money in the Madras Mint at that time:—

"Honorable Sir and Sirs,

"It is a great concern to me to observe by an extract of the General Letter from England, that the Honorable Company should have the least shadow of reason to suspect that I have been any way negligent in my duty towards them; for I do assure your Honors, that I have at all times used my utmost care and diligence, as much as in me lay, to keep the minters to their weight and standard in all the moneys that have been coined since my time; and that I never discovered any attempt to adulterate the coin, but in the affair of Rangum with which I took care to acquaint this Honorable Board.

"The methods of coinage in the Tower of London differ much from what is used here; it being impossible to adulterate the gold and silver there after the Assay Master has tried them, being cast into bars, before the assays are taken. Those bars afterwards run through flatting mills, the money cut out with an engine, milled and stamped, but no more melted. The constant method here has been, first to melt the gold or silver, and break it into small grains or powder; the muster is taken by the Assay Master; after which (if of the proper standard), the grains or powder is distributed among a great number of coolies in several work-houses or godowns: who weigh every rupee and pagoda separate, and afterwards deliver them to other coolies to melt. Different persons receive them to flat, and others to stamp. By which method of working, your Honors must be very sensible, that, if it was not for some confidence which must be put in the undertakers, and the fear of punishment in such as should be detected, my utmost care and vigilance could not prevent from adulterations. The only check upon them, and what I frequently

---

[1] *Pudameni*, signifying new coinage, so called in contra-distinction to the *palaya mani* or ancient coinage.

make use of after the first trial, is to take muster of their moneys in their presence, to assay after it is finished, to let them see I have a watchful eye over them.

"What I have already said, with the present flourishing state of the mint, will I humbly hope induce my Honorable Masters to believe that I have not been any way negligent in my duty hitherto, and shall take my utmost care that they have no cause of complaint in future.

"I am,

"Honorable Sir and Sirs,

"Your most obedient and humble Servant,

"SIDNEY FOXALL."

Writing in 1794 concerning the method employed in coining money at the Bombay Mint at that time Lieutenant Moor says:[1] "Tippoo, from his coins being regularly stricken and milled, must have a regular die, which is an apparatus unknown in other parts of India. In Bombay there is no mechanical process either for ascertaining the value of the piece, or of giving it the impression. The manner is as follows: the metal is brought to the mint in bars the size of the little finger, where a number of persons seated on the ground provided with scales and weights, a hammer, and an instrument between a chissel and a punch: before each man's birth is fixed a stone by way of anvil. The bars are cut into pieces, by guess, and if, on weighing, any deficiency is found, a little particle is punched into the intended rupee; if too heavy, a piece is cut off, and so until the exact quantity remains. These pieces are then taken to a second person, whose whole apparatus consists of a hammer and a stone anvil, and he batters them into something of a round shape, about seven-eighths of an inch diameter, and one-eighth thick; when they are ready for the impression. The die is composed of two pieces, one inserted firmly into the ground, the other, about eight inches long, is held in the right hand of the operator, who squatting on his heels (the posture in which all mechanics and artists work; the posture, indeed, in which every thing is done in India, for if a man has a dram given him, he finds it convenient to squat upon his heels to drink it), fills his left hand with the intended coins, which he with inconceivable quickness slips upon the fixed die with his thumb and middle finger, with his forefinger as dexterously removing them when his assistant, a second man with a mall, has given it the impression, which he does as rapidly as he can raise, and strike with the mall on the die held in the right hand of the coiner. The diameter of the die is about an inch and a half, inscribed with the Great Moghul's names, titles, date of the Hejra, his reign, &c., but as the coins are not so large, they do not, consequently, receive all, nor the same impression. The rupee is then sent to the treasury, ready for currency, as no milling, or any farther process is thought necessary."

In 1742 a grant of liberty to coin Arcot rupees was given to the Company, and the following is a translation of a Sunnud under

---

[1] Narrative of Little's Detachment, App. note ii, pp. 499, 500.

the seal of Nabob Sadutalla Khan Bahadur, Subah of Arcot, dated the 4th November 1742:—

"To the Mutasadar of the country of Chennapatnam and Sircar of Trippasoor, belonging to the Carnatic of Golcondah and to their successors.

"Be it known unto all men that from the beginning of the year Fusly 1152, I have ordered a mint to be erected to coin pagodas and rupees in Chindadrepettah, belonging to Chinnapatnam; and the same to be under the power of Mr. Benyon, Governor of Chennapatnam, for the Company. Wherefore do you let the said Governor have and enjoy for the Company all the customs that may arise in the said mint. Observe this as a strict taukeed and perform it accordingly. Dated Ramazan 17th in the 25th year of the reign of the Great Mogul Mahomed Shah."

Translation of the contents written on the back of the foregoing Sunnud.—"Ordered that a mint may be erected in Chindadreepettah belonging to Chinnapatnam for coining pagodas and rupees, and it may be commenced from the beginning of the year Fusly 1152, and to be under the power of Mr. Benyon, Governor of Chennapatnam, for the Company.

"His Excellency's order by his handwriting is to draw a Sunnud to the following purpose:

"'That Andiappah Naick, Dubash of the Governor of Chennapatnam, represented that the Governor desires liberty to erect a mint in Chindadreepettah belonging to Chennapatnam for coining pagodas, rupees, &c., and that we should free them from paying us the customs arising thereby, and let the same be applied to the said Governor for the Company; a sunnud is granted for that purpose."

Entered in the Book 19th Moon Ramazan, in the 25th year of the reign of the Great Mogul Mahomed Shah, which is the 4th November 1742.

1746. In 1746 a French fleet, commanded by La Bourdonnais arrived off Madras, which surrendered, but was restored to the English by the treaty of Aix-la-Chapelle two years later.

1756. In 1756 Siráj-ad-daula (Surajah Dowlah), then a youth of only eighteen years, marched upon and took Calcutta with a large army, but the city was retaken by Clive and Watson at the beginning of the following year. "The establishment of an independent coinage in Bengal," says Ruding,[1] "was of later date than at the other presidencies. For some time subsequently to their purchase of the zemindary of Calcutta, the only indulgence granted to the Company was the privilege of having their bullion coined at the mints of the Nawab of Bengal, which were at Patna, Dacca, and Murshedabad. After the capture of Calcutta a right to establish a mint of their own was one of the stipulations in the treaty with Suraj-ad-Doula, dated 7th February 1757."

1758. In 1758 Clive was appointed by the Court of Directors the first Governor of all the Company's settlements in Bengal. After a war, which continued fitfully for many years, Colonel (afterwards Sir Eyre) Coote won the decisive victory of Wandewash over the

[1] Op. cit., vol. ii., p. 418.

French General Lally and invested Pondicherry, which capitulated in 1761.[1]

In the year 1760 George III came to the throne. Many of the coins struck during his long reign (1760-1820) are still met with in large numbers in the bazaars, but the following copper and lead coins are worthy of special reference on account of their scarceness :— 1760.

1. Copper Double and Single Pice.
   Obverse :—The English crown, with G.R. above, and BOMB and the date below.
   Reverse :—The Bale Mark of the Company. (pl. xv, 1).

2. Copper half Pice. Of the same type as No. 1.

3. Bombay Pice.
   Obverse :—The Bale Mark of the Company.
   Reverse :—1 PICE BOMBAY, and the date (1773 and 1777). (pl. xv, 3).

4. Copper half Pice.
   Obverse :—The Bale Mark of the Company.
   Reverse :—½ (pl. xix, 9).

5. Lead double Pice.
   Obverse :—The English crown, with G.R. above, and BOMB below.
   Reverse :—The motto AVSPICIO REGIS ET SENATVS ANGLIÆ, and the date.

6. Lead Pice. Of the same type as No. 5.

7. Lead half Pice.
   Obverse :—The Bale Mark of the Company.
   Reverse :—½ PICE. (pl. xix, 10).

8. Lead quarter Pice. Of the same type as No. 7, but with the value ¼.

9. Copper quarter Pice.
   Obverse :—C.C. 1813.
   Reverse :—PI ¼ CE.
   (pl. xx, 3).

10. Copper. Two Annas.
    Obverse :—PATNA POST TWO ANNAS and the date.
    Reverse :—Value of the coin in Persian.

11. Copper. One Anna.
    Same as No. 10, except the value ONE ANNA.
    (pl. xx, 8).

---

[1] Notes on Pondicherry from Yule and Burnell, op. cit.
"Pondicherry. This name of what is now the chief French settlement in India, is *Pudu-ch'chēri*, 'New Town,' more correctly *Pudu-vai*, C.P. Brown however says it is *Pudi-cherū*, 'New Tank.' The natives sometimes write it Phulcheri."

1780. "An English officer of rank, General Coote, who was unequalled among his compeers in ability and experience in war, and who had frequently fought with the French of Phoolcheri in the Karnatik, and had as often gained the victory over them......" *H. ob. Hyder Naik*, 413.

1763. On the 15th of January 1763 Major Carnac, who commanded the English forces, marched against the prince, Sháh Álum, and attacked and beat him. "He pursued the prince very closely for some days, till the latter found himself so straightened, that he offered to throw himself upon the protection of the English, which was accepted, and on the 8th of February he joined the English camp, and proceeded with them to Patna. The province of Allahabad, including the district of Corah, estimated at the yearly revenue of twenty-two lacks of rupees, was assigned to him in guarantee by the Company; and, in addition, to render his establishment splendid, the British Governor, in behalf of the Company, agreed to pay into his Majesty's treasury the annual sum of twenty-six lacks of rupees from the revenues of Bengal." [1]

Describing a rupee of Sháh Álum struck in 1176 (A.D 1762-3), and bearing on one side the inscription

ضرب كلكته سنه جلوس ... ۴

"struck at Calcutta in the 4th year of the auspicious reign," Marsden says: [2] "This rupih was evidently struck at the period when Sháh Alum, after the defeat of his army, consented to place himself under the protection of the English Government, and to receive an assignment of certain revenues for his support. It is perhaps the earliest that expresses the name of Calcutta, and its weight accords with the regulated standard. The work is creditable to the new mint."

1765. In 1765 it was agreed by the articles of a Treaty and Agreement concluded between the Governor and Council of Fort St. William on the part of the English East India Company and the Nabob Nudjum ul Dowla "that the books of the Circar shall always be kept, and the business conducted at Moorshedabad, and that shall as heretofore be the seat of my government, and wherever I (Nabob Nudjum ul Dowla) am, I consent that an English gentleman shall reside with me to transact all affairs between me and the Company, and that a person of high rank shall also reside on my part at Calcutta to negotiate with the Governor and Council.

"I will cause the rupees, coined in Calcutta, to pass in every respect equal to the Siccas [3] of Moorshedabad, without any deduction of Batta; and whosoever shall demand Batta shall be punished. The annual loss on coinage, by the fall of Batta, on the issuing of the new Siccas, is a very heavy grievance to the country; and after mature consideration, I will, in concert with the Governor and Council, pursue whatever may appear the best method for remedying it."

---

[1] Francklin's History of the Reign of Sháh Álum, p. 25.

[2] Numismat. Orient., 1825, pt. ii, p. 677.

[3] Note on the word Sicca from Yule and Burnell, op. cit.

"The term *Sicca* (sikkhá, from Arab. *sikka*, 'a coining die,'—and 'coined money,'—whence P. *sikka zadan* to coin) . . . ."

1683. "Having received 25,000 rupees Siccas for Rajamaul."—*Hedges*, MS., April 4.

1705. "Les roupies Sicca valent à Bengale 39 sols."—*Luillier*. 255.

1779. "In the 2nd Term, 1779, on Saturday, March 6th, 'Judgment was pronounced for the plaintiff. Damages fifty thousand Sicca rupees.'"

On the 12th of August 1765, the Emperor Sháh Álum granted to the Company "the Dewanee of the provinces of Bengal, Behar and Orissa as a free gift and Ultumgau, without the association of any other person, and with an exemption from the payment of the customs of the Dewanee, which used to be paid by the Court . . . . . ."

In 1765 pattern gold mohurs, half, and quarter mohurs, were struck, bearing on the obverse a shield and the inscription ENGLISH EAST INDIA COMPANY, and on the reverse the inscription BOMBAY 1765. These pattern pieces (pl. xx, 4) I have seen in the collections of the British Museum and Mr. H. Montagu. In 1770 a pattern gold mohur was struck, bearing on the obverse the inscription BOMBAY 1770 15 RUPS, and on the reverse a Persian inscription. (pl. xx, 5.)

In 1767 commenced the first of the Mysore wars, of which the 1767.
last terminated with the capture of Seringapatam and death of Tippoo Sultán in 1799. The interesting fact is mentioned by Lieutenant Moor[1] with reference to a Bombay half pice coined in England for the use of the island, on which is the Honorable Company's mark, that "this mark is put upon everything that the Company send to India, and Tippoo, seeing it on their musquets, has imitated it on his; and on the butt, lock, barrel, and bayonet, is the mark, in which, instead of V.E.I.C., *United East India Company*, we see *Hydr*, Tippoo's father's name, in Persian. He put it also upon his cannon."

In his work "The principles of money applied to the present state of the coin of Bengal," Sir James Steuart says: "It has been observed that this coin, called gold mohurs, had been formerly coined at Delhi, of the same weight and fineness with the Sicca rupee of Bengal and other countries of Hindustan; but that they passed conventionally, having no legal *denomination*. In 1766 . . . . . it was proposed as an expedient for augmenting the currency of specie to make a coinage of gold . . . . . . , and the directors of this operation, pitching upon fifteen Arcot rupees as the value of one gold mohur, instead of estimating the value of these fifteen Arcot rupees by the fine metal contained in them, estimated them by their current value, which was above the proportion of their intrinsic worth. Not satisfied with this first deviation from principles, they added to the mohur (already over-rated in its proportion to the fifteen silver Arcot rupees) no less than 8 per cent. extra denomination, entirely arbitrary. So when this gold currency came abroad, it proved to be no less than 17½ per cent. worse in payments than silver rupees of Bengal, Madras, Bombay, and Surat.

"The people of that country (Bengal) had been so long accustomed to silver coin, that they never would, except when forced to it, receive the mohurs in payment. So the Company was obliged to make a new regulation in 1769, little better than the former. At last the gold currency fell altogether to many per cent. below its intrinsic value."

---

[1] Narrative of Little's Detachment, App. p. 478, pl. ii, 14, 15.

In his 'Voyages to the East Indies' I. Splinter Stavorninus, Rear Admiral in the service of the States General, says [1] of the coinage of Bengal, which presidency he visited between the years 1768 and 1771: "The only current coins in *Bengal*, and the whole extent of *Indostan*, are gold and silver rupees. All foreign gold and silver, whether coined or in bullion, is carried to the mint, and transformed into rupees, which are stamped with Persian letters instead of any portrait or arms. They decrease every year in value, and at the end of nine years the *sicca* rupees are taken at the same rate as *Arcot* rupees. When the rupees first come from the mint, they are called *sicca* rupees of the first year. Those which are coined at *Moorshedabad* are the current coin in which the trade of the Company is carried on, and by which all the other rupees in circulation here are reduced. It is divided into sixteen *annas;* its intrinsic value in Dutch money is one gilder, four stivers and a half, and it is taken in the Company's books at twenty-five stivers; but in Indian currency at thirty-one stivers and a half, for which it is current at *Hougly*. It is the money of account, according to which the value of the other rupees is calculated at a discount or agio, which is called *batta*, of from six to twelve per cent., which undergoes continual fluctuations, by the management of the money-changers. The *Arcot* rupees, which are coined by the English at *Arcot*, and by the French at *Pondicherry*, go for thirty stivers, yet the last are reckoned from one to three per cent. better than the former.

"The gold rupee, which is called *mohur*, is worth fifteen silver *sicca* rupees.

"Halves, fourths, eighths, and sixteenths of rupees are likewise coined; the last, as above said, are called *annas*.

"Copper coin is not seen in *Bengal*. For change they make use of the small sea-shells called cowries,[2] eighty of which make a *poni*, and sixty or sixty-five *ponis*, according as there are few or many cowries in the country, make a rupee. They come from the *Maldive* Islands. The money-changers sit upon all the *bazars* with quantities of them to furnish the lower orders with change for the purchase of necessaries. One hundred thousand rupees make what is called a *lack*, and one hundred lacks or ten millions of rupees a *crore*."

As regards the coinage current at Surat Stavorninus says: [3] "The coins that are current here are of gold, silver, and copper.

---

[1] Ed. London, 1798, vol. i, p. 460.

[2] Note on cowries from Yule and Burnell, op. cit.

1753. "Our Honorable Masters having expressly directed ten tons of cowries to be laden in each of their ships homeward bound, we ordered the Secretary to prepare a protest against Captain Cooke for refusing to take any on board the Admiral Vernon." M. *Long*. 41.

1780. "We are informed that a copper coinage is now on the carpet...... it will be of the greatest use to the public, and will totally abolish the trade of cowries, which for a long time has formed so extensive a field for deception and fraud." Hicky's *Bengal Gazette*.

1803. "I will continue to pay without demur, to the said Government, as my annual peskush or tribute 12,000 *kahuns* of cowries in three instalments as specified herein below." *Treaty Engagement* by the Rajah of Kitta Keonghur, a tributary subordinate to Cuttack, 16th December 1803.

[3] Op cit., vol. iii, p. 8.

The coin of gold of the country is the *mohur*, which is gold of twenty-three carat; it goes here for fifteen silver rupees, though its value is not constantly the same, but is settled according as gold is at a high or at a low price. All foreign gold coins are only taken according to their weight and intrinsic value.

"Ducats are likewise met with here, but no one is obliged to receive them in payment contrary to his inclination; they are distinguished into three sorts: the Venetian ducats, which are worth from $4\frac{1}{4}$ to $4\frac{5}{16}$ rupees, or f. 6-7 to 8 stivers; all other European ducats, to which they give the appellation of *images*, and which are current at from $4\frac{1}{8}$ to $4\frac{3}{16}$ rupees, or f. 6-3 to 5 stivers; and the third or last sort, those of *Constantinople* or *Stambouli*, among which are comprehended all other Turkish, Arabian, and Persian ducats, and which go at from $3\frac{7}{8}$ to $3\frac{15}{16}$ rupees, or f. 5-16 to 18 stivers. The value of these coins is lowered or enhanced in proportion as more or less gold is imported.

"The silver rupee is the standard coin of the country, the only one which is struck in the empire of Hindostan, and is current all over it; its real value in Dutch money is scarcely four and twenty stivers, but here, among the Europeans, it is calculated at thirty stivers; every rupee contains sixteen *annas*, but the calculation by *annas* is not so common here as in *Bengal;* the fractions of rupees are generally settled by *pice*, which is the only copper coin here, and of which more or less go to a rupee in proportion as copper is at a low or at a high price; when I was at Surat, sixty-four *pice* were given for a rupee; it is said that there are also leaden *pice*, but I saw none of them.

"In the same way as cowries are made use of in *Bengal*, as the lowest medium of exchange, almonds, which are called *badams*, are employed for that purpose here; the comparative value whereof is, as may easily be conceived, more liable to variation than any other representative medium.

"No other money is current here, and all foreign coins are taken according to their weight and assay; but the Mexican dollars, or pieces of eight, known among the natives by the appellation of *raal lakria*, must, if weight, contain seventy-three *waals:* their value is uncertain, running from f. 318 to f. 324 per hundred, and some times, but seldom, a little higher."

A double rupee, bearing the date ۱۱۹۴ (A.D. 1780), is described by Marsden[1] bearing on the obverse the inscription

سکه مبارك عالم گیر بادشاه غازی

and on the reverse the inscription

ضرب مچهلی پٹن سنہ جلوس ۲۱

"Struck at *Mechli-pattan* (Masulipatam) in the 21st year of the auspicious reign," concerning which he says: "This extraordinary coin presents a still more unaccountablo anomaly than any that has yet been noticed in the produce of the Anglo-Indian Mint. The numeral characters for the year 1194 are distinct, and, with due regard to consistency, it is of the 21st year of the reign, which can be no other than that of *Shâh Alum.* But it bears the

---

[1] Numismat. Orient., 1825, part ii, p. 685.

name (and his only) of *Alum-gīr* ; being either that of his father, who reigned not quite six years, and was put to death in 1173, or of the great *Aureng-zéb*, who died in 1118. Whether this discreditable anachronism proceeded from inattention or design, it would now be difficult to ascertain. The piece is a well executed double rupih, conied at a city within the English jurisdic-
1792-4. tion on the Coast of Coromandel, usually named Masulipatam."

In the years 1792—4 the following proof copper coins, which never came into circulation, were struck:—

1 and 2. Pice and Half Pice.

Obverse:—The Bale mark of the Company with the date 1792 below.

Reverse:—A balance with the word عدل between the scales.

These coins are hexagonal in shape.

3. *Obverse* and *Reverse*:—The Persian legend سکہ کمپنی ۱۷۹۳ عیسوی in the centre within a thick rim incused ENGLISH EAST INDIA COMPANY.

The edge is inscribed with the legend ENGLISH UNITED EAST INDIA COMPANY. (pl. xx, 6).

4. *Obverse*:—The crest of the Company with the value 48 TO ONE RUPEE and the motto AUSPICIO REGIS ET SENATVS ANGLIÆ incused upon a thick rim.

Reverse:—Similar to No. 3.

No. 5. *Obverse*:—The Bale mark of the Company with the date 1794 below.

Reverse:—سکہ کمپنی ۱۷۹۳ عیسوی without a thick rim, or English legend.

1793. In 1793 a regulation was passed, by which the gold and silver coin in Bengal, Behar, and Orissa was reformed, and the currency of any gold or silver coin in those provinces, but the nineteenth sun gold mohur, and their respective division into halves and quarters was prohibited.

In this regulation it is stated that "upon the mints at Patna, Dacca, and Moorshedabad being withdrawn soon after the commencement of the Company's administration, the proprietors and farmers of land in the interior parts of the country, who were bound by their engagements to pay the public revenue in sicca rupees, experienced considerable difficulty in obtaining those rupees from the coinage of them being confined to Calcutta, at which place the only mint that remained in the provinces was established; they were, in consequence, compelled to collect the rents from the ryots in the species of sonaut, or other old rupees, of which there happened to be the greatest number in their respective districts, and which they were permitted to pay into the public treasuries at a fixed exchange. In consequence of the ryots being required to pay their rent in a particular sort of rupee, they of course demanded it from the manufacturers in payment for their grain or raw materials; whilst the manufacturers, actuated by similar principles with the ryots, required the same species of rupee from the traders who came to purchase their cloth or other commodities. The various sorts of old rupees, accordingly, soon became the established currency of particular districts ; and, as a necessary consequence, the value of each rupee was enhanced in the district in which it was current, from being in demand for all transactions. As a further consequence, every other sort of rupees brought into the district was rejected, from being a different measure of value from that by which the inhabitants had become accustomed to estimate their property ; or, if it was received, a discount was exacted upon it, equal to what the receiver would have been obliged to pay upon exchanging it at the house of a shroff for the rupee current in the district, or to allow upon passing it in payment to any other individual. Thus if a sicca rupee of the nineteenth sun, which is intrinsically worth about seven per cent. more than an Arcot, was offered in payment in the Dacca Province, it was either refused, or received nearly at the same value as an Arcot; whilst the holders of Arcots, or other sorts of rupees, who carried them into districts in which they were not current were subject to similar loss . . . . . . The money-changers are the only description of people who derive any benefit from this disordered state of the coin. The loss falls upon Government and the public at large, and must be perpetual, unless the various old and counterfeit rupees now current in the different parts of the country can be thrown out of circulation, and one species of rupee made the general standard measure of value in all transactions between individuals and between Government and its subjects. The sicca rupee of the nineteenth sun is the established coin of the country, and the rupee in which the public revenues are payable. It was with a view to render it the general measure of value, that Government determined, in the year 1773, that all rupees coined in future should bear the impression of the nineteenth sun or year of reign of the Sháh Alum, and no other species of rupee (with the exception of some Arcots) has since been coined in the Calcutta Mint. The rupees of the eleventh, twelfth, and fifteenth sun were indeed directed to be considered current equally with the nineteenth sun sicca rupee ; but this was a temporary measure, intended to be continued in force only until there should be a sufficiency of the nineteenth sun sicca rupee introduced into circulation ....The preceding remarks evince, that it is in the interest of individuals of every description, except the money-changers, to co-operate with the Government to render the nineteenth sun sicca rupee generally current, and the standard of value throughout the country. Among the measures considered necessary to effect this important object, the following were the principal: First, to direct the officers employed in the provision of the investment, and manufacture of salt, and all commercial transactions of the Company, to make their agreements with individuals for sicca rupees of the nineteenth sun.........Secondly, to oblige individuals to estimate their property by the nineteenth sun sicca rupee.........Thirdly, to prohibit the receipt of any rupees, excepting siccas of the nineteenth sun, at the public treasuries after the date above alluded to.........Fourthly, to establish mints at the cities of Patna, Dacca, and Moorshedabad, to coin precisely the same rupee as that struck at Calcutta......... By the operation of these rules the various sorts of old and light rupees must, in course of time, fall to their intrinsic worth compared with the sicca of the nineteenth sun, as they will produce no more in the mint, and to which they will necessarily be brought to be converted into siccas, as they will be nowhere passable or in demand as coin, from being nowhere a measure of value. The rules by which the gold coin has been regulated have been productive of evils, similar to those which have prevailed with regard to the silver coin. Under the native administration, and until the year 1766 the gold mohur was not considered as a legal tender of payment in any public or private transaction, nor was the number of rupees for which it was to pass current ever fixed by the Government. It was struck for the convenience of individuals, and the value of it in the markets fluctuated like other commodities, silver being the metal which was the general measure of value throughout the country. In the year 1766, the value of the gold coin with respect to the silver was first fixed, and the former coin declared a legal tender of payment. A gold mohur was struck and ordered to pass for fourteen sicca rupees. But as this coin (calculating according to the relative value of the two metals) was much below the worth of the silver in the number of rupees for which it was ordered to pass, it was found impossible to render it current, and it was accordingly called in, and a new gold mohur, being that now current, was issued in 1769, which was directed to pass as a legal tender of payment for sixteen sicca rupees. The intrinsic worth of this coin was estimated to be equal to the nominal value of it, or as nearly so as was deemed necessary to render it current at the prescribed rate. But whether owing to the effect of the orders for the introduction of the over-rated gold coin of 1766, the considerable value of the new gold mohur, and the want of divisions of it, so as to render the coin calculated for the dealings of the lower orders of the people in the interior part of the country, or other causes, the currency of it has been almost entirely confined to Calcutta, where it has been received and paid in all public and private payments at the fixed value of sixteen sicca rupees. But this partial currency of the gold coin has enabled the money-changers to practice an abuse upon the public and individuals of a nature similar to that which has prevailed regarding the silver ....The means which appear best calculated to render the gold mohur generally current are to declare it receivable at all the public treasuries and in all public payments throughout the provinces, at the rate of sixteen sicca rupees; to make it a legal tender of payment in private transactions; to coin a great proportion of halves and quarters; and lastly, to impose a duty upon all gold bullion sent to the mint to be coined so as to prevent too large a proportion of gold being introduced into circulation, by diminishing, in some degree, the advantage at present derived from the importation of it in preference to silver."

To guard, as far as possible, against the counterfeiting, clipping, drilling, filing, defacing, or debasing the coin, it was enacted by Section VII of Regulation XXXV that "the edges of both the gold and silver coin are to be milled, and the dies are to be made of the same size as the coin, so that the whole of the impression may appear upon the surface of it."

As regards the coins of the nineteenth sun, which are repeatedly referred to in the above Regulation, Marsden says[1] in the course of his observations on a gold mohur, bearing on the obverse the date 1197 (A.D. 1781-2), and on the reverse the inscription

ضرب مورشداباد سنه جلوس ... ١٩

"struck at Moorshidábád in the 19th year of the auspicious reign."

"The legend adopted by Sháh Alum at his succession is continued on this *muhr* and the subsequent coinage in gold and silver, professing to be from the mint of Murshidábád, the modern capital of the province of Bengal, but which, in fact, were executed at Calcutta, under the immediate authority of the East India Company's Government. So early, indeed, as the year 1757, we find a treaty with the Nabob *Serajáh ed-daulah*, in which it is stipulated that sikkas (rupihs) may be coined at Allenagore (*Allah-nagar?*) or Calcutta, in the same manner as at Murshidábád. A similar article appears in a treaty with Jafir Ali Khán in 1763, and with Najim ed-daulah in 1764; but all these were superseded by the treaty of 1765, negociated by Lord Clive, then Governor of Bengal, in which a grant is made to the Company by Sháh Alum, of the Déwáni or plenary collection and administration of the revenues of that province. This *muhr* of 1196, as well as the nearly similar pieces of 1197, 1198, and 1201 are, in point of workmanship, respectable coins, and exceed in weight, by about 20 grains, the ancient gold of the empire; but present a fresh instance of that total disregard of the consistency and fidelity of dates, which has been already noticed as marking the money struck under European control; for although actually the coinage of the twenty-third, twenty-fourth, and twenty-eighth years of the monarch's reign, as indicated by the corresponding years of the *hejrah*, they all express uniformly the *nineteenth* year. This anachronism, repeated through every successive coinage of the same mint, has confounded the investigations of writers on Indian numismatics, and cannot be too strongly reprobated." This "anachronism," or "glaring absurdity," as it is also called by Marsden, is referred to by T. C. Tyschen[2] in the following words:—

"Mira est in his numis annorum imperii cum annis Hegiræ discordia: etenim cum Schah Alem regnum inierit a 1175, annus ejus 19 erat Heg 1193. Contra annus Heg 1202 esset imperii 28 a 1203, imp. 29 . . . . . . Videntur Angli typis veteribus aversæ partis aliquando uti, de annis miseri imperatoris rectè numerandis parùm curiosi. Further Mr. Stanley Lane-Poole says in the Introduction to the Coins of the Sultáns of Dehli in the British Museum[3]: "Daulat Khan Lódí and Khizr Khán, in the general confusion which accompanied the invasion of India by Timúr, preferred rather to trade upon the traditional credit of their predecessors than to make any demands upon the people's trust in their personal solvency, and thus issued their coins in the name of Fíróz III or Muhammad III, the mints of which issues cannot be held to offer a very trustworthy evidence of the extent of their striker's dominion, which, however, we know from other sources

---

[1] Numismat. Orient., 1825, part ii, p. 688.

[2] De Numis Indicis Comment, p. 192.

[3] 1884, p. xvii.

to have been limited to a small district immediately surrounding Dehlí. Neither of these two puppets was a king in any real sense, and to such it mattered little whose superscription was placed on the public money,—his duty was confined to authorising the legality of the new issues by so much of his attestation as was implied in the annual date recorded on the reverse..... a system, indeed, which the East India Company, of their own free will, imitated with much credit and simplicity by striking their rupees in the name of Sháh 'Alum and other defunct monarchs of Dehlí whose money had of old obtained good repute in the local bázárs. But as the progressive annual dates, which were needed to test the good faith of Oriental princes, came in process of time to be a source of confusion and an opportunity for money-changers, the Government adopted the expedient of selecting the best current coin of the day and based their standard upon its intrinsic value; and so the immutable date of the XIX *san* (year) of Sháh 'Álum came to figure upon our much prized 'Sicca Rupees.' [1]"

A rupee is described by Marsden,[2] bearing on the obverse the inscription

سکہ زد بر هفت کشور سایہ فضل الہ
حامی دین محمد شاہ عالم بادشاہ ۱۱۹۹

and on the reverse the inscription

ضرب کلکتہ سنہ جلوس ... ۲۴

concerning which he says: "It seems extraordinary that at the period when a handsome, well-executed coinage of gold and silver was issuing from the Mint of Calcutta (though nominally from that of Murshid-âbâd), a rupih so rude as this should make its appearance in the same capital..... Another specimen of the same coinage, on which the year of the era is obliterated, has the twenty-fifth year of the reign; as has the half rupih of the same class, weighing 3 dw. 17½ grains." Concerning a gold mohur struck in the name of Sháh Alum in 1202 (A.D. 1787-88) he says[3]: "In the workmanship of this coin we observe the first instance of milling on the edges in the European manner. There is a difference also in the style of engraving the characters, which have here a flat surface."

As regards the several varieties of coin produced by modifications of weight, standard, or die, from time to time in the Calcutta and subordinate mints of the Bengal Presidency, which bear the same legend and date, the following mode of discriminating them is pointed out by Prinsep[4]:—

"(1) The old standard sikká rupee of 1793—1818 has an oblique milling.

"(2) The new standard sikká rupee of 1818—1832 has a straight milling.

---

[1] E. Thomas: *Chronicles*, pp. 329, 330; *International Numismata Orientalia*, vol. i, part 1; *Ancient Indian Weights*, p. 53 f.

[2] L. c., p. 689.

[3] L. c., p. 690.

[4] *Useful Tables*. Ed. by Edward Thomas, 1858, pp. 2, 3.

"(3) The new sikká rupee, struck under the present regulation, has a plain edge without milling, and a dotted rim on the face.

The distinctions of the oblique and straight milling apply also to the old and new gold mohur.

Of the up-country or Farrukhábád coins—

"(4) The old standard Farrukhábád rupee (or '45th Sun Lucknow rupee' of Regulation XLV, 1803) has an oblique milling.

"(5) The Benares rupee, coined 1806—1819, has also an oblique milling.

"(6) The new standard Farrukhábád rupee, coined at the Farrukhábád Mint, 1819—24, and at the Benares Mint, 1819—30, and now at the Ságar Mint, has an upright milling.

"(7) The Farrukhábád rupee, coined under the new regulation at the Calcutta Mint, has a plain edge, and a plain rim on the face.

"The coins struck before 1793 at the old mints of Patna, Murshidábád, and Dacca, the Benares rupee anterior to 1806, and the coins of all the native independent states, are known by their having no milling. The Company's coin up the country is thus generally called *kaldár*, 'milled or made by machinery,' in contradistinction to the unmilled or native coins, which are fashioned and stamped with the hammer and anvil."

About the same time as the passing of Reg. XXXV, 1793, the Surat rupee of the Moghul Emperor was adopted as the currency of the Bombay Presidency. By an agreement with the Nawáb of Surat the rupees coined by both were to circulate at par, and they were mutually pledged to preserve its standard. The Nawáb's rupees, however, were soon found to contain 10, 12, and even 15 per cent. of alloy; in consequence of which the Bombay rupees were melted down, and recoined at Surat; the coinage of silver in the Bombay Mint was suspended for twenty years, and the Súrátis alone were seen in circulation. At length in 1800 the Company ordered the then Surat rupee to be struck at Bombay, and thenceforth it became fixed at 179 grains' weight, 164·74 pure. The mohur was also equalised in weight thereto.

By Regulation XLV of 1803 it was enacted that— 1803.

(Section II). A silver coin, to be denominated the Lucknow sicca rupee of the forty-fifth sun (pl. vii-1), struck in the mint of Furruckhabad, corresponding in weight and standard with the sicca rupee at present struck at Lucknow, in the dominions of the Nawáb Vizier, and thence denominated the Lucknow rupee, is hereby declared to be the established and legal silver coin in the provinces ceded by the Nawáb Vizier to the English East India Company.

(Section IV). A mint shall be established at, or in the immediate vicinity of the town of Furruckhabad, in which Lucknow sicca rupees of the forty-fifth sun, and of the prescribed weight and standard, and half and quarter rupees of the same standard and proportionate weight, will be coined.

(Section V). The Lucknow forty-fifth sun sicca rupee, as established by this regulation, shall be of the same size and form as the nineteenth sun sicca rupee, struck in the mint at Calcutta, and shall bear the following impression:—

Obverse

الہ حامی دین محمد سایہ فضل شاہ عالم بادشاہ سکہ زد بر ہفت کشور

Reverse

میمنت مانوس سنہ ۲۵ جلوس ضرب فرخ آباد

(Section VI). The half and quarter rupee shall be proportionately less in size than the rupee according to their respective value, and shall bear the same impression as the rupee.

(Section XII). The Mint Master at Calcutta shall cause a private mark to be put on all dies, which may be prepared for the mint at Furruckhabad, but in such a manner as not to be distinguishable by the naked eye, or by persons unacquainted with it. These marks shall be varied as often as the Mint Master at Calcutta shall judge proper upon new dies being made.

1811. In 1811 a coinage from Spanish dollars took place at the Madras Mint, consisting of double rupees, single rupees, halves and quarters, and one, two, three, and five fanam pieces. A silver coinage of half and quarter pagodas of dollar silver fineness also took place then. The silver half pagoda weighed 326·73 grs. troy, and was equal to $1\frac{3}{4}$ Arcot rupee.

1812. The following statement, dated Fort St. George, 24th April 1812, shows the denomination of gold and silver coins manufactured in the Madras Mint from April 1807 to December 1811:—

Gold.	Single Fanams.
Double Pagodas.	Double Rupees.
Single ,,	Single ,,
	Half ,,
Silver.	Quarter ,,
Half Pagodas.	One-eighth ,,
Quarter ,,	Four annas.
Five Fanams.	Two ,,
Double ,,	

The five, double, and single fanam pieces, are thin coins, but there is in the Madras Museum collection a thick five fanam piece (pl. XVI, 9) with oblique milling, and a thick double fanam is mentioned by Atkins. These coins are very scarce, and are either, as has been suggested, of older date than the others, or were struck as patterns.

The English inscription on the coins is sometimes blundered, reading, *e.g.*, DOUBLE FANVM or EANAM.

The silver four-anna and two-anna pieces are now exceedingly scarce, and a two-anna piece is referred to by Atkins as having been probably fabricated about the same time, in which the English inscription is in script character.

In a proclamation, dated Fort St. George, 19th June 1812, it is stated that "the coinage of double rupees, half and quarter pagodas has ceased, but these coins shall still continue to pass in circulation, and be issued and received at all the public treasuries at the same rate and value as heretofore.

"The coinage of rupees, half rupees, and quarter rupees of English standard fineness shall be commenced at the mint of this presidency forthwith, and shall severally weigh as follows, and contain the following proportions of pure silver and of alloy. The rupee shall weigh 180 grains English troy weight, and shall contain $166\frac{1}{2}$ grains of pure silver, and $13\frac{1}{2}$ grains of alloy. The half rupee shall weigh 90 grains English troy weight, and shall contain $83\frac{1}{4}$ grains of pure silver, and $6\frac{3}{4}$ grains of alloy. The quarter rupee shall weigh 45 grains English troy weight, and shall contain $41\frac{5}{8}$ grains of pure silver, and $3\frac{3}{8}$ grains of alloy.

"The above rupees, containing each $\frac{9}{400}$ of a grain more of pure silver than the Arcot rupees which have been issued from the Madras Mint under the proclamation of the 15th of July 1807, half rupees and quarter rupees shall pass in general circulation, and shall be received and issued at all the public treasuries under this presidency at the same rate with the Arcot and Company's rupees now in circulation, that is, at 350 rupees to 100 star pagodas."

A letter to the Chief Secretary to Government, dated Fort St. **1813.**
George, 7th January 1813, states that "considerable quantities of the new rupees, halves, and quarters, having now been coined, the issue of two-anna pieces from the mint will shortly commence ..... We are of opinion that the two-anna pieces, though hitherto unknown in the circulation of this presidency, will readily incorporate with the existing currency; integral numbers of these coins measuring with the pagoda, half pagoda and quarter pagoda, as well as with the rupees and its sub-divisions of halves and quarters. Thus twenty-eight two-anna pieces are equivalent to one pagoda, fourteen to the half, and seven to the quarter pagoda."

The term *Soolakie* or *Soolackie* as applied to coins is explained by a letter to the Chief Secretary to Government, Fort St. George, dated 18th January 1813, wherein it is stated that "there are two modes of rendering coins Soolakie ..... The one is adopted for the most part by the petty village surrafs in those territories (the Nizam's) who, being in general very inexpert in ascertaining the fineness of the metal, invariably punch a hole in the rupee to convince themselves that it is good silver; but as this expedient is not sufficient to guard against the frauds of coiners, who frequently counterfeit rupees of copper covered with a coat of silver, with one or two such holes in them, it is usual for the surrafs, when they have the slightest suspicion that the metal is base, to punch a fresh hole in it. In consequence, it is by no means uncommon to see rupees with eight or ten such marks indented upon them. The other kind of Soolakie coins are made so by the surrafs of large towns who undertake to *shroff* the money belonging to individuals for a certain percentage, under an agreement to make good any coins that may afterwards turn out to be counterfeit. In order that the coins that have undergone such examination may be recognised, each principal suraff has a private stamp or mark of his own, which he affixes to the edge or some other part of the coin. The existence of one or more such marks gives a sort of sanction to the currency, as the credit of those who have put their stamp to it is a pledge for its goodness. Hence many rupees have forty or fifty such impressions, and at last become completely defaced. Neither of these modes of making the rupee Soolakie diminishes at all the weight of it, but, according to long custom, its value in exchange becomes greatly reduced when it is imported into the Company's territories."

It appears from a letter addressed to the Board of Revenue by the Collector of Tinnevelly that by an old order of Government it was provided that all payments made to the troops in that province should be solely in *Cully* fanams (which are stated to have been coined originally by the Hindu Government in that province) at the fixed exchange of sixteen and a half per star pagoda. This order was rescinded in the course of the year 1812.

The following list is of interest as showing the various kinds of gold and silver coins which were melted and recoined at the Madras Mint in the years 1807 to 1813[1]:—

Timmanaidoo Pagodas.
Sultawny ,,
Vencataputty ,,
Doorgee ,,
Jemsherry ,,
Feroke ,,
Ahamuddy ,,
Aununtaroy ,,
Madras ,,
Sunnakurk or Madras Pagodas.
Mittee or ,,
Porto Novo Pagodas.
Bahadari ,,
Pulliput ,,
Siddeke ,,
Timmanaidoo Half Pagodas.
Sharkany ,,
Gajaputty ,,
Darvady ,,
Naidoo Pertaup ,,
Subderally ,,
New Subderally ,,
Commengy ,,
St. Thomé Pagodas.
Kurky ,,
Atchootaroy ,,
Elephant ,,
Ekary ,,
Old Ekary ,,
Old Mahomed Shaye ,,
New ,, ,, ,,
,, Hurpanully ,,
Old ,, ,,
,, Sravanore ,,
New ,, ,,
Old Arnee ,,
Vandavash ,,
Pulicat ,,
Vencataputty ,,
Bombay ,,

Bunder Pagodas.
Cacanadie ,,
Rassee Rapadum ,,
Poondanull and Longvet ,,
Pulk Bunder Kurky ,,
Peddatala Bengalore ,,
Star Pagodas soldered with rings.
Sataury or Sravanaroy Pagodas.
Tanjore Fanams.
Kauket or Aparunjee ,,
Rassee ,,
Timmanaidoo ,,
Canteroy ,,
New Veroy ,,
Old ,, ,,
Aununtaroy, Double ,,
,, Single ,,
Gopally ,,
New Gopally ,,
Old ,, ,,
Travancottah Cully ,,
Arealore ,,
Woodiary ,,
Cully ,,
Chuckree ,,
Calicut ,,
Tinnavelly ,,
New Gold Mohur.
Old ,,
One-third Old Gold Mohur.
,, New Gold Mohur.
Sunnamola Mohur.
Bombay ,,
Akburry ,,
Dilhe ,,
Rassee ,,
Soorat Jayanagur ,,
Sultauny ,,
Wallace ,,
Poonah ,,

[1] The spelling is retained as it occurs in the Mint Records.

Venetions or Shanar Cash.	Chellavany Rupees.
Alkoss Cash.	Narrain Pettah ,,
Guinea Cass.	Company's Soolaky ,,
Mydores.	Cunnanore ,,
St. Thomé Cash.	Gurnamully ,,
Gold Rupees.	Sultauny ,,
Spanish Dollars.	Emaumy ,,
Cut ,,	Chandoly ,,
German Crowns.	Masulipatam ,,
American Dollars.	Bombay ,,
Duccatoons.	Elephant ,,
Pondicherry Rupees.	Half Pagodas.
,, ,, 2nd sort.	Quarter ,,
Soolaky ,,	Sravanore Rupees.
Arcot ,,	Sicca ,,
Nabob Arcot ,,	Arcot ,,
Arcot Soolaky ,,	Bunder ,,
Nokurrah ,,	Kaukenadoo ,,
Mysore ,,	Pulicat ,,
Mallarthaye ,,	Four Annas.
Sunnamola ,,	Bungapully Rupees.
Soorat ,,	Chuckrums.
Rassee ,,	Tellicherry Fanams.
Adony ,,	Various other ,,
Kurnal ,,	

Under the heading July 21, 1813, Ruding says[1]: "The coins which usually circulated in the East Indies had not, as it appears, received any sanction from Government, until an Act which was passed at this time declared it to be expedient for the protection of property and trade in the East Indies, that, etc., etc.; and also that further provisions should be made for the punishment of the crimes of, etc., etc., and of counterfeiting the current coin, and uttering such counterfeit coin in the East Indies; it therefore enacted that if any person within the local limits of the criminal jurisdiction of any of His Majesty's Courts at Fort William, Fort St. George, Bombay, or Prince of Wales' Island, or if any person, personally subject to the jurisdiction of the said courts, at any place in the East Indies, or any place between the Cape of Good Hope and the Straits of Magellan, where the United Company of Merchants of England trading to the East Indies should have a settlement, factory, or other establishment, should counterfeit, or procure to be counterfeited, or willingly act or assist in counterfeiting any of the gold or silver coins of any of the British Governments in India, or any gold or silver coin usually current and received as money in payments in any part of the British possessions in the East Indies, it should and might be lawful for the court, before which any such person should be convicted of any such offence by due course of law, to order and adjudge that such person should be transported to such place beyond the seas, and for such term of years as the said court should direct. The punishment for uttering such counterfeit coin, knowing it to be such, to be upon conviction, for the first offence six months' imprisonment with hard labour during that time at the discretion 1813.

1. Op. cit., vol. ii, p. 111.

of the court, and surety to be given for good behaviour for six months more, to be computed from the end of the first six. For the second offence two years' imprisonment with hard labour as before, and surety to be given for two years after the expiration of the term of imprisonment. For the third offence transportation for life. A certificate, under the hand of the proper officer of the court, to be a sufficient proof of the former conviction.

"On conviction (upon the oath of one or more credible witness or witnesses, before one of His Majesty's justices of the peace, or if there should be no justice of the peace duly qualified to act in the place where such offence should be committed, before one of his majesty's court there) of having in possession more than five pieces of such counterfeit coin, without lawful excuse, the proof of which to lie upon the party accused, the whole of such counterfeit pieces to be forfeited, and to be cut to pieces and destroyed, and the offender to pay for every such piece not more than forty, nor less than twenty sicca rupees, in the currency of the place where such offence should be committed; one moiety of which to go to the informer or informers, and the other moiety to the poor of the presidency, settlement, or place where such offence should be committed, and in case the penalty should not be forthwith paid, the offender to be committed to the common gaol or house of correction, there to be kept to hard labour for the space of three calendar months, or until such penalty should be paid."

1815. In the 17th clause of a Regulation enacted 31st March 1815 for establishing certain rules for the business of the Madras Mint, it is stated that: "The coins now fabricated in the Madras Mint are of the following denominations: of gold *double pagodas*, each weighing three pennyweights, nineteen grains, and seven-eleventh parts of a grain, troy, of English standard, and of the value of two pagodas; *single pagodas*, each weighing one pennyweight, twenty-one grains, and nine-eleventh parts of a grain, troy, of English standard, and of the value of one pagoda: of silver *single rupees*, each weighing seven pennyweights and twelve grains, troy, of English standard, and of the value of twelve fanams sixty-eight cash, and four-seventh parts of a cash; *half rupees*, each weighing three pennyweights and eighteen grains, troy, of English standard, and of the value of six fanams, thirty-four cash, two-seventh parts of a cash; *quarter rupees*, each weighing one pennyweight and twenty-one grains, troy, of English standard, and of the value of three *Fanams*, seventeen cash, and one-seventh part of a cash; and *two-anna* pieces, each weighing twenty-two and a half grains, troy, of English standard, and of the value of one fanam, forty-eight cash, and four-seventh parts of a cash.

The inscriptions on the single and half rupee were—

Obverse

۱۱۷۲ سکہ مبارک بادشاہ غازی عزیزالدین محمد عالم گیر

Reverse

ضرب ارکاٹ سنہ ٦ جلوس میمنت مانوس

The inscriptions on the quarter rupee and two-anna piece were—

Obverse

۱۱۷۲ سکہ عالم گیر بادشاہ

Reverse

سنہ ٦ ضرب ارکاٹ

In a letter from the British Resident at Bangalore, dated 13th September 1816, concerning the Surat Rupees in circulation in the Province of Mysore it is stated that: "The Surat Rupee was originally imported into the Mysore country by the troops of Hyder Ali Khan, and by the soucars who returned from Malabar with his army after the capture of Calicut in or about the year 1766, but the currency was very limited until the conquest of Seringapatam, when that coin became somewhat more common in these provinces. As there was not any considerable commercial intercourse between Malabar and Canara and Mysore for several years after the fall of Seringapatam, the amount of the circulation in Soorat Rupees was never extensive until 1808." 1816.

In 1817 considerable correspondence took place as to the establishment of a mint by the French Company at Pondicherry. It was proposed that, with a view to simplifying accounts and removing any inconvenience which might arise from the establishment of the French Mint, the rupees to be coined at Pondicherry should be of precisely the same weight and value as those struck at Madras and at that time current in the territories of the Honorable Company. But to this proposition the Madras Government replied to the effect that it seemed scarcely necessary to express the expectation of the Governor-General in Council that the impression on the French coin should be such as to render it easily distinguishable from the coinage of the British Government, and that, were the mintage at Pondicherry to be after the pattern of the coins struck by the British Government, as there seemed grounds for imagining might have been in contemplation, the British Government would in effect be made to answer for the intrinsic work of a currency, which it would have no means of regulating. In conformity with the instruction of the British Government, the following specimens of the coins struck at Pondicherry were forwarded by the British Consul on June 12th, 1817:— 1817.

One Rupee.
Half „
Double Fanam.
Single „ of which
eight were equivalent to a Rupee.
Half Fanam.
One Doodee.
Half „
One Cash, of which
sixty-four were equivalent to a Fanam.

A letter from the Director of the Pondicherry Mint, bearing the same date, states that "I have the honor to send you eight specimens of the species (of coins) we have coined since the restoration of the place of Pondicherry to the French Government, viz.:—

"One Rupee. A small crescent has (ever) been added to the stamp as a mark of its being a French Rupee.

One Half Rupee.
One Double Pondy Fanam.
One Single " "
of which eight make a Rupee.

One Half Pondy Fanam.
One Doodoo or Quadruple Cash.
One Half Doodoo or Double Cash.
One Single Cash, 64 of which make a Fanam.

"We have not yet coined any gold species. The French old pagoda or crescent pagoda has the same weight and the same degree of fineness as the Star Pagoda. Many years before the Revolution the Mint of Pondicherry had ceased coining crescent pagodas. It had confined itself to coining 'three Sawmy'[1] Pagodas, otherwise improperly called Madras Pagodas.

"They were designed for the trade of Punjum cloths at our factory of Yanan. This last kind of species we will probably coin in a short time."

With respect to the crescent, which is mentioned in the above letter as being marked on the Pondicherry rupee, the British Commissioner remarks in a letter, dated 7th May 1817: "Adverting to a former letter respecting the French coinage, wherein I stated that the legend on it would be entirely different from that on ours, I beg to observe that the information I then conveyed to you was obtained in conversation with Count Du Puy and M. Dayot. The French coinage being now current in Pondicherry, I perceive that the legend is the same, or nearly so, as that of the Company's rupees, and that the principal mark of distinction is a small crescent on one of the sides. The intrinsic value of the coin I understand to be somewhat greater than that of ours."

By Regulation XXV of 1817 "for fixing the weight of the pice struck at the Calcutta mint, and for giving general circulation to pice struck at any of the mints subordinate to this presidency," the copper paisá struck at the Benares mint, weighing 98¼ grains, which were intended at first for circulation in the province of Benares only, and were distinguished with a trident or trisúla, were made current throughout the Bengal provinces at par with the Farrukhábád paisá.[2]

The following extracts from the Minutes of Consultation, dated 16th September 1817, bear upon the proposed new gold and silver coinage: "In considering this important subject," it is stated,

---

[1] Pagode a trois figures.

[2] Notes on *pice* or *paisá*. From Yule and Burnell, op. cit.

C. 1590. "The dám . . . . . . is the fortieth part of the rupee. At first this coin was called *paisah*."—*Ain.*, 31.

1615. "Pice, which is a copper coyne; twelve drammes make one pice. The English shilling, if weight, will yeeld thirtie-three *pice* and a halfe." *W. Peyton* in *Purchas*, 1, 530.

1673. "*Pice*, a sort of copper money current among the poorer sort of people . . . . . the Company's accounts are kept in book-rate *pice*, viz., 32 to the mam. [*i.e.*, mamoodie] and 80 pice to the rupee." *Fryer*, 205.

1689. "Lower than these (pice) bitter almonds here (Surat) pass for money, about sixty of which make a *pice*." *Ovington*, 219.

1726. "1 *ana* makes 1½ stuyvers or 2 *peys*." *Valentijn*, v. 179.

"the Board have referred particularly to the letter from the Honorable Court, dated the 25th of April 1806, which contains the ground work of all their subsequent orders concerning it. In that letter the Honorable Court explained their object to be to establish a general currency for the whole of India. They stated that the standard currency forming the money of account ought to be of one of the precious metals only, but not to the exclusion of the other; that the metal ought to be silver; and that no ratio ought to be fixed between the standard silver coin and the gold coin, but that gold should be left to find its own value. The Court further desired that the gold coin should be denominated a gold rupee,[1] and that the gold and silver rupees should be the same in weight, fineness, form and inscription. They also desired that half and quarter gold and silver rupees, and annahs should be coined, and stated that a copper coinage of six-pice, three-pice, and one-pice pieces would be sent from England.

"The Mint Committee report that they are aware of no objection to the immediate execution of the arrangements proposed by the Honorable Court, and they accordingly recommend that, with the exception of single annahs, the gold and silver coinage should forthwith commence in pursuance of the Honorable Court's orders. They propose also that the rupee should become the money of account, and that the accounts of Government should be converted from gold into silver at the present ratio of 1 to 13·875, or one pagoda for three rupees and a half. The money of account at Madras has heretofore been the gold pagoda, which used also to form the actual currency. When the silver rupee was introduced into the currency, it was settled that three rupees and a half should represent one pagoda. In consequence of the pagoda being undervalued at that rate, it has gradually disappeared from circulation, and the rupee now forms the actual currency, and, though not the money of account, has become the standard of value.

"With respect to the form and impression of the new gold and silver coins, these will finally be settled either in Bengal or in England. As the currency is intended for general use throughout India, it will be deserving of consideration whether the impression ought not to be in English, and whether the form ought not to resemble that of English rather than of Indian coins."

A proclamation, dated Fort St. George, 9th December 1817, states that "The Right Honorable the Governor in Council, in furtherance of the orders of the Honorable the Court of Directors, is pleased to publish for general information, that hereafter the standard circulating medium is to be the Madras silver rupee, in which all issues of pay and allowances, civil and military, and all public contracts are to be reckoned, made, and executed, and that the coinage of star pagodas will hereafter be discontinued.

---

[1] There is in the Madras Museum a single specimen of the little coin (pl. xi-10), which is commonly called the Bombay gold rupee, concerning which Marsden says (Num. Or., 1825, pt. ii., p. 696): "Of the same year of the reign (of Sháh Álum, 1218 or 1219), and evidently from the same mint, are some very small gold coins, weighing each about 12 grs., and which must be considered as gold ánás or sixteenth parts of a *muhr*. In appearance they resemble rather the gold fanams of the Karnatik, than fractional denominations of Hindustani coins."

" The Right Honorable the Governor in Council is also pleased to declare that all pay and allowances, both civil and military, having been heretofore rated in pagodas and converted into Arcot rupees at 350 per 100 star pagodas shall continue to be the same, and that all payments made from the public treasuries, and received into them in payment of revenue, that have heretofore been made in pagodas, shall continue to be at the rate of 350. A: Rs. equivalent to 100 star pagodas.

" The Right Honorable the Governor in Council is pleased to declare his intention to prepare for circulation the fractional parts of the rupee, viz. :—Annas and pice, of which 16 annas are equal to one rupee, and 12 pice to one anna.

" For this purpose the new coinage of silver will consist of the silver rupee, the half rupee or 8-annas piece, and the quarter rupee or 4-annas piece, and the Right Honorable the Governor in Council is pleased to command that these shall circulate, and be received in payment at their established value.

" The Right Honorable the Governor in Council having abrogated the use of the gold star pagoda, has been pleased, for public convenience, to substitute the gold rupee, bearing the same inscription as the silver rupee, and of equal weight, viz., 180 grains, containing of fine gold 165 grains and alloy of silver 15 grains, which gold rupee will be issued and received in all payments of revenue at the rate of fifteen silver rupees for one gold rupee. . . . .

" The established and acknowledged circulating medium in specie of the Presidency of Fort St. George is hereby declared to be hereafter as follows :—

	Pure gold.	Alloy.	Total.
Gold rupee	Grs. 165	Grs. 15	Grs. 180
Half gold rupee	„ $82\frac{1}{2}$	„ $7\frac{1}{2}$	„ 90
Quarter „ „	„ $41\frac{1}{4}$	„ $3\frac{3}{4}$	„ 45
	Pure silver.		
Silver rupee	Grs. 165	„ 15	„ 180
„ half rupee	„ $82\frac{1}{2}$	„ 7	„ 90
„ quarter „	„ $41\frac{1}{4}$	„ $3\frac{3}{4}$	„ 45
„ eighth „ or double anna ...	„ $20\frac{5}{8}$	„ $1\frac{7}{8}$	„ $22\frac{1}{2}$
Single anna	„ $10\frac{5}{16}$	„ $\frac{15}{16}$	„ $11\frac{1}{4}$

" As it will not be practicable at once to recall from circulation the whole of the star pagodas and their fractional parts, the silver fanams and copper cash, the Right Honorable the Governor in Council is pleased to announce his resolution that they shall still continue to be received as often as they are tendered, in payment, until the whole can be withdrawn ; that three rupees and a half shall be considered as representing the star pagoda, and that one star pagoda shall be equivalent to 45 fanams ; that one rupee shall pass as heretofore for 12 fanams 68 cash, and 1 fanam for 80 cash.

"The copper coinage in circulation is also hereby declared to be continued until a sufficient quantity of copper pice can be prepared, adapted in weight to its relative value with the superior denomination of coin. . . . . its fractional parts."

It appears from the records that, in the course of the year 1817, an order was passed directing Collectors not to receive Pondicherry rupees in payment of revenue, but this order was rescinded on the receipt of a letter from the Collector of South Arcot to the effect that the old Pondicherry rupees, fanams, and cash had always been received into the district treasuries of that division, and that, if they were not received, it would tend much to impede the collections both in the Land and *Sayer* department; besides which it would fall very hard on the cultivators, for they would be obliged to pay a certain *vutum*, in order to get the village shroffs to exchange the Pondicherry coins for the Company's, and this would completely put the ryots at the mercy of the village bankers. It was accordingly resolved that the old Pondicherry rupee should be received in payment of revenue, so long as it continued to be distinguishable from the new one, specimens of which had been assayed, and found to manifest a striking variation both in their weight and fineness. The prohibition of the circulation of the Pondicherry rupee is referred to in a letter from the Collector of Salem regarding the receipt and payment of revenue in *Cantaroy* fanams, in reply to which it was stated in a letter, dated 24th February 1818, that "The Collector refers to the orders prohibiting the circulation of the Pondicherry rupee in the territories of the Hon'ble Company, and we are aware of no reason why a preference should be given the currency of the Mysore Government, particularly when the Hon'ble Company are at the great expense of mint establishments and recoinage. We would therefore recommend that the Collector of Salem be instructed not to receive in future Cantaroy fanams in payment of revenue, they being the coinage of the Mysore mint, which has issued so large a quantity of late, encouraged no doubt by the fallacious value given to them in the Hon'ble Company's territory, as to have proved a great source of inconvenience in the Ceded Districts. The same orders should be extended to the other Collectors in that quarter."

In the preamble of Regulation XIV, 1818, "for altering the standard of the Calcutta sicca rupee[1] and gold mohur, and for further modifying some of the rules in force respecting these coins," it is stated that "the high standards established for the gold mohur and *sicca* rupee, having been found productive of many inconveniences, both to individuals and the public, inasmuch as they are ill-calculated to resist the wear and defacement to which coins are necessarily exposed, and as they are only to be obtained by having recourse to the expensive process of refining, 1818.

[1] Extract from a letter from the Assay Master, Fort St. George, dated 4th January 1821 :—

"The people of these territories appear to call all coins which are issued by the Bengal Government *sicca* rupees; thus there are Cutke siccas, Nagapoor siccas, Jayapoor siccas, Bajeeron siccas, Naraînpetta siccas, Benares, Farrukhâbâd, and others, but the Wallis rupees are understood to be the Calcutta sicca, the finest and heaviest of all."

diminishing consequently the productiveness of most of the sorts of bullion imported into the Company's territories; and it being desirable also that as much uniformity as can be established between the currencies circulating at the different presidencies should be introduced, consequently that an approximation of the Calcutta coins to the standard of those current at Madras and Bombay should be effected, it has been resolved to rescind the provisions of former regulations relative to the standard of the gold mohur and nineteenth sun *sicca* rupee, and to coin in future money of the proportions hereafter to be specified.

"As a reduction in the value of the sicca rupee, from its being in great measure the money of account, both in private and public transactions, would necessarily change the terms of all existing contracts, and might be productive of embarrassment and trouble, it has been determined to leave the rupee unaltered in this respect; and the new Calcutta *sicca* rupee will consequently contain the same quantity of fine silver as that heretofore struck; and, being of the same intrinsic value, will circulate on the same terms. The mint proportions of silver and gold being, it is believed, inaccurately estimated at present, and it being also desirable that an uniformity in this respect should be introduced at the three Presidencies of Calcutta, Madras and Bombay, it has been thought advisable to make a slight deduction in the intrinsic value of the gold mohur to be coined at this presidency, in order to raise the relative value of fine gold to fine silver, from the present rates of 1 to 14·861 to that of 1 to 15. The gold mohur will still continue to pass current at the present rate of sixteen rupees."

With respect to the new coinage at the Madras mint, which has already been referred to, two points for consideration remained after specimens of the gold coins had been minted, viz., whether they should be left plain or milled, and whether they should bear the date of the year in which they were minted. Specimens of the gold coins were forwarded to Government for approval, and a letter from the Secretary to Government to the Mint Committee, dated 26th January 1819, states that "The Right Honorable he Governor in Council concurs in your opinion that it is desirable to make a difference between the impressions of the gold and silver rupees, and also to alter the Persian inscription which those coins bear. The Governor in Council accordingly sanctions the specimens of gold coins submitted . . . . ., except the English denominations under the Company's arms, which ought to be omitted. The Governor in Council desires that the coins may be milled, but not dated, as the shroffs might take advantage of the dates to impose a batta on the coinage of particular years." The draft of a proclamation on the proposed alteration of the impression of the gold coins, submitted to Government on the 9th of March 1819, stated that "The Right Honorable the Governor in Council has been pleased to resolve that the inscriptions on the gold rupee, the gold half rupee and the gold quarter rupee shall be different from those on the silver rupee, the silver half rupee, and the silver quarter rupee, and has accordingly directed that the gold rupee shall in future be impressed on the face with the Honorable Company's arms and the words

ENGLISH EAST INDIA COMPANY, and on the reverse with the words English Company's rupee in the Persian character; that the gold half rupee shall bear the Company's crest and the words ENGLISH EAST INDIA COMPANY on the face, and the words English Company's half rupee in the Persian character on the reverse; that the gold quarter rupee shall bear the Company's crest and the words ENGLISH EAST INDIA COMPANY on the face, and the words English Company's quarter rupee in the Persian character on the reverse.

By Regulation XI of 1819 the coinage of the Benares rupee 1819.
was discontinued, and the Farrukhábád rupee declared the local currency of the province of Benares. "The Benares mint," Prinsep says:[1] "had been established by Rájá Balwant Singh in 1730. It remained under native management for twenty years after the province was ceded to the Company in 1775. The rupee had the full weight of one hundred and seventy-five grains, and was $2\frac{1}{4}$ per cent. better than the present rupee, or about equal to the Dihlí rupee of that date. It fell in value subsequently about four ánás per cent. and there, of course, remained under English management until it was abolished."

In a letter to Government, dated 8th March 1820, the Madras 1820.
Mint Committee recommended that "the gold rupee should be divided into thirds instead of halves and quarters. The third would be of the value of five rupees, which is a most convenient sum for computation. A coin of that value, we have no doubt, would be in great request, and thus would both contribute to the convenience of the public, and, by promoting the circulation of gold, would maintain its relative value to the standard coin of the Government." The Mint Master was ordered to prepare a specimen of a *third*, to be submitted for the sanction of the Governor in Council. The main reason of the recommendation of the Mint Committee was that, as the gold rupee was equal in value to fifteen silver rupees, the half equal to seven rupees and a half, and the quarter to three rupees and three quarters, these fractional parts did not correspond to any exact number of the coins next inferior in denomination, and were of a value so inconvenient as to prevent their ever being much in use.

The following letter was addressed to Government by the Accountant-General, Fort St. George, on 28th February 1820:—

"By the report of the balance of the general treasury, dated the 20th instant, it is stated that there are no silver annas remaining, and, as it is expedient that there should be an ample supply of that coinage in substitution for the old and new Madras fanams which should be withdrawn from circulation, I beg to recommend that instructions be issued to the Mint Master to convert a greater portion of his silver balance into annas and to proceed upon the recoinage of the half and quarter pagoda, of dollar standard, including the five double and single fanam pieces.

"There is also in circulation a rupee of the coinage of 1807, of dollar standard, which should also be called in and recoined, as

---

[1] Op. cit., p. 26.

well as the new Arcot rupee, which is of British standard, or 11 ozs. 2 dwts.

"The old Arcot rupee is of a standard of superior fineness to the others, the recoinage of which may be a subject for consideration."

Directions were accordingly given to coin a sufficient number of double annas and quarter and half rupees, and then to recoin all the fanam pieces.

1821. The preamble of Regulation V, 1821, "for settling the rates at which Benares and Farrukhábád rupees shall be received in payment of the revenue of malguzars, whose engagements are expressed in Gohurshahee or Tirsolee rupees" states that "it is enacted by Regulation XI, 1819, that the Farrukhábád rupees shall be received within the province of Benares at par with the Benares rupees; but no provision has been made for regulating the exchange in account between the said rupees and the Gohurshahee and Tirsolee rupees, in which it appears that the engagements of many malguzars are expressed; moreover, the batta to be taken from such malguzars has hitherto been arbitrarily fixed, and considerable abuses have consequently prevailed. The intrinsic value of the coins having been now ascertained by a careful assay, whence it has appeared that the rupee denominated Chorah Gohurshahee exceeds, and the other descriptions of Gohurshahee equal the Farrukhábád rupee in value, and that the latter coin is 3-11-7 per cent. superior in value to the Tirsolee rupee, the Revenue officers have been directed to adjust their demands on the said malguzars according to the results of the assay, subject to the general principle of receiving the Farrukhábád rupee at par with the Benares rupee, and without any demand of batta on account of its inferiority in value below the local currency."

1823. It is stated in a letter from A. D. Campbell, Esq., Magistrate of Bellary, to the Madras Government, dated 27th April 1823, that a Brahmin, an inhabitant of Gudival in the Hyderabad territory, had tried to pass off 250 rupees of a suspicious nature, purporting to be of the Company's new coinage, in Kurnool, and stated, on examination, that they were forged by a goldsmith residing in the village of Muroor in the Hyderabad country. The Nabob was applied to, and detectives were sent to the goldsmith, who showed them all his utensils, and forged some coins in their presence. The practical suggestion was made by Mr. Campbell that the inscription on the Company's coin should be partly in English, in order to render the forgery of it more difficult, as, though the English soldiers would still continue to imitate the coin, natives would find it much more difficult to imitate exactly English characters than the native letters which were familiar to them. The further suggestion was made that a private mint mark might be placed on the coin, to be communicated to Collectors or their principal shroffs as a check upon forgery.

In 1823 a pice piece (fifty-three to the pound) with its half and quarter, were executed by W. Wyon for the East Indies, by the authority of the Secretary of State and the Master of the Mint. The obverse of these coins bore the arms of the Company and the motto AUSP. REGIS. & S. ANGLIAE, and the reverse a Persian inscription.[1]

The mint at Farrukhábád was abolished by Regulation II, 1824, it being considered no longer necessary to continue it, inasmuch as provision had been made by Regulation XXVI, 1817, for the coinage of the Farrukhábád rupee at any of the mints established by Government. 1824.

Early in 1824 specimens were prepared in the Madras mint of a rupee, which, while superior in workmanship to the current rupee, was stated to be also much better adapted for the currency of the Madras Presidency, and very difficult to counterfeit. It appears from a letter from the Registrar of the Zillah Court, Chingleput, to Government, dated 15th December 1823, that the most usual artifices by which coins were imitated or counterfeited at that time consisted in hollowing the centre of the old thick Company rupee, and filling up the cavity with lead, or striking off the impression from both sides of a thin Company rupee on copper, and covering the surface with about one-tenth of an inch of silver, and thereby making it only distinguishable from the original by its weight. But a still more lucrative speculation was carried on by gilding the silver rupee, which was of the same weight, and bore the same superscription as one species of the gold mohurs.

In the year 1825 the following correspondence took place with regard to the coinage of Prince of Wales' Island:— 1825.

From

THE SECRETARY TO GOVERNMENT,
Fort William,

To

THE SECRETARY TO GOVERNMENT,
Fort St. George.

SIR,

I am directed by the Right Honorable the Governor-General in Council to transmit to you the accompanying copy of correspondence relative to the supply of copper coinage required by the Penang Government, and to request that the Honorable the Governor in Council will be pleased to cause the coinage in question to be prepared at Fort St. George, if practicable, and transmitted to Penang.

2. Specimens of coins are herewith transmitted.

I have the honor to be,
Sir,
Your most obedient servant,

9th June 1825. HOLT MACKENZIE.

---

[1] Ruding, op. cit., vol. ii., p. 129.

From

THE ACTING SECRETARY TO GOVERNMENT,
Fort Cornwallis,

To

THE SECRETARY TO GOVERNMENT,
Fort St. William.

SIR,

The copper coin sent out by the Honorable Court of Directors, having been all issued from the treasury, and great inconvenience being likely to arise before a supply can be received from England, I am directed to forward specimens of the coins in use, the pice and half pice, in the hope that it may be found practicable to manufacture the same at the mint in Calcutta. These coins are issued, the first at 100, the second at 200 to the dollar, and pass at Singapore, and all over the Malay Peninsula, where they are much sought after. A coinage of a double pye, 50 to the dollar, bearing the same stamp, would also be convenient, should the measure be found practicable, and not attended with inconvenience. The transmission of the above coin to the amount of 10,000 dollars in value would prove extremely useful to the general condition of the island.

I have, &c., &c.,

9th April 1825. E. I. BLUNDELL.

The mint records show that, in consequence of this correspondence, new punches and dies were made, and 130,300 double pice, 136,700 single pice, and 145,000 half pice struck for the Penang Government.

As regards the earlier coinage of Pulo Pinang or Prince of Wales' Island, Marsden says: [1]

"There are in the collection a few specimens of small silver coins struck in Bengal for the use of the English settlement at this place. On one side is the customary mark of the East India Company, with the date 1788, and, on the other, in the Arabic character the barbarous words جزيرة پرنس ابويلس

"'Jezirah Prans ab Wailis,' for 'Prince of Wales' Island.' The weight of the large coin is 4 dwts. 4½ grs. and of the smaller, 1 dwt. 18 grs. There is also a small specimen in copper with the same inscription and date of 1787." Further Ruding figures [2] two coins bearing on the obverse the arms of the Company and the date 1810, and on the reverse the inscription 'Púlú Pinang,' surrounded by an ornamental border.

In a letter from the Bombay Government to the Secretary to Government, Fort St. George, dated Bombay Castle, 12th August 1824, it is stated that "The Honorable the Governor in Council has authorised those Bombay or Surat rupees termed Chapee, Soolakee, and Gabree rupees, which may be found in the consignments of treasure from Malabar, to be received at this presidency, the two first at a discount of 3 per cent. and the last at a discount

---

[1] Op. cit., p. 809, pl. liv, mccxxviii.

[2] Op. cit., vol. ii, p. 405, pl. xvi, figs. 9, 10.

of 2 per cent. to cover the charges of recoinage." The meaning of the term 'Soolakee' has been already explained (p. 45) and the terms 'Chapee' and 'Gabree' are explained in a letter from the Collector of South Canara to the Accountant-General, Fort St. George, dated 26th March 1825, wherein it is stated that "The Chapee rupees are so called on account of their being impressed with a stamp, which they receive at the treasuries of the Native States where they have been circulated, and this stamp or chop does not in any way take away from their weight or value; on the contrary it may be considered an additional proof of their being genuine, as it is only after being shroffed in those treasuries that the mark is affixed by the treasurers.

"The Chapee-Soolakee has the additional mark of a nail, or other pointed instrument driven into the coin, to ascertain in the first instance that it is silver of the proper standard.

"The Gabree rupee is so called from the circumstance of a small piece of the metal having been rubbed or knocked off the coin in the course of circulation. It has its origin in general in the rupee being originally short of weight from the mould not being completely filled, when the rupee was struck, and a small portion of silver equal to the quantity deficient being subsequently added on the part imperfectly stamped. This piece of silver not being fused with the metal is liable to be rubbed off, and the coin from which it has been removed is called Gabree, and is more or less deficient in weight according to the size of the piece of silver that has been displaced and lost, which, however, is always very small, seldom exceeding the value of $\frac{3}{200}$ part of a rupee, or 1½ per cent."

The following correspondence bears on the currency at this time in the Tenasserim Provinces:— 1829.

From

THE CIVIL COMMISSIONER,

Tenasserim Provinces,

To

THE CHIEF SECRETARY TO GOVERNMENT,

Fort William.

13*th January* 1829.

SIR,

A number of Madras pagodas and other coins, amounting in value to Madras rupees 19,328-13-0, having been collected in the treasuries at Tavoy and Mergui, and the common currency of these provinces being Madras rupees, I beg leave to transmit these coins, which the Burmese inhabitants are unwilling to receive, in order that the same may be sent to the mint at Calcutta and coined into rupees. I beg to enclose a list of the different coins and a receipt of the same.

I take this opportunity of soliciting that application may be made to the Government of Fort St. George to remit to me a supply of copper coinage to the extent in value of 20,000 Madras rupees for the use of these provinces in which the want of some suitable currency is very much felt.

I have, &c., &c.,

From

THE SECRETARY TO GOVERNMENT,
Fort William,

To

THE SECRETARY TO GOVERNMENT,
Fort St. George.

23*rd January* 1829.

SIR,

I am directed by the Governor-General in Council to transmit to you the accompanying copy of a letter from Mr. A. D. Maingy, Civil Commissioner for the Tenasserim Provinces, dated the 13th instant, and to request that the Right Honorable the Governor in Council will be pleased to order a supply of copper money to the extent of 20,000 Madras rupees to be consigned to that gentleman by the earliest convenient opportunity.

I have, &c., &c.,

1833. In 1833 a regulation (No. VII) was passed for altering the weight of the new Farrukhábád rupee, and for assimilating it to the legal currency of the Madras and Bombay Presidencies, for adjusting the weight of the Calcutta sicca rupee, and for fixing a standard limit of weight for India.

In the preamble of this regulation it is stated that "by a Resolution of the Governor-General in Council, dated the 10th of September 1824, the Farrukhábád rupee was ordered to be coined of one hundred and eighty grains, one hundred and sixty-five fine and fifteen alloy, and was declared the legal currency of the Saugor and Nerbuddah territories. It is considered expedient to adopt this weight and standard for the Farrukhábád rupee at the Calcutta as well as at the Saugor mint, instead of that described in section V, Regulation XI, 1819, from which it differs very slightly, and to make the Farrukhábád currency correspond in weight and intrinsic value with the new currency of the Madras and Bombay Presidencies. It is likewise convenient to make a trifling alteration in the weight of the Calcutta sicca rupee, as prescribed by clause 1, section 1, Regulation XIV, 1818. It is further convenient to introduce the weight of the Farrukhábád rupee as the unit of a general system of weights for Government transactions throughout India under the native and well-known denomination of the tola." [1]

---

[1] Note on tola. From Yule and Burnell, op. cit.

"Tola, s., an Indian weight (chiefly of gold or silver) not of extreme antiquity. Hind. *tola* (Sansk. tuta, a balance, *tul* to lift up, to weigh). The Hindu scale is 8 *rattis* = 1 másha, 12 *máshas* = 1 *tola*. Thus the *tola* was equal to 96 *rattis*.

1563. "I knew a Secretary of Nizamoxa, a native of Coracon, who ate every day three *tollas* of opium, which is the weight of ten cruzados and a half."

1610. "A *tole* is a rupee *challany* of silver, and ten of these *toles* are the value of one of gold." *Hawkins*, in *Purchas*, 1, 217.

1615-16. "Two *tole* and a half being an ounce." *Sir T. Roe*, in *Purchas*, 1, 545.

In section ii of the same regulation it is stated that "the use of the sicca weight of 179·666, hitherto employed for the receipt of bullion at the mint, being in fact the weight of the Moorshedabad rupee of the old standard, which was assumed as the sicca currency of the Honorable Company's Provinces of Bengal, Behar and Orissa, shall be discontinued, and in its place the following unit, to be called the tola, shall be introduced, which, from its immediate connection with the rupee of the Upper Provinces and of Madras and Bombay, will easily and speedily become universal through the British territories.

"The tola or sicca weight to be equal to one hundred and eighty grains troy, and the other denominations of weight to be derived from this unit, according to the following scale, viz. :—

8 rattis = 1 masha = 15 troy grains.
12 mashas = 1 tola = 180 troy grains.
80 tolas (sicca weight) = 1 seer = $2\frac{1}{2}$ lbs. troy.
40 seers = 1 mun, or bazar maund = 100 lbs. troy."

This system of weights was ordered to be adopted at the Mints and Assay Offices of Calcutta and Saugor, respectively, in the adjustment and verification of all weights for Government or public purposes, sent thither for examination.

The Mysore mint, which was abolished in 1843, was removed from Mysore to Bangalore in 1833, in which year it appears from the following letter to the Madras Government to have been the intention to have the copper coinage supplied by the Madras mint.

COMMISSIONER'S OFFICE,

Bangalore, 23*rd August* 1833.

SIR,

I am directed by the Commissioners for the affairs of Mysore to . . . . . . explain that, in making the application contained in my letter of the 20th June last, the Commissioners acted under an impression that an ample stock of copper coin received from Europe might probably be in store at Madras, and disposable for the use of Mysore.

As this however is not the case, and as the Commissioners find that they can have the coin made at Bangalore (a course of proceeding which does not appear to them liable to any serious objection) on more advantageous terms than those on which it could be supplied from Madras, they direct me to state that it is not their intention to avail themselves of the offer, which the Right Honorable the Governor in Council has had the goodness to make to them of the Madras mint on this occasion.

I have, &c., &c.,

In 1833 the abolition of the Madras mint was recommended by the Calcutta Mint Committee, and the following extract from a letter, dated 29th January 1834, shows the feeling of the Court of Directors on this subject :—

"The grounds upon which the Calcutta Mint Committee have come to the conclusion that the Madras mint may be abolished without injury to the public interests are as follows: It appears from their report that since 1882-83 the annual average importation of bullion into the territories of your Government by sea has been about 44 lakhs, while the average annual export has amounted to 63 lakhs, showing an excess of export by sea to the amount of 19 lakhs. From this fact they are led to conclude that the local currency, as far as required for domestic purposes, has not been derived from foreign bullion. They next proceed to inquire whether any large source of supply is furnished to your mint by the inland trade, and they state that the average import of bullion from the interior does not much exceed 4 lakhs of rupees a year, so that, unless the receipts from the Government revenue itself afford the materials of the coinage which takes place in the mint, very little of the business carried on there can arise from the coinage necessary to meet the internal demands of the Madras territories. The recoinage from the Government revenue they consider must be very small, as even in the Calcutta mint it does not amount to 3½ lakhs of rupees a year on an average.

"The average amount of the coinage at the Madras mint from 1815 to 1820 was 50 lakhs a year, and, from 1817 to 1828, 68 lakhs, but during the latter part of the period, viz., from May 1825 to May 1828 it was only 42 lakhs.

"The net annual export of bullion from Madras, it has been seen, is 19 lakhs of rupees, and as there are no mines in the country and the import from the interior in the course of trade is only 4 lakhs a year, the immediate inference would be that nearly the whole of the net export of 19 lakhs must have been made in the current coin of the country. But it appears in fact to have been even much larger. The Calcutta Mint Committee state that the average annual export of silver coin, intending, it is to be presumed, Madras rupees, for the last 4 years has been nearly 50 lakhs; consequently the bullion imported has been re-exported in the shape of coin, and the mint has been employed very unnecessarily in charging its . . . . at a gratuitous wastage and expense. The Committee then observe that the export of coin from Madras was chiefly on public account. In 1824-25 and 1825-26 large sums were sent to Ava for the purpose of paying the Madras troops employed in the war, and a large supply goes also annually to Bombay, which, now that an effective mint has been established at that presidency, might as well be sent in the shape of bullion. The average amount of coinage required for domestic circulation under the Madras Presidency will therefore, it is said, not be more than 10 or 15 lakhs a year, which, if it were coined at the Calcutta mint and forwarded thence to Madras, would render it practicable to effect an annual saving, by abolishing the Madras mint, to the extent of at least 60,000 rupees a year.

"We have carefully considered the facts and reasonings brought forward by the Calcutta Mint Committee upon this subject, and we think that the conclusion to which they have come is a just one. We cannot indeed admit the propriety of their statement that the Madras mint 'has been employed very unnecessarily in changing the form of the bullion imported at a gratuitous wastage and expense,' because it is evident that the conversion of that bullion into coin was required for important public purposes; but it seems quite clear that this coinage may for the future be conducted at the Calcutta and Bombay mints without leading to any material inconvenience, and at a great saving of expense to the State. Such an arrangement has become still more desirable than ever from this circumstance, of which you probably are aware, that the machinery of the new Calcutta and Bombay mints (the erection of which has occasioned such a large outlay of money) was fabricated upon a scale sufficient to enable those two mints combined to supply the whole of the coinage necessary for British India, and the present coinage at the new Calcutta mint is not by any means so extensive as to employ the powers of which the machinery is capable. In addition to the facts stated by the Calcutta mint as above referred to, we observe by a more recent account received from you that the value of the coinage in your mint, which had fallen in the years 1825—1828 to an average of 42 lakhs of rupees, was in 1828-29 not quite 27 lakhs, and in 1829-30 was little more than 22 lakhs."

In obedience to the orders of Government, in consequence of this letter, the Madras Mint Committee called on the mercantile community, both European and Native, requesting the former to state "whether, in the event of the accommodation which the mint has heretofore afforded being withdrawn, it would, in their opinion, affect the commercial interest of the Madras Presidency, and, if so, in what manner and to what extent. The native merchants were requested to state whether they thought the abolition of the mint would injure the trade of the port, and in what manner and to what extent." The concurrent opinion of the entire mercantile community, with the exception of Messrs. Parry, Dare and Co., was that very serious injury would be done to the commercial interests of the presidency by abolishing the mint, and the Mint Committee came to the conclusion that "the existence of the mint is essential to the interests of the public; that its continuance is inseparably connected with the prosperity of this settlement, and necessary to the due administration of its finances; and, should it be abolished, and Government should find it expedient to re-establish it, such a measure would be attended with much expense and difficulty, arising from the dispersion of the present establishment and the impracticability hereafter to collect them again in the public service, or to find properly qualified persons to supply their place."

In 1834 pattern rupees were struck, bearing the following devices and legends:— 1834.

1. *Obverse.*—Bust of the King (William IV) r, and legend GULIELMUS. IIII. D.G. BRITT. ET. IND. REX. surrounded by a wavy line.

Reverse.—In the centre ONE RUPEE with lotus flower above, and date 1834 below, surrounded by a wreath; around EAST INDIA COMPANY, and the value in Persian, Nágarí, and Bengálí.

(pl. xx-7.)

2. Similar to No. 1, except the legend on the obveres GULIELMUS. IIII. D.G. BRITANNIAR. REX. F.D.

3. Similar to No. 2, but thicker and smaller.

4. Similar to No. 1, except the legend on the obverse WILLIAM. IV. KING.

5. *Obverse.*—Similar to No. 4.

Reverse.—A lion and palm tree and the legend BRITISH INDIA.

6. *Obverse.*—A lion and palm tree, and the legend BRITISH INDIA.

Reverse.—In the centre ONE RUPEE with lotus flower above, and date 1834 below, surrounded by a wreath; around EAST INDIA COMPANY, and the value in Persian, Nágarí, and Bengálí.

1835. On March 31st, 1835, a letter was addressed to the Governor-General by the Calcutta Mint Committee relative to the promulgation of a new uniform coinage for British India, in which it is stated that: "We have now the honor to submit specimens of a rupee bearing the device of Flaxman's lion, selected by Lord William Bentinck as in his lordship's opinion the best adopted for the coin of British India.

"2. The Mint Master explains in his letter accompanying these specimens, that, in consequence of their being struck from the matrix die and not in the regular coinage presses, they are defective on the edge for want of the collar.

"3. Mr. Saunders has also at our request furnished specimens of the King's head rupee, in order that your Honor in Council may judge of the two together. One of the latter specimens has the straight milling of the English coin, which we are inclined to prefer to the plain edge.

"4. The opinion we formerly ventured to express in favor of the device of His Majesty's head is by no means lessened by the present comparison. An emblematical design, however appropriate it may be for the *reverse* of a handsome medal or medallic coin, such as we would make of the gold mohur, seems to us by no means so well suited for the *obverse* of the current coins as the effigy of the reigning monarch, and in regard to the danger of forgery there can be no doubt that a correct drawing of the human head, which all the world is in the constant habit of observing so as to tell at a glance the slightest difference of feature, is both easier to recognise and more difficult to imitate than the contour of an animal seldom or never seen by the majority of mankind. This argument cannot be better illustrated than by the fact that the lion was engraved in twenty-six days, while the head occupied upwards of one month and ten days.

"5. We beg leave to submit an impression in pure gold of the King's head with the lion as a reverse, proposed as a double gold mohur of 360 grains standard.

"6. Captain Forbes has submitted a memorandum on the expediency of requesting the Honorable Court of Directors to procure well-executed matrix dies of such devices as may finally be adopted from Mr. Wyon, the Chief Engraver of the London Mint.

" 7. This would doubtless be an excellent guide for our native engravers, but we do not think it necessary to suspend the introduction of the new device until it is obtained, the present matrices being in our opinion quite good enough for the purpose.

" 8. It would be highly desirable, however, to procure a good collection of modern medals and coins from England to serve as models for our native school of die engravers, and it will be particularly requisite to be furnished from the London mint with proof impressions of the King's head, especially on the occasion of a new sovereign. The present head is copied from an English gold coin procured in the bazar, and considerably rubbed on the surface.

" 9. It may be satisfactory to inform your Honor in Council that we have ascertained from Colonel Presgrave, Mint and Assay Master at Saugor, that he will be able to strike the new coin in his mint, if provided with collar dies instead of those now furnished to him.

" 10. There is then no obstacle to the introduction at once of the new currency, if only reasonable time be allowed for the preparation or multiplication of dies (of which unfortunately the supply on hand is small). The coinage of *sicca* rupees has been for some time suspended as a preliminary measure.

" 11. With reference to this last point and to the adoption of the 180 grain rupee as the universal coin of British India, we beg leave to call the attention of your Honor in Council to the expediency of changing at the same time the rupee of account in the general books of this presidency.

" 12. The maintaining of the sicca rupee in account after its coinage has been abolished would be evidently impolitic, and even now, from the erroneous valuation given to the Farrukhábád rupee in exchange (104½ to 100 siccas), considerable inconvenience is experienced in adjusting accounts between the Mint and the Accountant-General's offices, and the Collectors of the upper provinces. Should the new unit be adopted, it will be advisable to convert all *sicca* values and amounts into it at the intrinsic par of $\frac{16}{15}$ to avoid the confusion of the fictitious exchange hitherto employed."

In reply to this letter the Secretary to Government was ordered to inform the Mint Committee that:

" 1. The rupee having on one side the device of His Majesty's head, and on the reverse the inscription EAST INDIA COMPANY, together with the nominal value of the coin in English, Persian and Nágarí, and the representation of a lotus flower and myrtle wreath, has been approved by the Governor-General in Council as the model for the future coinage of the rupee of British India. Your suggestion for introducing on this coin the straight milling of the English currency is also approved and sanctioned.

" 2. The Governor-General in Council does not contemplate suspending the introduction of the new device until matrix dies can be obtained from England. You will be therefore pleased to communicate with the Madras, Bombay and Saugor mints, with the view of effecting a change in the rupee currency throughout British India with all convenient expedition.

"3. It will be, of course, necessary as subservient to the measure to change the rupee of account on the general books of this presidency as suggested by you. The Governor-General in Council, on the adoption of the new unit, approves of the conversion of all *sicca* value and amounts into it at the intrinsic par of $\frac{16}{15}$.

"4. I am directed to call for further reports and suggestions from you as to a corresponding change in the gold and copper currency of British India, which it will be advisable to submit at your earliest convenience."

In a further letter from Government, the Mint Committee of Calcutta was informed that "It has this day (22nd April 1835) resolved to inscribe on the reverse of the new silver coinage the denomination of value in the English and Persian languages only, and to have no difference whatever in the dies of the several presidencies. The year (1835) of the die will represent the era of the alteration of the coins, and will not need to be changed until a new coin shall be ordered to be struck. On the face of the coin with His Majesty's head it will be sufficient to stamp the name of the Sovereign WILLIAM IV, without the word *King*." But in a further letter, dated 13th May 1835, it is stated that "the selection of the Governor-General in Council has fallen upon the specimen with the inscription WILLIAM IV KING, as none of the others without the word *King* are approved. The above legend is accordingly to be adopted for the obverse of the new coin."

The details of the new coinage were finally laid down by Act XVII, 1835, wherein it was enacted "that from the 1st day of September 1835, the undermentioned silver coins *only* shall be coined at the mints within the territories of the East India Company; a rupee to be denominated the Company's rupee; a half rupee, a quarter rupee, and a double rupee; and the weight of the said rupee shall be 180 grains troy, and the standard shall be as follows:—

$\frac{11}{12}$ or 165 grains of pure silver;
$\frac{1}{12}$ or 15 grains of alloy;

and the other coins shall be of proportionate weight and of the same standard.

"And that these coins shall bear on the obverse the head and the name of the *reigning* sovereign of the United Kingdom of Great Britain and Ireland, and on the reverse the designation of the coin in English and Persian, and the words EAST INDIA COMPANY in English with such embellishment as shall from time to time be ordered by the Governor-General in Council.

"And that the Company's rupee, half rupee, and double rupee shall be a legal tender in satisfaction of all engagements, provided the coin shall not have lost more than 2 per cent. in weight, and provided it shall not have been clipped or filed, or have been defaced otherwise than by use.

"And that the said rupee shall be received as equivalent to the Bombay, Madras, Farrukhábád and Sonat rupees, and to fifteen-sixteenths of the Calcutta sicca rupee; and the half and double rupee respectively shall be received as equivalent to the half and double of the abovementioned Bombay, Madras, Farrukhábád and Sonat rupees, and to the half and double of fifteen-sixteenths of the Calcutta sicca rupee . . . .

"And that the undermentioned gold coins only shall henceforth be coined at the mints within the territories of the East India Company:—

First, a gold mohur of 15 rupee-piece, of the weight of 180 grains troy, and of the following standard, viz.:—

$\frac{11}{12}$ or 165 grains of pure gold.
$\frac{1}{12}$ or 15 grains of alloy.

Second, a five-rupee piece equal to a third of a gold mohur.

Third, a ten-rupee piece equal to two-thirds of a gold mohur

Fourth, a thirty-rupee piece, or double gold mohur.

"And the three last-mentioned coins shall be of the same standard with the gold mohur, and of proportionate weight.

"And that these gold coins shall bear on the obverse the head and name of the reigning sovereign of the United Kingdom of Great Britain and Ireland, and on the reverse the designation of the coin in English and Persian, and the words EAST INDIA COMPANY in English, with such embellishment as shall from time to time be ordered by the Governor-General in Council, which shall always be different from that of the silver coinage.

"And that no gold coin shall henceforward be a legal tender of payment in any of the territories of the East India Company.

"And that it shall be competent to the Governor-General in Council, in his executive capacity, to direct the coining and issuing of all coins authorised by this Act; to prescribe the devices and inscriptions of the copper coins issued from the mints in the said territories, and to establish, regulate, and abolish mints, any law hitherto in force to the contrary notwithstanding."

In the same year (1835) an Act (No. XXI) was passed, by which it was enacted "that from the 20th day of December 1835 the following copper coins only shall be issued from any mint within the Presidency of Bengal:—

1. A pice weighing .. .. .. 100 grs. troy,
2. A double pice weighing .. .. 200 ,,
3. A pice, or one-twelfth of an anna weighing .. .. .. 33⅓ ,,

with such devices as shall be fixed for the same by the Governor-General in Council."

By the same Act it was further enacted "that from the said 20th of December 1835, the said pice shall be legal tender for $\frac{1}{64}$ of the Company's rupee, and the said double pice for $\frac{1}{32}$ of the Company's rupee and the said pie for $\frac{1}{192}$ of the Company's rupee. Provided always that, after the said 20th of December 1835, no copper coin shall in any part of the territories of the East India Company be legal tender, except for fractions of a rupee."

In the following year (1836) it was enacted by Act XIII, that "from the 1st January 1838, the Calcutta sicca rupee shall cease to be a legal tender in discharge of any debt, but shall be received by the Collectors of land revenue, and at all other treasuries, by weight, and subject to a charge of 1 per cent. for recoinage. 1836.

"And that from the 1st of June 1836, Section V, Regulation XXV, 1817, of the Bengal Code that the pice struck at the mints of Benares and Farrukhábád agreeably to the provisions of Regulation X, 1809, and Regulation VII, 1814, and Regulation XXI, 1816, shall be considered as circulating equally with the pice of Calcutta coinage throughout the provinces of Bengal, Behar and in Orissa, and shall in like manner be received as a legal tender in payment of the fractional parts of a rupee of the local currency at the rate of sixty-four pice for each rupee, shall be repealed; and the said pice shall be a legal tender only within the provinces and places for which they were respectively coined....."

In a letter from the Government of India to the Madras Mint Committee, dated 17th December 1836, in which the question, whether the Madras mint should be restored temporarily or permanently and for the coinage of what metal, is discussed at great length, it is stated that "the coinage of silver having been shewn not to be necessary on the one hand and of doubtful practicability on the other, the only question that remains respects the copper coinage of the Madras Presidency, the supply of which is stated to be deficient in the extreme. The coinage of copper has been suspended in the Calcutta mint for two reasons—*first*, because of the urgent demand for silver in replacement of the sicca currency of Bengal, and *secondly*, because the price of copper has risen so much beyond previous averages, that the coinage ceased to yield the same profit as heretofore........ The mint of Calcutta having an excess of power available, and the expectation of ability to purchase copper on reasonable terms, the question recurs, whether this coinage shall be prosecuted for replacement of the existing copper currency of Bengal and the North-West Provinces, or part of the coinage shall be diverted to supply the wants of Madras.

"The determination of this question must rest on the decision that may be come to in respect to the expediency and possibility of continuing in circulation the old pyce, which the Government have latterly restored to credit. If this currency be not recalled and displaced, a small addition to the existing currency is all that can be required to keep the copper circulation steady at its legal tender par. But, if the copper currency of Bengal is to be entirely renovated, there will be no spare power in the mint to give to the striking of copper for Madras.

"The Right Honorable the Governor-General of India in Council is inclined at present to the opinion that it will be necessary eventually to call in and replace the old pyce of the former Calcutta mint. On this account, therefore, as well as on the ground that the coinage of copper can be commenced at Madras at a small cost and without delay, Rs. 2,000 only being required to set up the machinery and an establishment to work it, and because also there will be no difficulty or loss hereafter in stopping such a coinage, when it shall be no longer required, His Lordship in Council sanctions the proposition of Mr. Braddock that this coinage shall immediately be undertaken with the means available, provided the copper can be purchased at the price stated as that of tenders made to this mint, viz., Rs. 42 per Indian mun[1] or 100 lbs. troy, or, if the metal can be furnished from the Government stores."

From 1837 till 1840, during which time the mint machinery was undergoing repairs, the Madras records are silent; but it appears from a letter from the Mint Master, dated 17th February 1840, that the repairs were at that time so far advanced as to render it necessary that the preparation of the dies for the ensuing coinage should be commenced as soon as possible, so that the coinage might be proceeded with as soon as possible. It was about the same time pointed out that new Company's silver rupees, half, and quarter rupees, were the coins which it would be most desirable to strike off on the first opening of the mint, simultaneously with copper single pie pieces.

In a letter from the Calcutta Mint Committee, dated 14th December 1839, it is stated that "Captain Smith in his report to the Madras Government having impugned the artistical execution of the coinage of this mint, so far as concerns the device of the Company's rupee hitherto coined, in the accuracy of which we, as well as the Mint Master, entirely agree, the Mint Master has reminded us that, in the original communications to the Honorable Court in 1819, the necessity for a properly-qualified die engraver was strongly pointed out to the Honorable Court, and that the appointment of an engraver, consequent upon that representation, was then not made only because the mint was not sufficiently advanced to require his services. We think it our duty to state that we have had every reason to be satisfied with our present engraver, of whose efforts to produce an effigy of Her present Majesty from a sovereign we have the honor to forward a specimen; but, as he is at present the only competent engraver available, and has resisted every solicitation of the officers of the mint to instruct others in his art who might take up his duty when he was unwell or eventually succeed him, we are bound in duty to declare our conviction that it has become absolutely necessary that an able engraver should be sent out by the Honorable Court to take upon him, jointly with Kasheenauth, the duty of die engraver, and of preparing plates of steel or copper as the Mint Master and the Accountant-General for the time being shall direct, and to instruct such persons in the art of engraving to be his assistants and successors, as the Mint Committee for the time being shall direct to be placed under his instructions for these purposes." 1839.

By proclamation, dated November 18th, 1840, the Governor-General in Council was pleased to notify that "from and after the 1840.

---

[1] Note from Yule and Burnell, op. cit.

"The values of the *man* as a weight, even in modern times, have varied immensely, *i.e.*, from little more than 2 lbs. to upwards of 160. The 'Indian maund' which is the standard of weight in British India, is of 40 *sers*, each *ser* being divided into 16 chitaks; and this is the general scale of sub-division in the local weights of Bengal and Upper and Central India, though the value of the *ser* varies. That of the standard *ser* is 80 *tolas* or rupee-weights and thus the *maund* = 82$\frac{2}{7}$ lbs. avoirdupois. The Bombay maund (*or man*) of 40 *sers* = 28 lbs.; the Madras one of 40 *sers* = 25 lbs. The Palloda *man* of Ahmadnagar contained 64 *sers*, and was = 163$\frac{1}{4}$ lbs. This is the largest *man* we find in 'the Useful Tables.' The smallest Indian *man* again is that of Colachy in Travancore and = 18 lbs. 12 oz. 13 drs."

11th day of November 1840 in respect to the mint of Calcutta, and from and after the 1st day of April 1841 in respect to the mint of Fort St. George and Bombay, those parts of Act XVII of 1835 which were suspended by Act XXXI of 1837 (on the accession of Queen Victoria), directing that certain silver coins issued from the mints within the territories of the East India Company shall bear on the obverse the head of the reigning sovereign of the United Kingdom of Great Britain and Ireland, will be again in force; and that the device of the silver coins which shall be coined from and after the said dates, respectively, in the mints of India, in conformity with Acts XVII of 1835 and XXI of 1838, will be as Act XVII of 1835 enacts, viz. :—

On the *obverse* the head of Her Majesty Victoria with the words VICTORIA QUEEN.

On the *reverse* the denomination of the coin in English and Persian in the centre encircled by a wreath and around the margin the words EAST INDIA COMPANY, 1840.

" The coin will be milled on the edge with a serrated or upright milling, like the rupee now current bearing the head of his late Majesty William IV.

" The weight, standard, fineness and value of the Company's rupees as defined in the Act are here repeated. Weight, 180 grains troy, or one tolah. Standard quality eleven-twelfths silver one-twelfth alloy value. The same as the Company's rupee of 1835, the Madras, Bombay, Farrukhábád and Sonat rupee, and equal to fifteen-sixteenths of the late sicca rupee.

" The other silver coins authorised to be issued from the Government mint by Act XVII of 1835, and Act XXI of 1838, viz. :—double, half, and quarter rupees, and two-anna pieces will bear in all respects a due proportion to this rupee."

1841. By a further proclamation, dated February 10th, 1841, the Governor-General in Council was pleased to notify "that the gold coins henceforth to be issued from the Government mints at the different presidencies in India in conformity with Act XVII of 1835 shall bear the following device:—

" On the *obverse* the head of Her Majesty Queen Victoria with the words VICTORIA QUEEN, 1841.

" On the *reverse* a lion and a palm tree in the centre, with the designation of the coin in English and Persian below, and around the margin the words EAST INDIA COMPANY.

" The coin will be milled on the edge like the rupee. The weight and standard will be according to the Act as follows: Weight of the gold mohur or fifteen-rupee piece, 180 grs. troy; standard of ditto, $\frac{11}{12}$ or 165 grs. pure gold, $\frac{1}{12}$ or 15 grs. alloy.

" The other gold coins, viz., the five-rupee, ten-rupee, and thirty-rupee or double gold mohur pieces, will be of the same standard as the gold mohur or fifteen-rupee piece, and of proportionate weight."

1843. In a letter, dated 7th April 1843, the Assay Master to the Madras Mint wrote to the effect that he once proposed to Lord William Bentinck, when Governor-General, a spelter or zinc coinage of money which, as the method of rendering that metal malleable had become generally known, might have been effected at a small expense, and been made with considerable profit to the Company, superseded the use of cowrie shells, and most likely been melted down to form brass, as the copper was in various parts of the Company's dominions, thus affording a continued source of profit to the Company.

By Act XIII, 1844, it was enacted "that, from the 1st day of August 1844, the Trisoolee pice struck for the province of Benares, under the provisions of Regulations X of 1809 and VII of 1814, and at the Saugor mint, shall cease to be a legal tender within the province of Benares. 1844.

"And that until the said 1st day of August 1844, such Trisoolee pice shall be received on account of the Government, and shall be exchanged by take (that is to say, every Trisoolee pice paid in shall be received as one Company's pice and one Company's pice shall be given for every Trisoolee pice presented for exchange) at such treasuries or other places within the province of Benares as shall be pointed out for that purpose in any proclamation of the Lieutenant-Governor of the North-Western Provinces. . . . .

"And that it shall be lawful for the said Lieutenant-Governor, if he shall see fit, to order that in any case one Company's rupee shall be given for every sixty-four Trisoolee pice so presented for exchange, and that in every case one Company's rupee shall be given for every sixty-four Trisoolee pice accordingly."

In 1844 a further Act (No. XXII) was passed "for regulating the copper coinage of the mints in the territories of the East India Company," by which it was enacted "that from and after the passing of this Act the following copper coins only shall be issued from any mint within the territories of the East India Company :—

1. A pice weighing ... ... 100 grs. troy.
2. Double pice weighing ... ... 200 „
3. A pie or one-twelfth of an anna weighing ... ... $33\frac{1}{3}$ „

with such devices as shall be fixed for the same by the Governor-General in Council.

"And that from and after the passing of this Act the said pice shall be a legal tender throughout the territories of the East India Company for $\frac{1}{64}$ of the Company's rupee, and the said double pice for $\frac{1}{32}$ of the Company's rupee, and the said pie for $\frac{1}{192}$ of the Company's rupee."

In a minute by a member of the Madras Mint Committee on the question of the advisability of the practice of receiving uncurrent coins at the provincial treasuries, dated 1st April 1845, it is stated that "the practice of receiving uncurrent coins at the provincial treasuries at certain rates of exchange has existed almost from the period of the assumption of the country, and was adopted mainly, if not entirely, with the view of displacing the old currency by the new. . . . It would be desirable to ask the opinion of the Board of Revenue whether they considered the refusal generally in all districts to receive a foreign currency at the provincial treasuries in payment of revenue would be attended with any prejudicial effects; if not, I should make the refusal a general one. I would propose, however, that the prohibition should 1845.

be confined to the currency of native states and foreign European. The old Arcot rupees and all former coins issued from the Company's mints, including star pagodas and the Company's former rupees, as well as Bombay and sicca rupees, should continue to be received as hitherto. The Bombay-Soorat rupee, in which coin a considerable portion of the land revenue of the Bellary district is paid, is now classed, and I think improperly so, as uncurrent coin, and these should continue to be received at par, as they have hitherto been. We should under this system avoid all the evils attendant on the iniquitous practice adopted by Native Governments of debasing their coin from time to time, while all coins which have been issued from provinces now forming an integral portion of the British territory in India will continue to be received, till they wholly disappear from circulation.

"I would except, however, one coin from the general rule, namely, Spanish dollars. The rate of conversion at which they are received yields a large profit on recoinage. They are likely to be in demand at any time for remittance to China or on Eastern settlements, and they are by far the best form of bullion to send to England, if the Home treasury should be in need of specie remittances from this country. I think in 1838-1839 the Court of Directors particularly desired to have Spanish dollars in such cases."

In the same year a proposal was before the Madras Mint Committee as to the coinage of silver single anna pieces for the Ceylon Government.

1851. In March 1851 a proposal was made by the Assay Master, Fort St. George, that, in consequence of the general complaint of the want of currency suited to the exigencies of the lower orders throughout the territories of the East India Company, a zinc, or as it was commercially termed spelter coinage, representing the hundredth part of an anna, should be established, which would afford a profit equal to that of copper coinage, and would, it was thought, in time, supersede the use of cowries, the value of which fluctuated to the detriment of the vast multitude among whom it was current. It was also proposed that a trifling alteration might be made with regard to the copper coinage, a piece of the value of the tenth of an anna being substituted for the pie, and one of the value of the fifth of an anna for the three-pie pieces. But, as the abolition of the Madras mint was at that time under consideration, the proposals were not entertained.

A letter from the Mint Master, Calcutta, to the Mint Master, Madras, dated 30th June 1851, states that "in continuation of my letter intimating the dispatch of two matrices and six punches for the Queen Victoria rupee, I have now the honour to intimate that I have this day forwarded to the General Post Office for dispatch to you one box containing three obverse and three reverse punches for the Queen Victoria half rupee, as also three obverse and three reverse punches for the Queen Victoria quarter rupee.

"The obverse of the rupee punches last supplied and of the half rupee punches now forwarded have been obtained from original matrices engraved by Mr. Wyon of the Royal Mint, London, and transmitted to Calcutta by the Honorable the Court of Directors. The punches for the reverse have, however, been struck from matrices engraved by the Calcutta mint engraver, but are the same in design as those executed by Mr. Wyon, only having such a slight convexity as was found requisite to enable the dies formed by them to bring up the impressions on the coins.

"The punches for the quarter rupee have been obtained from the original English matrix, and they will therefore require to have the last two figures of the year (40) sunk in the die after it has been multiplied.

"The dies now in use in the mint for the whole, the half, and the quarter Victoria rupee bear date 1840, as has been considered desirable, to prevent the shroffs from charging a discount on the coins bearing this date, as they would do if the coins now issuing bore the date of the present year.

"Punches for the eight-rupee or the two-anna silver piece will be ready for dispatch by the next steamer."

In Notification, No. 26, dated Fort William, 22nd December 1852. 1852, it is stated that "by section 9, Act XVII of 1835, of the Government of India, it was enacted, that thenceforward no gold coin should be a legal tender of payment in any of the territories of the East India Company; and, accordingly, gold ceased from the date of the passing of the Act to be a legal tender of payment in the Company's territories in India.

"But, by a proclamation issued on the 13th January 1841, officers in charge of public treasuries were authorized freely to receive gold coins, struck in conformity with the provisions of the same Act XVII of 1835, at the rates indicated by the denomination of the pieces, until they should have passed certain limits of lightness, set forth in a table published with the proclamation, or until further orders; and gold coins have been thus received in liquidation of public demands up to the present date.

"Notice is now given . . . . . that on and after that date (1st January 1853), no gold coin will be received on account of payments due, or in any way to be made to the Government . . . . Gold will continue as heretofore to be received into any of the mints . . . . for coinage, under the Act and rules at present in force for the coinage of gold, but mint certificates for gold coins will be discharged in gold only, and no such certificate for gold will be accepted in any public treasury in liquidation of public demands, or on account of any payment to the Government whatever."

In 1854 an Act was passed "to amend Act No. XXI of 1853 1854. and Act No. XXII of 1844, and to authorise the issue of half pice," by which it was enacted that "after the passing of this Act, copper coins to be called half pice may be issued from any of the mints in the territories under the Government of the East India Company.

"A half pice shall weigh fifty grains troy, and shall be a legal tender in any part of the said territories for $\frac{1}{128}$th part of the Company's rupee, but shall not be a legal tender, except for fractions of a rupee."

Repealed by Act No. XIII, 1862.

1858. The charter of the Company was renewed for the last time in 1853, only, however, for so long as Parliament should ordain, and the number of Directors was reduced, and their patronage as regards appointments to the Civil Service was taken away, so as to make way for the principle of open competition. Five years later, on the 1st November 1858, at a durbar held at Allahabad, the royal proclamation was sent forth, which announced that Queen Victoria had assumed the Government of India, and so the career of the East India Company terminated after an existence of more than two-and-a-half centuries.

1862. So much of Act XVII, 1835, as provided that only the silver coins therein mentioned shall be coined, &c., and that they shall bear the words EAST INDIA COMPANY; also Act XXXI, 1837; Act XXII, 1844; and Act XI, 1854, except as to coin already issued, were repealed by Act No. XIII of 1862, by which it was enacted as follows:—

I. From the first day of November 1862, so much of the 1st and 2nd sections of Act XVII of 1835 (*relating to gold and silver coinage*), as provides that only the silver coins therein mentioned shall be coined at the mints within the territories of the East India Company, and that such coins shall bear on the reverse the words EAST INDIA COMPANY; also Act XXXI of 1837 (*relating to coinage*), Act XXI of 1838 (*relating to the silver coin*), Act XXII of 1844, and Act XI of 1854 (*relating to the copper coin*), shall be repealed, except as to any Act already done, or coin already coined or issued under the same.

II. From the first day of November 1862, except as provided by Act XVI of 1847 (*for establishing a copper currency in the Settlements of Penang, Singapore and Malacca*), in respect of cents, half cents and quarter cents, no silver or copper coins, except those mentioned below, shall be coined at the mints in British India:—

Silver Coins.

A rupee to be called the Government rupee.
A half rupee.
A quarter rupee or four-anna piece.
An eighth of a rupee or two-anna piece.

Copper Coins.

A double pice or half anna.
A pice or quarter anna.
A pie, being one-third of a pice, or one-twelfth of an anna.

III. The rupee so coined shall be of the same weight and standard as those provided for the Company's rupee by the said Act XVII of 1835, that is to say, the weight shall be 180 grains troy, and the standard as follows:—

$\frac{11}{12}$th or 165 grains of pure silver.
$\frac{1}{12}$th or 15 grains of alloy.

The other silver coins shall be of proportionate weight and of the same standard.

IV. The copper coins so coined shall be of the weight prescribed for coins of the same denominations respectively by Acts XXI of 1835 and XI of 1854, that is to say:—

The double pice shall weigh	.. ..	200 grs. troy.
The pice	.. ..	100 ,,
The half pice	.. ..	50 ,,
The pie	.. ..	$33\frac{1}{3}$,,

V. Until the Governor-General in Council shall otherwise order under the power hereinafter reserved, the silver and copper coins so coined shall bear on the obverse the likeness and the name of Queen Victoria and the inscription VICTORIA QUEEN, and on the reverse the designation of the coins in English, filled by the word INDIA, with such date and embellishments on each coins as the Governor-General in Council shall from time to time direct.

II.—CATALOGUE OF COINS IN THE MADRAS MUSEUM.

ENGLISH EAST INDIA COMPANY.

No.	Date.	Obverse.	Reverse.
		A. COINS WITH DATE.	
		MADRAS COPPER.	
1	1722	Orb and cross inscribed C.C. E., surrounded by a radiate border. [Pl. i, 1.]	Date 1722, with wavy line above and below, surrounded by a beaded circle.
2	1733	Bale-mark of the Company.	Date 1733. [Pl. i, 2.]
3	1733	"	" [Pl. i, 3.]
4	1736	"	Date 1736. [Pl. i, 4.]
5	1737	"	Date 1737, surrounded by a beaded circle. [Pl. i, 5.]
6	1755	Orb and cross inscribed C.C. E., surrounded by a radiate border.	Date 1755, with wavy line above and below. [Pl. i, 6.]
7	1755	"	" but traces of a beaded circle.
8	1755	"	"
9	1756	"	" but date *x*756. [Pl. i, 7.]
10	176*x*	"	" but date 176*x*.
11	176*x*	"	"
12	177*x*	"	" but date 177*x*.
13	177*x*	"	"
		BOMBAY COPPER DOUBLE PICE.	
14-15	1777	A crown with BOMB 1777 below it.	Bale-mark of the Company. [Pl. xv, 1.]

No.	Date.	Obverse.	Reverse.
		A. COINS WITH DATE—*continued.*	
		BOMBAY COPPER DOUBLE PICE—*continued.*	
16–25	177*x*	„ but date indistinct.	„ [Pl. xv, 2.]
		BOMBAY COPPER PICE.	
26	1777	Inscription 1 PICE BOMBAY 1777.	Bale-mark of the Company. [Pl. xv, 3.]
27–35	177*x*	„ but date indistinct.	„ [Pl. xi, 13.]
		MADRAS COPPER.	
36	1786	Orb and cross inscribed C.C. E., surrounded by a radiate border.	Date 1786, with wavy line above and below. [Pl. i, 8.]
		BOMBAY 20 CASH.	
		(*a*). GILT PROOF.	
37	1791	Bale-mark of the Company with date 1791 below.	A balance with the word عدل between the scales.
		(OBLIQUE MILLING.)	
		(*b*). BRONZE PROOF.	
38	1791	„	„
		BOMBAY 15 CASH.	
		BRONZE PROOF.	
39	1791	„	„
40	1791	„	„
		BOMBAY 10 CASH.	
		COPPER.	
41	1791	„	„ [Pl. i, 9.]

No.	Date.	Obverse.	Reverse.
		A. COINS WITH DATE—*continued.*	
		BOMBAY 5 CASH.	
		(*a*). GILT PROOF.	
42	**1791**	**Bale-mark of the Company with date 1791 below.**	**A balance with the word عدل between the scales.**
		(*b*). BRONZE PROOF.	
43	**1791**	,,	,,
		BOMBAY 20 CASH.	
		(*a*). COPPER.	
44	**1794**	,,	,, [Pl. i, 10.]
		(*b*). GILT PROOF.	
45	**1794**	,,	,,
		BOMBAY 10 CASH.	
		(*a*). COPPER.	
46	**1794**	,,	,,
		(*b*). GILT PROOF.	
47	**1794**	,,	,,
		BOMBAY 5 CASH.	
		GILT PROOF.	
48	**1794**	,,	,,

No.	Date.	Obverse.	Reverse.
		A. COINS WITH DATE—*continued.*	
		MADRAS $\frac{1}{48}$ RUPEE.[1]	
		(*a*). COPPER.	
49	1794	The arms of the Company with 48 TO ONE RUPEE below. The motto AUSPICIO REGIS ET SENATUS ANGLIÆ incuse upon a broad rim.	Bale-mark of the Company. The legend UNITED EAST INDIA COMPANY 1794 incuse upon a broad rim.
		The edge inscribed with the legend ENGLISH UNITED EAST INDIA COMPANY.	
		(*b*). GILT PROOF.	
50	1794	,,	,,
		(*c*). BRONZE PROOF.	
51	1794	,,	,,
		MADRAS $\frac{1}{96}$ RUPEE.	
		BRONZE PROOF.	
52	1794	,, but 96 TO ONE RUPEE.	,,
		MADRAS $\frac{1}{48}$ RUPEE.	
		COPPER.	
53	1797	Same as No. 49.	Same as No 49 except date.
		MADRAS $\frac{1}{96}$ RUPEE.	
		(*a*). COPPER.	
54	1797	Same as No. 52.	Same as No. 52 except date.

[1] This and the following coins of the same type are attributed by weight to the 'Cirkars in der Präsidentschaft Madras,' and Atkins writes concerning them: "In the following series an attempt has evidently been made to assimilate the Mohammedan with the Hindu monetary systems, as the 48th part of a Rupee is just equal to the Faluce or piece of 20 Cash. They were struck for the Circars, a large district on the coast of the Bay of Bengal to the north of the Carnatic country, and thus in a measure connecting Madras with Bengal."

No.	Date.	Obverse.	Reverse.
		A. COINS WITH DATE—*continued.*	
		(*b*). GILT PROOF.	
55	1797	Same as No. 52.	Same as No. 52 except date.
		MADRAS COPPER CASH.	
56	۱۲۱۲	Bale-mark of the Company surrounded by a beaded circle.	Date ۱۲۱۲. [Pl. i, 11.]
		TELLICHERRY SILVER.	
57	1799 ?	T. 99, and Persian inscription, surrounded by a beaded circle.	Persian inscription surrounded by a beaded circle. [Pl. ii, 1.]
58	1799 ?	,,	,, [Pl. ii, 2.]
		MADRAS COPPER.	
59	1801	Orb and cross inscribed C.C. E. surrounded by a radiate border.	Date *x*801 with wavy line above and below. [Pl. i, 12.]
60	1801	,,	,,
61	180*x*	,, [Pl. i, 13.]	,,
		MADRAS COPPER 2 DUBS.	
62	1801	۱۸۰۱ عیسوی دو فلوس هانربل کمپنی (" Christian year 1801. Two *falūs* of the Honorable Company ") surrounded by a serrated circle.	Inscription in Telugu " Two Dubs of the Company : " 2 DUBS : surrounded by a serrated circle. [Pl. ii, 3.]
		MADRAS COPPER ½ DUB.	
63	1801	۱۸۰۱ عیسوی فلوس هانربل کمپنی (" Christian year 1801. *Falūs* of the Honorable Company.")	Inscription in Telugu " Half Dub of the Company : " ½ DUB. [Pl. ii, 4, 5.]
64	1801	,,	,,

No.	Date.	Obverse.	Reverse.
		A. COINS WITH DATE—*continued.*	
		BOMBAY COPPER DOUBLE PICE.	
65	1802	Bale-mark of the Company with date 1802 below, surrounded by a serrated circle.	A balance with the word عدل between the scales, surrounded by a serrated circle.
66	1803	„ but date 1803.	„
		MADRAS COPPER 1 CASH.	
67	1803	Bale-mark of the Company.	Date 1803. [Pl. ii, 6.]
68	1803	„	„ [Pl. ii, 7.]
		MADRAS 1 CASH.[1]	
		(*a*). COPPER.	
69	1803	Lion l, carrying a crown, with date 1803 below. Plain rim on face.	كاس ("*kās*") 1 CASH. Plain rim on face. [Pl. ii, 8.]
70	1803	„	„
		(*b*). SILVER PROOF.	
71	1803	„	„
72	1803	„	„

[1] "These pieces occur as proofs in silver, bronzed, and gilt. They were made in England by Messrs. Boulton and Vatt, and it is said that No. 137 (= Nos. 69, 70) is the smallest coin ever struck in collar." Atkins.

No.	Date.	Obverse.	Reverse.
		A. COINS WITH DATE—*continued.*	
		MADRAS COPPER 10 CASH.	
73	1803	The arms of the Company with EAST INDIA COMPANY above, and date 1803 below : serrated rim on face.	ده کاس دو فلوس است ("Ten *kās* make two *falūs*") X CASH : serrated rim on face. [Pl. ii, 9.]
74	1803	,,	,,
		MADRAS COPPER 5 CASH.	
75	1803	,,	پنج کاس یکفلوس است ("Five *kās* make one *falūs*") V CASH : serrated rim on face. [Pl. ii, 10.]
76	1803	,,	,,
		BOMBAY 20 CASH.	
		GILT PROOF.	
77	1804	,, but date 1804.	A balance with the word عدل between the scales, and date ١٢١٩ beneath surrounded by a beaded circle.
		BOMBAY 10 CASH.	
		(*a*). COPPER.	
78	1804	,,	,, [Pl. ii. 11.]
		(*b*). GILT PROOF.	
79	1804	,,	,,

No.	Date.	Obverse.	Reverse.
		A. COINS WITH DATE—*continued.*	
		BOMBAY 5 CASH.	
		(*a*). COPPER.	
80	1804	The arms of the Company with EAST INDIA COMPANY above, but date 1804. [Pl. iii, 1.]	A balance with the word عدل between the scales, and date ١٢١٩ beneath; surrounded by a beaded circle.
81	1804	"	"
		(*b*). GILT PROOF.	
82	1804	"	"
		SILVER, TELLICHERRY.	
83	1805	A balance with the letter T between the scales, and date 1805 below.	Persian inscription. [Pl. iii, 2.]
84	1805	"	"
85	1805	" [Pl. iii, 3.]	"
		GOLD, TELLICHERRY.	
86	180*x*	T. 99, Persian inscription, and date 180*x*: surrounded by a beaded circle. [Pl. iii, 4.]	Persian inscription, surrounded by a beaded circle.
		MADRAS COPPER.	
87	1807	Bale-mark of the Company.	Date 1807. [Pl. iii, 5.]
88	1807	"	"

No.	Date.	Obverse.	Reverse.
		A. COINS WITH DATE—*continued.*	
		MADRAS COPPER 3 DUBS.	
89	1807	۱۸۰۷ عیسوی این سکہ سہ فلوس هانربل کمپنی یك فلم خورد است ("Christian year 1807. This coin, three *falūs* of the Honorable Company, makes one little fanam.")	In centre within circle, inscription in Telugu "Three new dubs and one little fanam." The same inscription in Tamil round margin. [Pl. iii, 7.]
		MADRAS COPPER ½ DUB.	
90	1807	۱۸۰۷ عیسوی نیم فلوس هانربل کمپنی ("Christian year 1807. Half *falūs* of the Honorable Company.")	In centre within circle inscription in Telugu "Company's half dub." The same inscription in Tamil round margin. [Pl. xv, 4.]
91	1807	"	"
		MADRAS COPPER 20 CASH.	
92	1808	The arms of the Company with EAST INDIA COMPANY above, and date 1808 below : serrated rim on face.	بیست کاس چهار فلوس است ("Twenty *kās* make four *falūs*") XX CASH : serrated rim on face. [Pl. iii, 6.]
93	1808	"	"
		MADRAS COPPER 10 CASH.	
94	1808	"	ده کاس دو فلوس است ("Ten *kās* make two *falūs*") X CASH : serrated rim on face.
95	1808	"	"

No.	Date.	Obverse.	Reverse.
		A. COINS WITH DATE—*continued.*	
		BENGAL 1 PIE.	
		COPPER PROOF.	
96	1809	The arms of the Company, with ONE PIE above, and date 1809 below: surrounded by a beaded circle.	The value of the coin "One Pai Sikka" in Persian, Nagárí, and Bengáli: surrounded by a beaded circle. [Pl. xv, 5.]
		BENGAL ½ PIE.	
		COPPER PROOF.	
97	1809	"	" but value of coin "Half Pai Sikka." [Pl. xv, 6.]
		BOMBAY COPPER PICE.	
98	1809	Bale-mark of the Company with date 1809 below.	A balance with the word عدل between the scales.
99	1810	" but date 1810.	"
100	1813	" but date 1813.	"
101	1815	" but date 1815.	"
102	1815	" "	"
		BOMBAY COPPER 4 PICE.	
103	1816	" but date 1816.	A balance with the word عدل and numeral 4 between the scales. [Pl. iii, 8.]
		BOMBAY COPPER DOUBLE PICE.	
104	1816	" " [Pl. iii, 9.]	" but no numeral.
		BOMBAY COPPER PICE.	
105	1816	" "	" [Pl. iii, 10.]

No.	Date.	Obverse.	Reverse.
		A. COINS WITH DATE—*continued.*	
		BOMBAY COPPER DOUBLE PICE.	
106	1819	Bale-mark of the Company, but date 1819.	A balance with the word عدل but no numeral.
		BOMBAY COPPER PICE.	
107	1820	„ but date 1820.	„
		BOMBAY COPPER PICE.	
108	1821	Bale-mark of the Company.	A balance with inscription in Nágarí पैसा ("*Paisá*") between the scales, and date ꣁꣃꣂꣁ below. [Pl. xv, 7.]
		BOMBAY COPPER ½ PICE.	
109	1821	„ and traces of date 18 *xx*.	A balance with inscription in Nágarí अर्धपैसा ("*Half Paisá*") between the scales, and date ꣁꣃꣂꣁ below. [Pl. iv, 1.]
		BOMBAY COPPER PICE.	
110	18*xx*	Bale-mark of the Company, date illegible.	A balance with the word عدل between the scales. [Pl. iv, 4.]
111	1825	Bale-mark of the Company with date 1825 below.	„ [Pl. iv, 2.]
112	1825	„	„
		BOMBAY COPPER ½ PICE.	
113	1825	„	„ [Pl. iv, 3.]
		BOMBAY COPPER ¼ PICE.	
114	1825	„	„

No.	Date.	Obverse.	Reverse.
		A. COINS WITH DATE—*continued.*	
		BENGAL COPPER 4 PAÍ.	
115	1825	The arms of the Company and date 1825: serrated rim on face.	Inscription 4 چهار[1] پائی ۱۲۴۰ سنہ within a wreath: serrated rim on face. [Pl. iv, 5.]
		BENGAL COPPER 2 PAÍ.	
116	1825	,,	,, but inscription 2 دو پائی سنہ ۱۲۴۰.[2] [Pl. iv, 6.]
117	1825	,,	,,
		BENGAL COPPER 1 PAÍ.	
118	1825	,,	,, but inscription 1 یك پائی سنہ ۱۲۴۰.[3] [Pl. iv, 7.]
119	1825	,,	,,
		BOMBAY COPPER ¼ ANNA.	
120	1833	The arms of the Company and date 1833: plain rim on face.	A balance with the word عدل between the scales, QUARTER ANNA above, and date ۱۲۴۹ below: plain rim on face. [Pl. iv, 8.]
121	1833	,,	,,
		BOMBAY COPPER 1 PIE.	
122	1833	The arms of the Company and date 1833: plain rim on face.	A balance with the word عدل between the scales, PIE above, and date ۱۲۴۸ below: plain rim on face. [Pl. iv, 9.]
123	1833	,,	,,
		BOMBAY COPPER ½ ANNA.	
124	1834	The arms of the Company with EAST INDIA COMPANY above, and date 1834 below: plain rim on face.	A balance with the word عدل between the scales, HALF ANNA above, and date ۱۲۴۹ below: plain rim on face. [Pl. iv, 10.]

[1] "Four *paí*, year 1240."
[2] "Two *paí*, year 1240."
[3] "One *paí*, year 1240."

No.	Date.	Obverse.	Reverse.
		A. COINS WITH DATE—*continued.*	
		GOLD.	
		DOUBLE MOHUR.	
125	1835	Bust of the King r: WILLIAM IV KING above, and date 1835 below: dotted rim on face.	Lion and Palm Tree: EAST INDIA COMPANY above, TWO MOHURS دو اشرفی[1] below: dotted rim on face.
		(STRAIGHT MILLING.)	[Pl. v, 1.]
		SINGLE MOHUR.	
126	1835	,,	,, but ONE MOHUR یک اشرفی[2]
			[Pl. v, 2.]
		SILVER.	
		1 RUPEE.	
127	1835	Bust of the King r: WILLIAM IV KING: dotted rim on face.	Inscription ONE RUPEE یک روپیہ[3] within a wreath EAST INDIA COMPANY 1835, around: dotted rim on face.
		(STRAIGHT MILLING.)	[Pl. v, 3.]
128	1835	,,	,,
		½ RUPEE.	
129	1835	,,	,, but inscription within the wreath HALF RUPEE هشت آنه[4]
		(STRAIGHT MILLING.)	[Pl. v, 4.]
130	1835	,,	,,

[1] "Two ashrafí."
[2] "One ashrafí."
[3] "One rupee."
[4] "Eight annas."

No.	Date.	Obverse.	Reverse.
		A. COINS WITH DATE—*continued.*	
		SILVER—*continued.*	
		¼ RUPEE.	
131	1835	Bust of the King r: WILLIAM IV KING: dotted rim on face.	Dotted rim on face, but inscription within the wreath ¼ RUPEE چهار آنه [1]
		(STRAIGHT MILLING.)	
			[Pl. v, 5.]
132	1835	,,	,,
		COPPER.	
		½ ANNA.	
133	1835	The arms of the Company and date 1835: plain rim on face.	Inscription دو پائی [2] HALF ANNA within a wreath: EAST INDIA COMPANY around: plain rim on face. [Pl. v, 6.]
134	1835	,,	,,
		¼ ANNA.	
135	1835	,,	,, but inscription within the wreath یك پائی [3] ONE QUARTER ANNA. [Pl. v, 7.]
136	1835	,,	,,
		$\frac{1}{12}$ ANNA.	
137	1835	,,	,, but inscription within the wreath $\frac{1}{12}$ ANNA ثلث پائی [4] [Pl. v, 8.]
138	1835	,,	,,

[1] "Four annas."
[2] "Two *pai*."
[3] "One *pai*."
[4] "One-third *pai*."

No.	Date.	Obverse.	Reverse.
		A. COINS WITH DATE—*continued.*	
		SILVER—*continued.*	
		1 RUPEE.	
139	1840	Bust of the Queen l: VICTORIA QUEEN: serrated rim on face.	Inscription ONE RUPEE يك روپيه within a wreath: EAST INDIA COMPANY 1840 around: serrated rim on face.
		(STRAIGHT MILLING.)	
140	1840	"	"
		½ RUPEE.	
141	1840	"	" but inscription within the wreath HALF RUPEE هشت آنه
		(STRAIGHT MILLING.)	
142	1840	"	"
		¼ RUPEE.	
143	1840	"	" but inscription within the wreath ¼ RUPEE چهار آنه
		(STRAIGHT MILLING.)	
144	1840	"	"
		GOLD.	
		SINGLE MOHUR.	
145	1841	Bust of Queen Victoria l: VICTORIA QUEEN: serrated rim on face.	Lion and Palm Tree: EAST INDIA COMPANY above, ONE MOHUR يك اشرفى below: serrated rim on face.

No.	Date.	Obverse.	Reverse.
		A. COINS WITH DATE—*continued.*	
		SILVER—*continued.*	
		2 ANNAS.	
146	1841	Bust of Queen Victoria l: VICTORIA QUEEN: serrated rim on face.	Serrated rim on face, but inscription within the wreath TWO ANNAS دو آنہ[1] and date 1841.
		(No MILLING.)	
147	1841	"	" [Pl. v, 9.]
		COPPER.	
		1 CENT.	
148	1845	Bust of the Queen l: and inscription VICTORIA QUEEN: plain rim on face.	Inscription ONE CENT within a wreath: EAST INDIA COMPANY, 1845, around: serrated rim on face.
149	1845	"	"
		½ CENT.	
150	1845	"	" but inscription within the wreath HALF CENT.
151	1845	"	"
		¼ CENT.	
152	1845	"	" but inscription within the wreath QUARTER CENT.
		SILVER.	
		1 RUPEE.	
153	1849	Bust of the Queen l: VICTORIA QUEEN: serrated rim on face.	Inscription ONE RUPEE ایک روپیہ within a wreath: EAST INDIA COMPANY, 1849, around: serrated rim on face.

[1] "Two annas."

No.	Date.	Obverse.	Reverse.
		A. COINS WITH DATE—*continued*.	
		½ RUPEE.	
154	1849	Bust of the Queen l: VICTORIA QUEEN: serrated rim on face.	Serrated rim on face, but inscription within the wreath HALF RUPEE هشت آنہ.
		(STRAIGHT MILLING.)	
		¼ RUPEE.	
155	1849	,,	,, but inscription within the wreath ¼ RUPEE چہار آنہ.
		(STRAIGHT MILLING.)	
		2 ANNAS.	
156	1849	,,	,, but inscription within the wreath TWO ANNAS.
		(NO MILLING.)	
		COPPER.	
		¼ ANNA.	
157	1853	The arms of the Company and date 1853: serrated rim on face.	Inscription پاؤ آنہ ONE QUARTER ANNA within a wreath: EAST INDIA COMPANY around: serrated rim on face.
		½ PICE.	
158	1853	,, but plain rim on face.	,, but inscription ½ PICE within the wreath and plain rim on face.
159	1853	,,	,,

No.	Mint : Date.	Obverse.	Reverse.
		B. COINS STRUCK IN THE NAME OF NATIVE PRINCES.	
		MURSHIDÁBÁD.	
		GOLD MOHUR.	
		(OBLIQUE MILLING.)	
1	Murshidábád ۱۲۰۲	حامی دین محمد سایهٔ فضل اله سکه زد بر هفت کشور شاه عالم بادشاه ۱۲۰۲ ("Defender of the Muhammadan faith, Reflection of Divine Excellence, the Emperor Sháh Alam has struck this coin to be current throughout the seven climes. 1202") (Prinsep.)	ضرب مرشد آباد سنه ۱۹ جلوس میمنت مانوس ("Struck at Murshidábád in the 19th year of his fortunate reign.") [Pl. vi, 1.]
1. 1	Murshidábád ۱۲۰۲	"	"
		GOLD MOHUR.	
		(STRAIGHT MILLING.)	
1. 2	Murshidábád ۱۲۰۲	"	"
		GOLD ONE-QUARTER MOHUR.	
		(OBLIQUE MILLING.)	
2	Murshidábád ۱۲۰۴	۱۲۰۴ سکه شاه عالم بادشاه ("1204 Coin of the Emperor Sháh Âlam.")	ضرب مرشد آباد سنه ۱۹ ("Struck at Murshidábád in the 19th year.") [Pl. vi. 2.]
3	Murshidábád ۱۲۰۴	"	"
		RUPEE.	
		(OBLIQUE MILLING.)	
4	Murshidábád *Sun* 19.	حامی دین محمد سایهٔ فضل اله سکه زد بر هفت کشور شاه عالم بادشاه ("Defender of the Muhammadan faith, Reflection of Divine Excellence, the Emperor Sháh Alam has struck this coin to be current throughout the seven climes.")	ضرب مرشد آباد سنه ۱۹ جلوس میمنت مانوس ("Struck at Murshidábád in the 19th year of his fortunate reign.")

No.	Mint: Date.	Obverse.	Reverse.
		B. COINS STRUCK IN THE NAME OF NATIVE PRINCES—*continued.*	
		RUPEE—*continued.*	
		(Straight Milling.)	
5	Murshidábád *Sun* 19.	Same legend as 4: dotted rim on the face.	Same legend as 4: dotted rim on the face. [Pl. vi, 3.]
6	Murshidábád *Sun* 19.	Same legend: but plain rim on face.	Same legend: but plain rim on face.
		HALF RUPEE.	
		(Straight Milling.)	
7	Murshidábád *Sun* 19.	Same legend: but serrated rim on face.	Same legend: but serrated rim on face. [Pl. vi, 4.]
		QUARTER RUPEE.	
		(Straight Milling.)	
8	Murshidábád ۱۲۰۴	۱۲۰۴ سکه شاه عالم بادشاه ("1204. Coin of the Emperor Sháh Alam:") serrated rim on face.	ضرب مرشد آباد سنه ۱۹ ("Struck at Murshidábád in the 19th year:") serrated rim on face. [Pl. vi, 5.]
		RUPEE.	
		(Without Milling.)	
9	Murshidábád *Sun* 19.	حامی دین محمد سایهٔ فضل اله سکه زد بر هفت کشور شاه عالم بادشاه ("Defender of the Muhammadan faith, Reflection of Divine Excellence, the Emperor Sháh Álam has struck this coin to be current throughout the seven climes.")	ضرب مرشد آباد سنه ۱۹ جلوس میمنت مانوس ("Struck at Murshidábád in the 19th year of his fortunate reign.") [Pl. vi, 6.]
10	Murshidábád *Sun* 19.	Same legend as 9: serrated rim on the face.	Same legend as 9: serrated rim on the face.

No.	Mint : Date.	Obverse.	Reverse.
		B. COINS STRUCK IN THE NAME OF NATIVE PRINCES—*continued.*	
		HALF RUPEE.	
		(Without Milling.)	
11	Murshidábád *Sun* 19.	Same as 9.	Same as 9. [Pl. vi, 7.]
		QUARTER RUPEE.	
		(Without Milling.)	
12	Murshidábád ۱۲۰۴	۱۲۰۴ سکہ شاہ عالم بادشاہ ("1204. Coin of the Emperor Sháh Álam.")	ضرب مرشد آباد سنہ ۱۹ ("Struck at Murshidábád in the 19th year.") [Pl. vi, 8.]
		FARUKHÁBÁD.	
		RUPEE.[1]	
		(Oblique Milling.)	
13	Farukhábád *Sun* 45.	حامی دین محمد سایۂ فضل الہ سکہ زد بر هفت کشور شاہ عالم بادشاہ ("Defender of the Muhammadan faith, Reflection of Divine Excellence, the Emperor Sháh Álam has struck this coin to be current throughout the seven climes.")	ضرب فرخ آباد سنہ ۴۵ جلوس میمنت مانوس ("Struck at Farukhábád in the 45th year of his prosperous reign.") [Pl. vii, 1.]
		RUPEE.	
		(Straight Milling.)	
14	Farukhábád *Sun* 45.	"	" [Pl. vii, 2.]
15	Farukhábád *Sun* 45.	"	"

[1] 45th sun Lucknow rupee of Reg. XLV, 1803.

No.	Mint : Date.	Obverse.	Reverse.
		B. COINS STRUCK IN THE NAME OF NATIVE PRINCES—*continued.*	
		RUPEE—*continued.*	
		(WITHOUT MILLING.)	
16	**Farukhábád** *Sun* 45.	Same legend as 13: plain rim on face.	Same legend as 13: plain rim on face. [Pl. vii, 3.]
17	**Farukhábád** *Sun* 45.	,,	,,
		HALF RUPEE.	
		(WITHOUT MILLING.)	
18	**Farukhábád** *Sun* 45.	,,	,, [Pl. vii, 4.]
19	**Farukhábád** *Sun* 45.	,,	,, [Pl. vii, 5.]
		QUARTER RUPEE.	
		(WITHOUT MILLING.)	
20	**Farukhábád** ١٢٠۴	١٢٠۴ سکه شاه عالم بادشاه ("1204. Coin of the Emperor Sháh Álam:") plain rim on face.	ضرب فرخ آباد سنه ۴٥ ("Struck at Farukhábád in the 45th year:") plain rim on face. [Pl. vii, 6.]
21	**Farukhábád** ١٢٠۴	,,	,,
		BENARES.	
		RUPEE.	
		(OBLIQUE MILLING.)	
22	**Benares** ١٢٢٩	حامی دین محمد سایهٔ فضل اله سکه زد بر هفت کشور شاه عالم بادشاه سنه ١٢٢٩ ("Defender of the Muhammadan faith, Reflection of Divine Excellence, the Emperor Sháh Alam has struck this coin to be current throughout the seven climes. 1229.")	ضرب محمد آباد بنارس جلوس میمنت مانوس سنه ١٧/۴٩ ("Struck at *Muhammadábád*, Benares, in the year ١٧/۴٩ of his fortunate reign.") [Pl. vii, 7.]

No.	Mint : Date.	Obverse.	Reverse.
		B. COINS STRUCK IN THE NAME OF NATIVE PRINCES—*continued.*	
		HALF RUPEE.	
		(OBLIQUE MILLING.)	
23	Benares ١٢٢٩	"	" [Pl. vii, 1.]
		QUARTER RUPEE.	
		(OBLIQUE MILLING.)	
24	Benares ١٢٢٩	١٢٢٩ سکہ شاہ عالم بادشاہ ("1229. Coin of the Emperor Sháh Alam.")	ضرب بنارس سنہ ١٧٤٩ ("Struck at Benares in the year 1749.") [Pl. vii, 8.]
		TRISOOLEE PICE.	
25	Benares *Sun* ٣٧	Value of the coin "*One pai*" in Persian and Bengálí: Mint mark a *trisula.*	شاہ عالم بادشاہ جلوس سنہ ٣٧ Mint mark a *trisula.* [Pl. xvi 1.]
26	Benares *Sun* ٣٧	"	"
27	Benares *Sun* ٣٧	"	"
28	Benares *Sun* ٣٧	"	"
29	Benares *Sun* ٣٥	"	شاہ عالم بادشاہ جلوس سنہ ٣٥ Mint mark a *trisula.* [Pl. xvi, 2.]

B. COINS STRUCK IN THE NAME OF NATIVE PRINCES—*continued.*

SURAT.

RUPEE.

(Straight Milling.)

No.	Mint : Date.	Obverse.	Reverse.
30	Surat ۱۲۱۵	سکه مبارک شاه عالم بادشاه غازی سنه ۱۲۱۵ ("The auspicious coin of the great Emperor Shah Álam, 1215:") surrounded by lined circle.	ضرب سورت سنه ۴۶ جلوس میمنت مانوس ("Struck at Surat in the 46th year of his propitious reign:") surrounded by lined circle. [Pl. viii, 2.]
31	Surat ۱۲۱۵	"	"

RUPEE.

(Without Milling.)

No.	Mint : Date.	Obverse.	Reverse.
32	Surat ۱۲۱۵	Same legend as 25: but serrated rim on face.	Same legend as 25: but serrated rim on face. [Pl. viii, 3.]
33	Surat ۱۲۱۵	"	"

HALF RUPEE.

(Without Milling.)

No.	Mint : Date.	Obverse.	Reverse.
34	Surat ۱۲۱۵	"	" [Pl. viii, 4.
35	Surat ۱۲۱۵	"	"

QUARTER RUPEE.

(Without Milling.)

No.	Mint : Date.	Obverse.	Reverse.
36	Surat ۱۲۱۵	Same legend as 27: but plain rim on face.	Same legend as 27: but plain rim on face. [Pl. viii, 5.]
37	Surat ۱۲۱۵	"	"

No.	Mint : Date.	Obverse.	Reverse.
		B. COINS STRUCK IN THE NAME OF NATIVE PRINCES—*continued.*	
		THICK GOLD MOHUR.	
38	Surat	. . . . . بادشاه . . . . A small crown.	. . . . جلوس ۳ . . . . . [Pl. xvi, 3.]
		THIN RUPEE.[1]	
39	Surat	. . . . . بادشاه غا	. . . . جلوس . . . . . [Pl. xvi, 4.]
		THICK RUPEE.	
40	Surat, 1825	. . . . بادشاه ۳ . . . . A small crown.	. . . . . . جلوس . . . . . Date 1825 incuse. [Pl. xvi, 5.]
41	"	"	"
		THICK HALF RUPEE.	
42	"	"	" [Pl. xvi, 6.]
		ARCOT.[2]	
		DOUBLE RUPEE.	
		(OBLIQUE MILLING.)	
43	Arcot ۱۱۷۲	۱۱۷۲ سکہ مبارک بادشاہ غازی عزیزالدین محمد عالمگیر ("The auspicious coin of the noble Monarch Ázíz-ud-dín Muhammad Álamgír, 1172:") serrated rim on face.	ضرب ارکاٹ سنہ ۶ جلوس میمنت مانوس ("Struck at Arkát in the 6th year of his propitious reign:") serrated rim on face. [Pl. ix, 1.]
44	Arcot ۱۱۷۲	"	"

[1] "The improved '*Surat*' Rupee, showing more of legend and better struck, coined both at Calcutta and Bombay, 1800 to 1818. Those struck at Bombay bear as mint mark a small crown." Atkins.

[2] Arcot rupees and their divisions were struck not only at the Madras Mint, but also at the Calcutta Mint, the latter being known as Calcutta-Arcot rupees, and distinguished from the former by bearing a rose as a mint mark instead of a lotus flower. Both types are represented in the following series. (*Vide* pl. ix, x.)

No.	Mint : Date.	Obverse.	Reverse.
		B. COINS STRUCK IN THE NAME OF NATIVE PRINCES—*continued.*	
		RUPEE.	
		(OBLIQUE MILLING.)	
45	Arcot ١١٧٢	Same legend as 33 : surrounded by a lined circle.	Same legend as 33 : surrounded by a lined circle. [Pl. ix, 2.]
46	Arcot ١١٧٢	"	"
		DOUBLE ANNA.	
		(OBLIQUE MILLING.)	
47	Arcot ١١٧٢	١١٧٢ سکہ عالمگیر بادشاہ ("1172. Coin of the Emperor Alamgír :") surrounded by a lined circle.	ضرب ارکاٹ سنہ ٦ ("Struck at *Arkát* in the 6th year :") surrounded by a lined circle. [Pl. ix, 3.]
48	Arcot ١١٧٢	"	"
		SINGLE ANNA.	
		(OBLIQUE MILLING.)	
49	Arcot ١١٧٢	"	" [Pl. ix, 4.]
50	Arcot ١١٧٢	"	"

B. COINS STRUCK IN THE NAME OF NATIVE PRINCES—*continued.*

RUPEE.

(STRAIGHT MILLING.)

No.	Mint : Date.	Obverse.	Reverse.
51	Arcot ۱۱۷۲	۱۱۷۲ سکہ مبارک بادشاہ غازی عزیزالدین محمد عالمگیر ("The auspicious coin of the noble Monarch, Áziz-ud-dín Muhammad Álamgír 1172 :") dotted rim on face.	ضرب ارکاٹ سنہ ۶ جلوس میمنت مانوس ("Struck at *Arkót* in the 6th year of his propitious reign :") dotted rim on face. [Pl. ix, 5.]
52	Arcot ۱۱۷۲	,,	,,

HALF RUPEE.

(STRAIGHT MILLING.)

No.	Mint : Date.	Obverse.	Reverse.
53	Arcot ۱۱۷۲	,,	,, [Pl. ix, 6.]
54	Arcot ۱۱۷۲	,,	,,

QUARTER RUPEE.

(STRAIGHT MILLING.)

No.	Mint : Date.	Obverse.	Reverse.
55	Arcot ۱۱۷۲	,,	,, [Pl. ix, 7.]
56	Arcot ۱۱۷۲	,,	,,

GOLD MOHUR.

(INDENTED CORD MILLING.)

No.	Mint : Date.	Obverse.	Reverse.
57	Arcot ۱۱۷۲	۱۱۷۲ سکہ مبارک بادشاہ غازی عزیزالدین محمد عالمگیر ("The auspicious coin of the noble Monarch Azíz-ud-dín Muhammad Álamgír, 1172 :") dotted rim on face.	ضرب ارکاٹ سنہ ۶ جلوس میمنت مانوس ("Struck at Arkát in the 6th year of his propitious reign:") dotted rim on face. [Pl. x, 1.]

No.	Mint : Date.	Obverse.	Reverse.
		B. COINS STRUCK IN THE NAME OF NATIVE PRINCES—*continued.*	
		GOLD MOHUR—*continued.*	
		(INDENTED CORD MILLING.)	
58	Arcot ۱۱۷۲	”	”
		HALF MOHUR.	
		(INDENTED CORD MILLING.)	
59	Arcot ۱۱۷۲	”	” [Pl. x, 2.]
		RUPEE.	
		(INDENTED CORD MILLING.)	
60	Arcot ۱۱۷۲	”	” [Pl. x, 3.]
61	Arcot ۱۱۷۲	”	”
		HALF RUPEE.	
		(INDENTED CORD MILLING.)	
62	Arcot ۱۱۷۲	”	” [Pl. x, 4].
		QUARTER RUPEE.	
		(INDENTED CORD MILLING.)	
63	Arcot ۱۱۷۲	۱۱۷۲ سکہ عالمگیر بادشاہ ("1172. Coin of the Emperor Alamgír:") dotted rim on face.	ضرب ارکاٹ سنہ ٦ ("Struck at Arkát in the 6th year:") dotted rim on face. [Pl. x, 5.]

No.	Mint : Date.	Obverse.	Reverse.
		B. COINS STRUCK IN THE NAME OF NATIVE PRINCES—*continued.*	
		GOLD MOHUR.	
		(No Milling.)	
64	Arcot ۱۲۱۴	سکه زد بر هفت کشور سایهٔ فضل اله حامی دین محمد شاه عالم بادشاه ("Defender of the Muhammadan faith, Reflection of Divine Excellence, the Emperor Sháh Alam struck this coin to be current throughout the seven climates.[1] 1214.")	ضرب ارکات سنه ۵۹ جلوس میمنت مانوس ("Struck at Arkát in the 59th (?) year of the auspicious reign.") [Pl. x, 6.]
		THICK RUPEE.	
		(Without Milling.)	
65	Arcot ۱۲۱۴	"	" but year 44. [Pl. x, 7.]
		THICK RUPEE.	
		(Without Milling.)	
66	Arcot	Traces of . . . . بادشاه	Lotus, and traces of سنه جلوس ارکات [Pl. x, 8.]
67	Arcot	"	"

[1] "When Timur, establishing his throne in India, overcame the Kings of Cashmeer, Bengal, Decan, Gudjraat, Lahore, Poorub, and Paishoor, he united the kingdoms, and called himself conqueror and sovereign of the seven climates or countries." Moor, Narrative of Little's Detachment, App. p. 472.

No.	Obverse.	Reverse.
	C. COINS WITHOUT DATE.	
	GOLD.	
	MADRAS THREE-SWAMI PAGODA.[1]	
1	Standing figures of Venkatesvara and his two wives.	Granulated surface. [Pl. xi, 1.]
2	”	”
3	”	”
	MADRAS PORTO NOVO OR SCOTT PAGODA.	
4	Figure of Vishnu.	Granulated surface. [Pl. xi, 2.]
	COPPER.[2]	
5	”	”
	GOLD.	
	MADRAS OLD STAR PAGODA.	
6	Figure of Vishnu with a star above the head.	Granulated surface with a 5-rayed star. [Pl. xi, 3.]
7	”	”
8	”	”
	BRASS.	
9	”	”

[1] Pagoda = $3\frac{1}{2}$ rupees; 1 rupee = 12 Fanams; 14 paisa = 75 cash.
[2] This is the only copper coin of this type which I have ever seen or heard of, and was obtained from Mr. Desika Chari. *Auct.*

No.	Obverse.	Reverse.
	C. COINS WITHOUT DATE—*continued.*	
	MADRAS NEW DOUBLE STAR PAGODA.	
10	The gopuram of a temple surrounded by stars in centre: inscription round margin TWO PAGODAS. دو هون [1]	Figure of Vishnu surrounded with dots in centre: inscription round margin "Two Pagodas" in Tamil and Telugu.
	(OBLIQUE MILLING.)	[Pl. xi, 4.]
11	"	"
	MADRAS NEW SINGLE STAR PAGODA.	
12	" but inscription PAGODA هون [2]	" but inscription "Pagoda" in Tamil and Telugu. [Pl. xi, 5.]
	(OBLIQUE MILLING).	
	MADRAS SINGLE MOHUR.	
13	Arms of the Company and inscription ENGLISH EAST INDIA COMPANY: dotted rim on face.	کمپنی انگریز بہادر اشرفی ("Ashrafi of the Honorable English Company:") dotted rim on face.
	(STRAIGHT MILLING.)	[Pl. xi, 6.]
14	"	"
	MADRAS ½ MOHUR.	
15	Lion l. holding crown, and inscription ENGLISH EAST INDIA COMPANY: dotted rim on face.	کمپنی انگریز بہادر نیم اشرفی ("Half ashrafi of the Honorable English Company:") dotted rim on face.
	(STRAIGHT MILLING.)	[Pl. xi, 7.]
	MADRAS ¼ MOHUR.	
16	"	کمپنی انگریز بہادر پاو اشرفی ("Quarter ashrafi of the Honorable English Company:") dotted rim on face.

[1] "Two hún." [2] "Hún."

No.	Obverse.	Reverse.
	C. COINS WITHOUT DATE—*continued.*	
	(STRAIGHT MILLING.)	
		[Pl. xi, 8.]
	MADRAS 5 RUPEES.	
17	Shield with lion l holding crown, and inscription ENGLISH EAST INDIA COMPANY: dotted rim on face.	پنجروپیه کمپنی انگریز بهادر ("Five Rupees of the Honorable English Company:") dotted rim on face.
	(STRAIGHT MILLING.)	
		[Pl. xi, 9.]
18	,,	,,
19	,,	,,
	BOMBAY GOLD RUPEE.	
20	. . . . بادشاه غازی	. . . . سنه جلوس . . . .
		[Pl. xi, 10.]
	SILVER.	
	MADRAS ? CHARLES II.	
21	Figure of Vishnu.	Two linked C's.
		[Pl. xi, 12.]
22	,,	,,
23	,,	,,
24	,,	,,
		[Pl. xi, 12.]
25	,,	,,
26	,, but surrounded by beaded circle.	,, but surrounded by beaded circle.
		[Pl. xv, 8.]
27	,,	,,

No.	Obverse.	Reverse.
	C. COINS WITHOUT DATE—*continued.*	
	COPPER.	
	BOMBAY DOUBLE PICE.	
28	A crown.	Motto [AU] SPICIO [REG] IS ET [SENATUS] ANG [LIAE. [Pl. xv, 9.]
29	"	"
	BOMBAY PICE.	
30	"	" [Pl. xv, 10.]
31	"	
	BOMBAY ?	
32	A crown with wreath below.	Undecipherable Persian inscription. [Pl. xvi, 7.]
	LEAD.	
	BOMBAY DOUBLE PICE.	
33	A crown with G.R. above, BOMB below.	Motto AUSPICIO REGIS ET SENATUS ANGLIÆ. [Pl. xvi, 8.]
	COPPER.	
	MADRAS.	
34	Orb and cross inscribed within a beaded circle. C.C. E.	Undecipherable inscription within a beaded circle. [Pl. xv, 11.]
	BOMBAY PICE.	
35	Bale-mark of the Company.	1 PICE BOMB. [Pl. xi, 13.]
	MADRAS.	
36	"*Srí.*" (Tamil).	"Kumpaní" (Tamil). [Pl. xii, 1.]
37	"	"

No.	Obverse.	Reverse.
	C. COINS WITHOUT DATE—*continued.*	
	COPPER—*continued.*	
38	Bale-mark of the Company: surrounded by a beaded circle.	Crossed lines and symbols. [Pl. xii, 2.]
39	,,	,,
40	,,	,,
41	,,	,,
42	,,	Persian inscription. [Pl. xii, 3.]
43	Bale-mark of the Company.	Bale-mark of the Company.
	MADRAS 40 CASH.	
44	این چهل کاس است ("This is Forty Cash") XL CASH: serrated rim on face.	Inscription in Tamil and Telugu, "This is Forty Cash:" serrated rim on face. [Pl. xii, 4.]
45	,,	,,
	MADRAS 20 CASH.	
46	این بیست کاس است ("This is Twenty Cash") XX CASH.	Inscription in Tamil and Telugu, "This is Twenty Cash." [Pl. xii, 5.]
	MADRAS 10 CASH.	
47	این ده کاس است ("This is Ten Cash.") X CASH.	Inscription in Tamil and Telugu, "This is Ten Cash." [Pl. xii, 6.]

No.	Obverse.	Reverse.
	C. COINS WITHOUT DATE—*continued.*	
	COPPER—*continued.*	
	MADRAS 10 CASH—*continued.*	
48	این ده کاس است ("This is Ten Cash") X CASH.	Inscription in Tamil and Telugu "This is Ten Cash."
49	,,	,,
	MADRAS 5 CASH.	
50	این پنج کاس است ("This is Five Cash") V CASH.	Inscription in Tamil and Telugu "This is Five Cash." [Pl. xii, 7.]
51	,,	,,
	MADRAS 2½ CASH.	
52	این دو و نیم کاس است ("This is Two-and-a-half Cash") 2½ CASH: surrounded by a circle of dots.	Inscription in Tamil and Telugu "This is Two-and-a-half Cash:" surrounded by a circle of dots. [Pl. xii, 8.]
53	,,	,,
	MADRAS ¼ DUB.	
54	Inscription in Tamil "Quarter Dub of the Company."	Inscription in Telugu "Quarter Dub of the Company." [Pl. xiii, 6.]
	BENGAL TWO PA'Í SIKKA.	
55	سنہ جلوس ۳۷ شاہ عالم بادشاہ ("In the 37th year of the reign of the Emperor Sháh alam.")	Inscription in Bengálí, Persian, and Nágarí "Two Pá'í Sikka." [Pl. xii, 10.]
	BENGAL ONE PA'Í SIKKA.	
56	,,	Inscription in Bengálí, Persian, and Nágarí "One Pa'í Sikka." [Pl. xiii, 1.]
57	,,	,,
58	,, but plain rim on face.	,, but plain rim on face. [Pl. xiii, 2.]

C. COINS WITHOUT DATE—*continued.*

COPPER—*continued.*

No.	Obverse.	Reverse.
59	سنه جلوس ۳۷ شاه عالم بادشاه (" In the 37th year of the reign of the Emperor Sháh Alam :") but plain rim on face.	Inscription in Bengalí, Persian, and Nágarí "One Pa'í Sikka :" but plain rim on face.
60	,, but lined circle on face.	Inscription in Persian and Nágarí' " One Pa'í Sikka :" lined circle on face. [Pl. xiii, 3.]

BENGAL ½ PA'Í SIKKA.

No.	Obverse.	Reverse.
61	,,	Inscription in Persian and Nágarí " Half Pa'í Sikka :" lined circle on face. [Pl. xiii, 4.]

BENGAL ½ ANNA.

No.	Obverse.	Reverse.
62	Inscription in English and Bengálí "Half Anna :" serrated rim on face.	Inscription in Persian and Nágarí " Half Anna :" serrated rim on face. [Pl. xiii, 5.]

BENGAL 1 PIE.[1]

No.	Obverse.	Reverse.
63	Inscription in English and Bengálí, " One Pie : " serrated rim on face.	Inscription in Persian and Nagárí " One Pie :" serrated rim on face. [Pl. xii, 9.]
64	,,	,,

SILVER.

MADRAS 4 ANNAS.

No.	Obverse.	Reverse.
65	Centre, چهار آنه روپیه ;[2] around, FOUR ANNAS.	Centre, "Four Annas" (Telugu) : around, " Four Annas " (Tamil) and a star.

(Oblique Milling.)

No.	Obverse.	Reverse.
66	,,	,, [Pl. xiii, 7.]

[1] " The pá'í or third of a paisá has ...... merely the name "one pá'í, which makes it liable to be confounded with the " one pá'í sikká, " and on this account, perhaps, it has not found ready currency. The natives reckon only sixty-four paisá to the rupee, while the English accounts divide the áná into twelve pá'í ; to distinguish them, this latter (hitherto an imaginary coin) was called the pá'í of account." Prinsep.

[2] " Four annas *rupia*."

No.	Obverse.	Reverse.
	C. COINS WITHOUT DATE—*continued.*	
	SILVER—*continued.*	
	MADRAS 2 ANNAS.	
67	Centre, دو آنه روپیه [1]; around, TWO ANNAS.	Centre, "Two Annas" (Telugu) around, "Two Annas" (Tamil) and a star.
	(OBLIQUE MILLING.)	[Pl. xiii, 8.]
68	,,	,,
	MADRAS ½ PAGODA.	
69	The gopuram of a temple surrounded by stars in centre: inscription round margin HALF PAGODA نیم هون پهولی.[2]	Figure of Vishnu surrounded by dots in centre: inscription round margin "Half Star Pagoda" in Tamil and Telugu.
	(OBLIQUE MILLING.)	[Pl. xiv, 1.]
70	,,	,,
	MADRAS ¼ PAGODA.	
71	,, but inscription QUARTER PAGODA پاو هون پهولی[3].	,, but inscription "Quarter Star Pagoda" in Tamil and Telugu.
	(OBLIQUE MILLING.)	[Pl. xiv, 2.]
72	,,	,,
	MADRAS 5 FANAMS.	
73	Centre, پنج فلم; [4]; around, FIVE FANAMS.	Centre, "Five Rukalu" (Telugu); around, "Five Panams" (Tamil) and a star.
	(OBLIQUE MILLING.)	[Pl. xiv, 3.]

[1] "Two annas *rupia*."
[2] "Half *puli* hun."
[3] "Quarter *puli* hun."
[4] "Five falams."

No.	Obverse.	Reverse.
	C. COINS WITHOUT DATE—*continued.*	
	SILVER—*continued.*	
74	Centre, پنج فلم ; around, FIVE FANAMS.	Centre, "Five Rukalu" (Telugu); around, "Five Panams" (Tamil) and a star.
75	"	"
76	"	" but no star.
	(THICK COIN.)	
		[Pl. xvi, 9.]
	MADRAS DOUBLE FANAM.	
77	Centre, دو فلم [1]; around, DOUBLE FANAM.	Centre, "Two Rukalu" (Telugu); around, "Two Panams" (Tamil) and a star.
	(OBLIQUE MILLING.)	
		[Pl. xiv, 4.]
78	"	"
79	"	"
	MADRAS FANAM.	
80	Centre, فلم [2]; around, FANAM.	Centre, "Ruka" (Telugu); around, "Panam" (Tamil) and a star.
	(OBLIQUE MILLING.)	
		[Pl. xiv, 5.]
81	"	"
82	A star in centre: surrounded by the word FANAM and a wreath.	A star in centre: surrounded by the words "Ruka" (Telugu) and "Panam" (Tamil).
		[Pl. xiv, 6.]
83	"	"

[1] "Two falams."

[2] "One falam."

ADDENDA.

During the revision of the later proof sheets, I had the opportunity of examining a large number of coins from the Ganjam district, out of which the following coins of the Company have been added :—

P. 93. Nos. 145·1 and 145·2. Gold Mohur. (Lion and Palm Tree). 1841.

P. 96. No. 4·1. Murshidábád rupee, oblique milling.

" " Nos. 4·3 and 4·2. Murshidábád ½ rupee, oblique milling.

" " Nos. 4·4 and 4·5· Murshidábád ¼ rupee, oblique milling.

P. 97. No. 7·1. Murshidábád ½ rupee, straight milling.

" " No. 8·1. Murshidábád ¼ rupee, straight milling.

P. 98. No. 12·1. Murshidábád ¼ rupee, without milling.

" " No. 13·1. Farukhábád ½ rupee, oblique milling.

P. 102. Nos. 41·1 and 41·2. Thick Surat rupee, without date incuse.

" " Nos. 42·1—42·7. Old sun 19 sikka rupees, and ½ rupees.

P. 106. Nos. 65·1—65·31. Arcot rupees of the same type as No. 65, with various dates.

" " Nos. 67·1—67·3. Arcot ½ and ¼ rupees of the same type as No. 67.

INDEX TO PLATES.

PLATE I.

Fig.	Metal.	Date.	Description of Coin.	Page.
1	Ae.	1722	Madras.	79
2	,,	1733	,,	28, 79
3	,,	,,	,,	79
4	,,	1736	,,	28, 79
5	,,	1737	,,	79
6	,,	1755	,,	28, 79
7	,,	1756	,,	28, 79
8	,,	1786	,,	28, 80
9	,,	1791	Bombay. 10 Cash.	80
10	,,	1794	,, 20 ,,	81
11	,,	١٢١٢	Madras. Cash.	83
12	,,	1801	Madras.	83
13	,,	180x	,,	83

PLATE II.

Fig.	Metal.	Date.	Description of Coin.	Page.
1	Ar.	1799 ?	Tellicherry.	21, 83
2	,,	,,	,,	21, 83
3	Ae.	1801	Madras. 2 Dubs.	83
4	,,	,,	,, ½ Dub.	83
5	,,	,,	,, ,, ,,	83
6	,,	1803	,, 1 Cash.	84
7	,,	,,	,, ,, ,,	84
8	,,	,,	,, ,, ,,	84
9	,,	,,	,, 10 ,,	85
10	,,	,,	,, 5 ,,	85
11	,,	1804	Bombay. 10 ,,	85

PLATE III.

Fig.	Metal.	Date.	Description of Coin.	Page.
1	Ae.	1804	Bombay. 5 Cash.	89
2	Ar.	1805	Tellicherry.	21, 86
3	,,	,,	,,	21, 86
4	Au.	180*x*	,,	22, 86
5	Ae.	1807	Madras.	86
6	,,	1808	Madras. 20 Cash.	87
7	,,	1807	,, 3 Dubs.	87
8	,,	1816	Bombay. 4 Pice.	88
9	,,	,,	,, 2 ,,	88
10	,,	,,	,, Single.	88

PLATE IV.

Fig.	Metal.	Date.	Description of Coin.	Page.
1	Ae.	1821	Bombay. ½ Pice.	89
2	,,	1825	,, Single Pice.	89
3	,,	1826	,, ½ ,,	89
4	,,	18*xx*	,, Single ,,	89
5	,,	1826	,, 4 Paí.	90
6	,,	,,	,, 2 ,,	90
7	,,	,,	,, 1 ,,	90
8	,,	1833	,, ¼ Anna.	90
9	,,	,,	,, 1 Pie.	90
10	,,	1834	,, ½ Anna.	90

PLATE V.

Fig.	Metal.	Date.	Description of Coin.	Page.
1	Au.	1835	Double Mohur.	91
2	,,	,,	Single ,,	91
3	Ar.	,,	1 Rupee.	91
4	,,	,,	½ ,,	91
5	,,	,,	¼ ,,	92
6	Ae.	,,	½ Anna.	92
7	,,	,,	¼ ,,	92
8	,,	,,	$\frac{1}{12}$,,	92
9	Ar.	1841	2 Annas.	94

PLATE VI.

Fig.	Metal.	Date.	Description of Coin.	Page.
1	Au.	١٢٠٢	Murshidábád. Mohur.	96
2	,,	١٢٠٣	,, ¼ ,,	96
3	Ar.	*Sun.* 19	,, Rupee.	97
4	,,	,,	,, ½ ,,	97
5	,,	١٢٠٣	,, ¼ ,,	97
6	,,	*Sun.* 19	,, Rupee.	97
7	,,	,,	,, ½ ,,	98
8	,,	١٢٠٣	,, ¼ ,,	98

PLATE X.

Fig.	Metal.	Date.	Description of Coin.	Page.
1	Au.	١١٧٢	Arcot. Mohur.	104
2	,,	,,	,, ½ ,,	105
3	Ar.	,,	,, Rupee.	105
4	,,	,,	,, ½ ,,	105
5	,,	,,	,, ¼ ,,	105
6	Au.	١٢١٣	,, Mohur.	106
7	Ar.	,,	,, Rupee.	106
8	,,	,,	,, ,,	106

PLATE XI.

Fig.	Metal.	Date.	Description of Coin.	Page.
1	Au.		Madras. 3 Swámi Pagoda	107
2	,,		,, Porto Novo ,,	13, 22, 107
3	,,		,, Old Star ,,	13, 14, 107
4	,,		,, New double Star ,,	14, 108
5	,,		,, Single ,, ,,	14, 108
6	,,		,, Mohur.	108
7	,,		,, ½ ,,	108
8	,,		,, ¼ ,,	109
9	,,		,, 5 Rupees.	109
10	,,		Bombay. Gold Rupee.	51, 109
11	Ar.		Madras ? Charles II.	20, 109
12	,,		,, ,, ,,	21, 109
13	Ae.	177x	Bombay. Pice.	80, 110

PLATE XII.

Fig.	Metal.	Date.	Description of Coin.	Page.
1	Ae.		Madras.	110
2	,,		,,	111
3			,,	111
4	,,		Madras. 40 Cash.	111
5	,,		,, 20 ,,	111
6	,,		,, 10 ,,	111
7	,,		,, 5 ,,	112
8	,,		,, 2½ ,,	112
9	,,		Bengal. 1 Pie.	113
10	,,		,, 2 Paí Sikka.	112

PLATE XIII.

Fig.	Metal.	Date.	Description of Coin.	Page.
1	Ae.		Bengal. 1 Paí Sikka.	112
2	,,		,, ,, ,,	112
3	,,		,, ,, ,,	113
4	,,		,, ½ ,, ,,	113
5	,,		,, ⅓ Anna.	113
6	,,		Madras. ½ Pie.	112
7	Ar.		,, 4 Annas.	113
8	,,		,, 2 ,,	114

PLATE XIV.

Fig.	Metal.	Date.	Description of Coin.	Page.
1	Ar.		Madras. ½ Pagoda.	114
2	,,		,, Single ,,	114
3	,,		,, 5 Fanams.	114
4	,,		,, Double Fanam.	115
5	,,		,, Single ,,	115
6	,,		,, ,, ,,	115

PLATE XV.

Fig.	Metal.	Date.	Description of Coin.	Page.
1	Ae.	1777	Bombay. Double Pice.	33, 79
2	,,	177*x*	,, ,, ,,	80
3	,,	1777	,, Single Pice.	33, 80
4	,,	1807	Madras. ⅓ Dub.	87
5	,,	1809	Bengal. Proof. 1 Pie.	88
6	,,	,,	,, ,, ½ ,,	88
7	,,	1821	Bombay. Pice.	89
8	Ar.		Madras? Charles II.	20, 109
9	Ae.		Bombay. Double Pice.	110
10	,,		,, Single ,,	110
11	,,		Madras.	110

PLATE XVI.

PLATE XVII.

PLATE XVIII.

PLATE XIX.

PLATE XX.

Fig.	Metal.	Date.	Description of Coin.	Page.
1	Ae.	173*x*	George II. Pice.	28
2	,,	1742	,, ,, ,,	28
3	,,	1813	George III. ¼ Pice.	33
4	Au.	1765	Bombay. Pattern Mohur.	35
5	,,	1770	,, ,, ,,	35
6	Ae.	1793	Proof. Copper.	38
7	Ar.	1834	Pattern. Rupee.	63
8	Ae.		Patna Post. One Anna.	63
9		1822	Benares. Pattern.	

Plate. I.

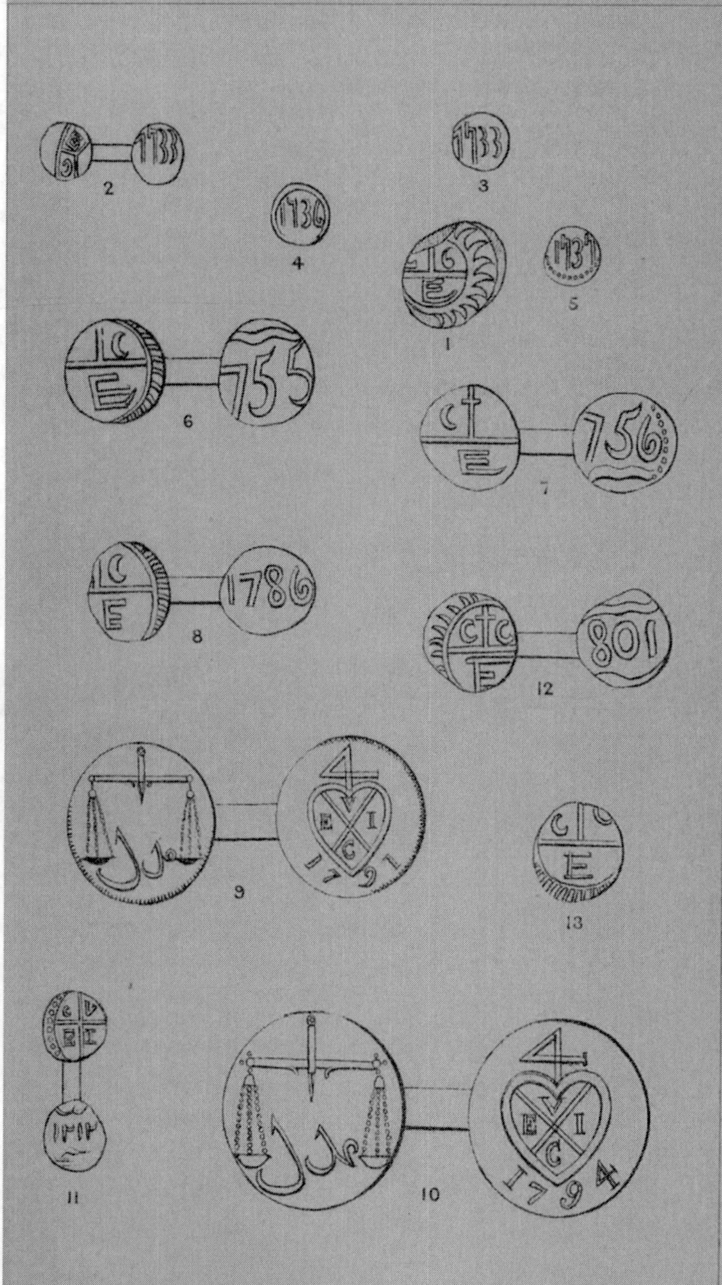

Plate II.

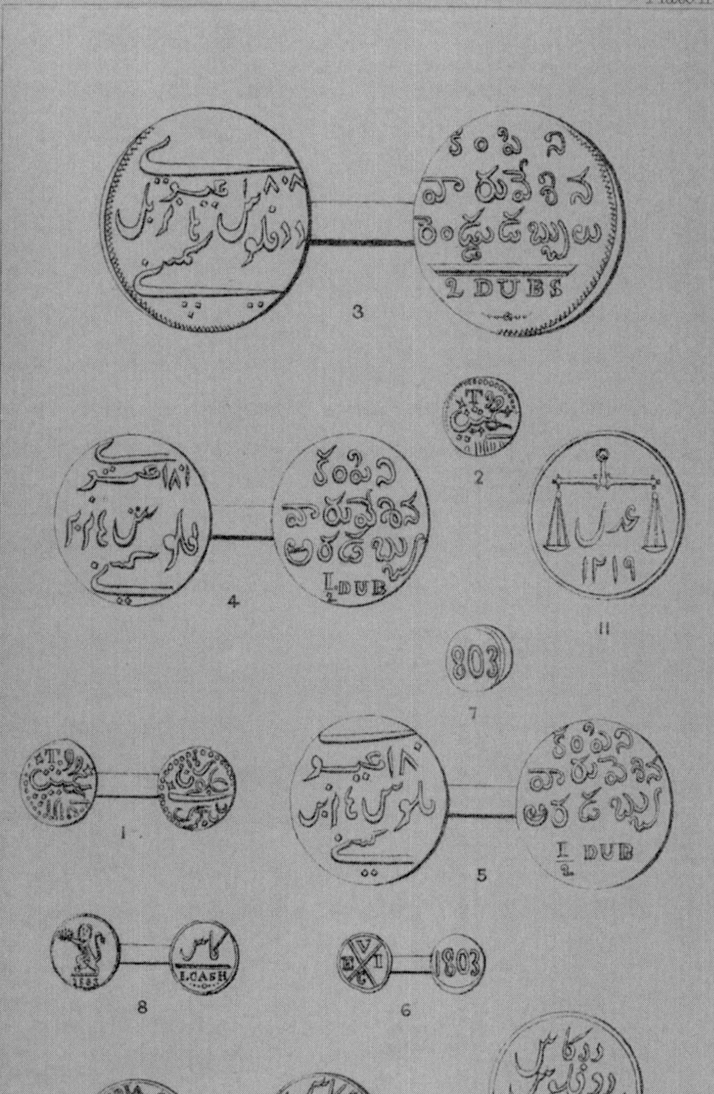

Plate III.

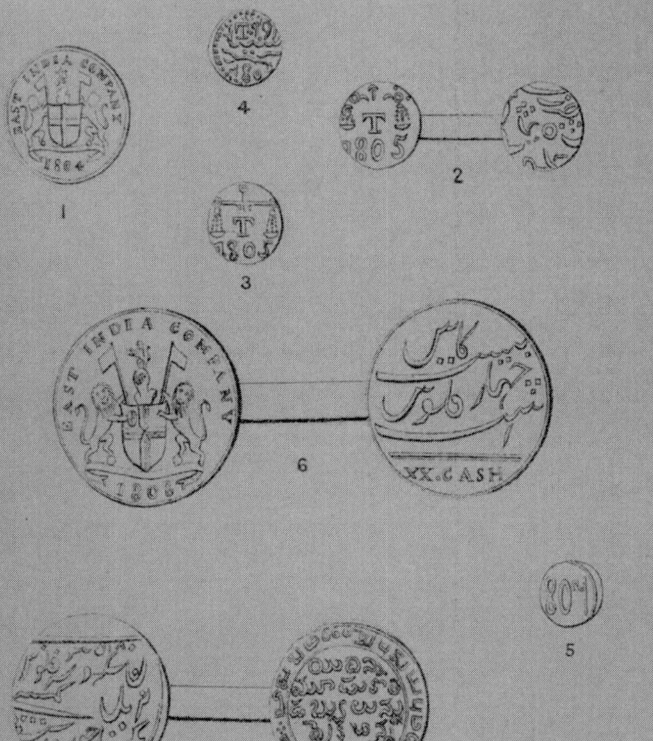

3
5
6
7
1
2
4
QUARTER ANNA
8
PIE
9
HALFANNA
10

Plate V.

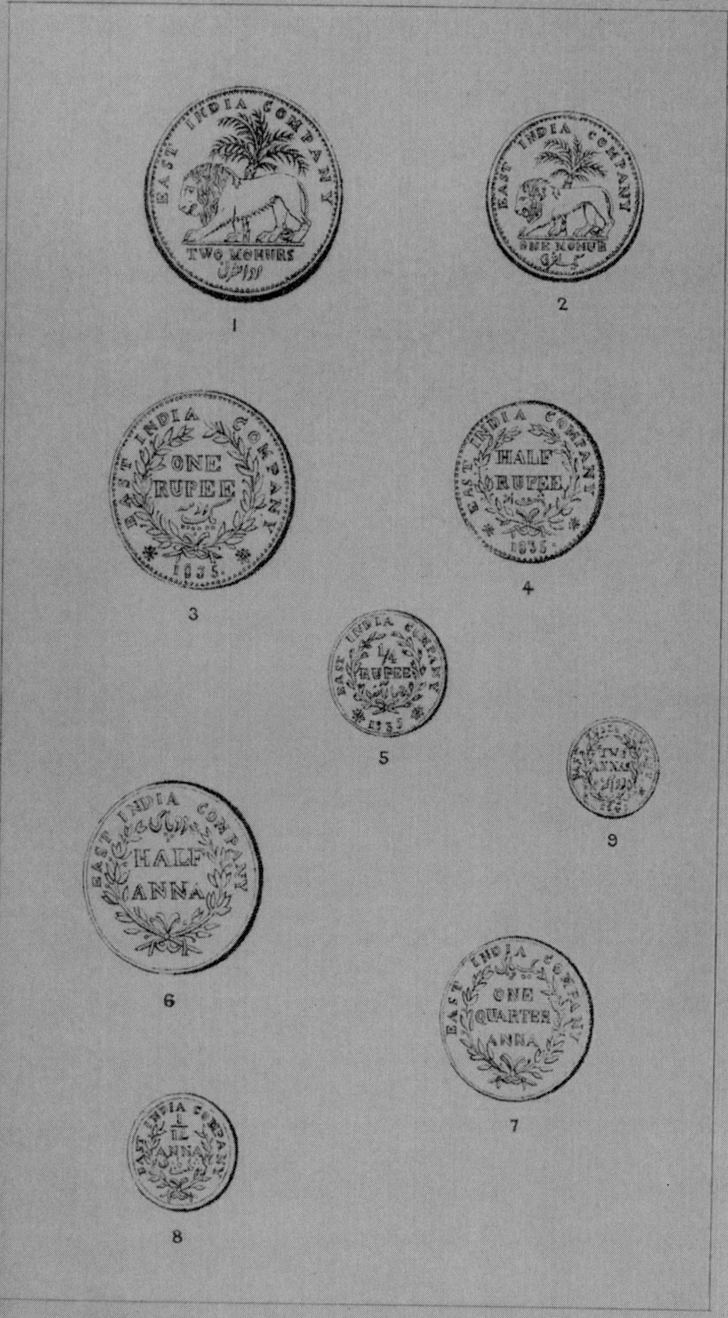
EAST INDIA COMPANY
TWO MOHURS
1
EAST INDIA COMPANY
ONE MOHUR
2
EAST INDIA COMPANY
ONE RUPEE
1835.
3
EAST INDIA COMPANY
HALF RUPEE
1835
4
EAST INDIA COMPANY
1/4 RUPEE
1835
5
EAST INDIA COMPANY
HALF ANNA
6
EAST INDIA COMPANY
ONE QUARTER ANNA
7
EAST INDIA COMPANY
1/12 ANNA
8
9

Plate. VI.

1

2

3

4

5

6

7

8

Plate. VII.

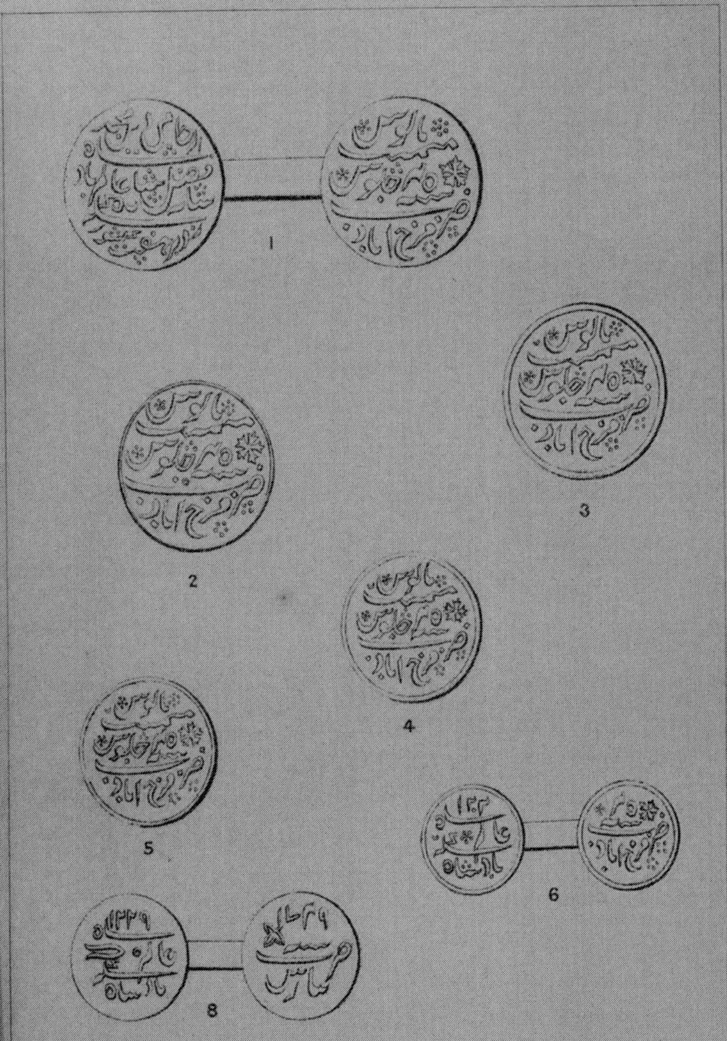

Plate VIII.

1

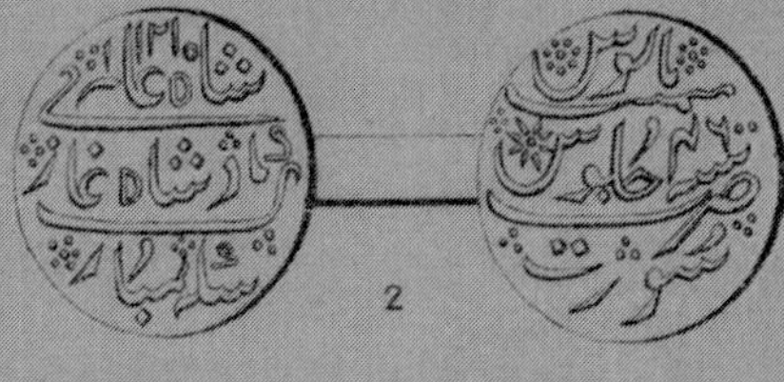

2

3

4

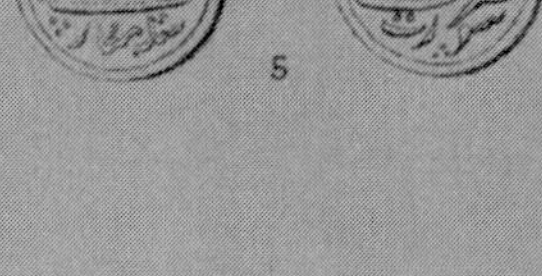

5

Plate IX.

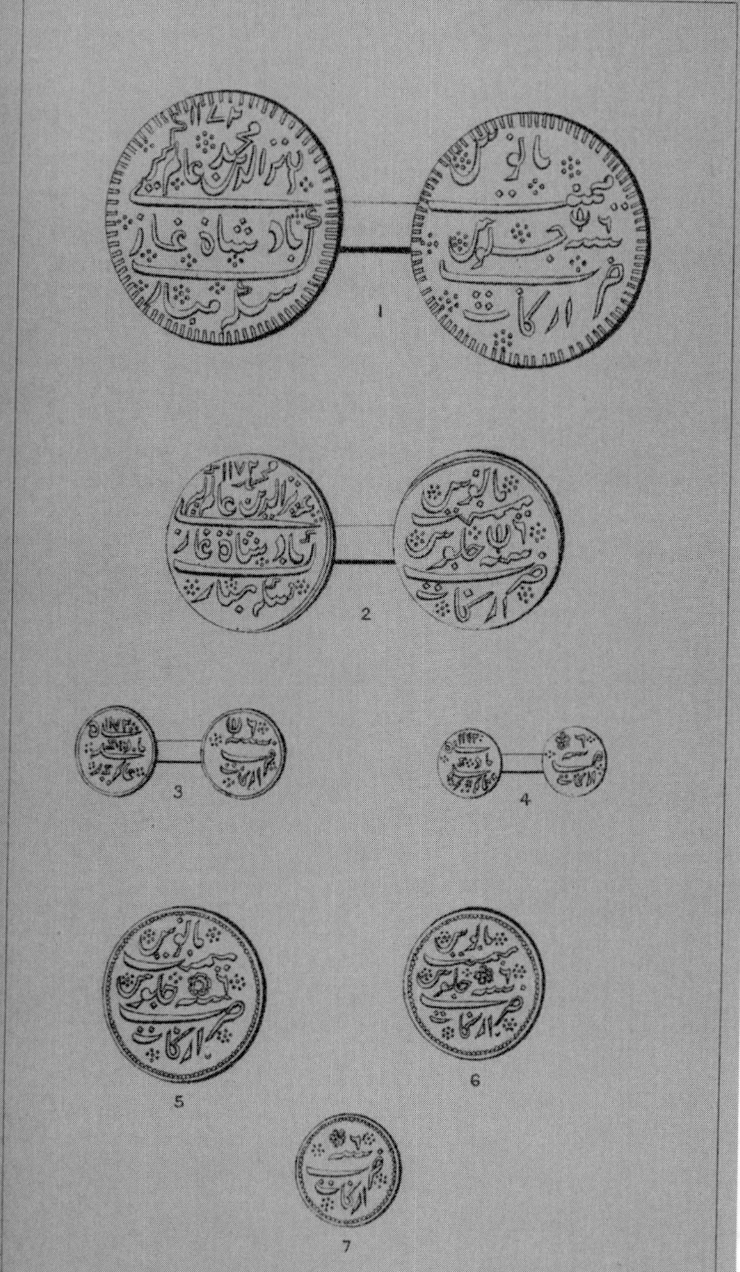

Plate X.

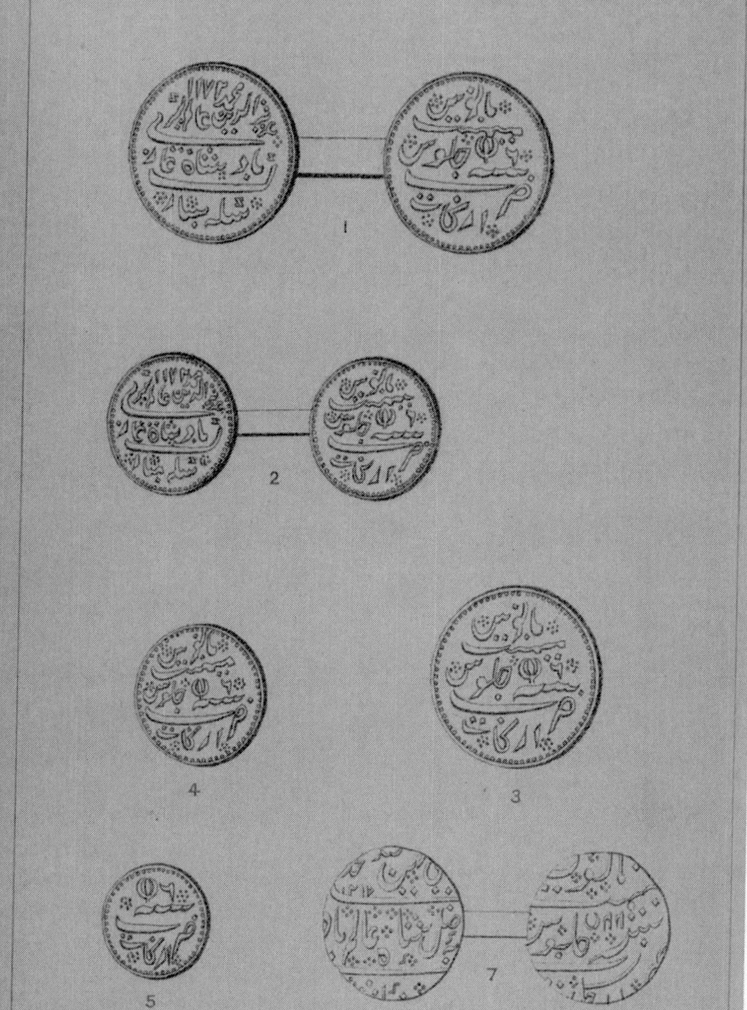

Plate XI.

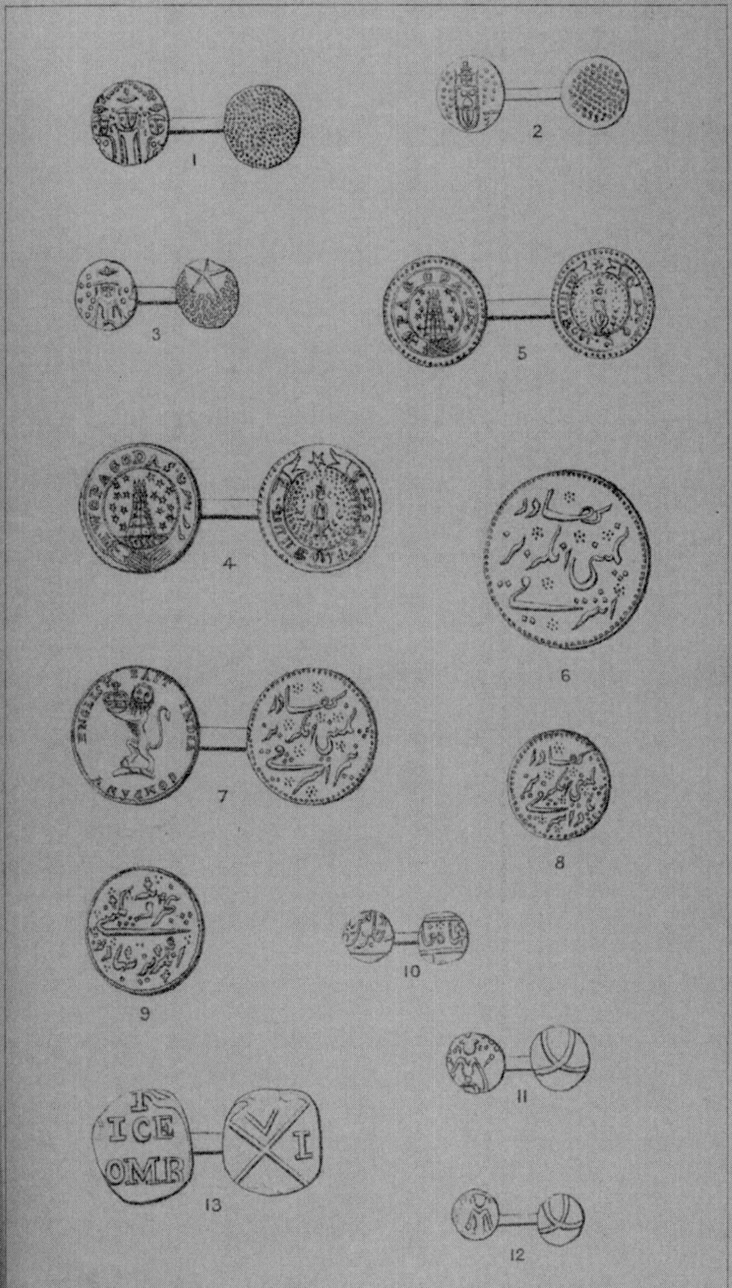

Plate XII.

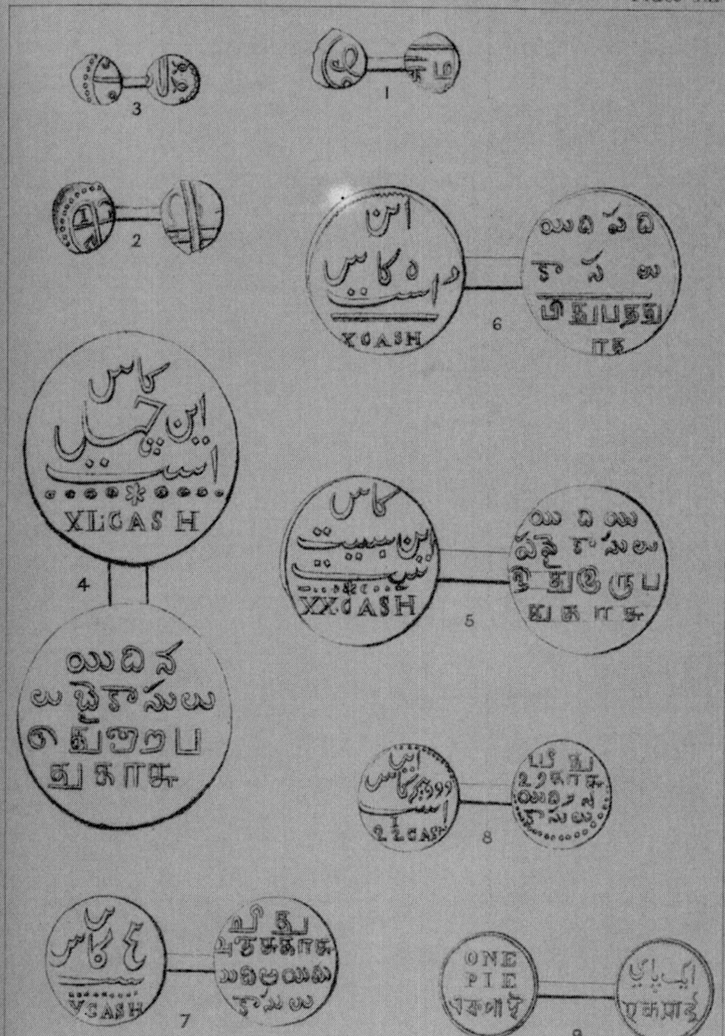

Plate XIII.

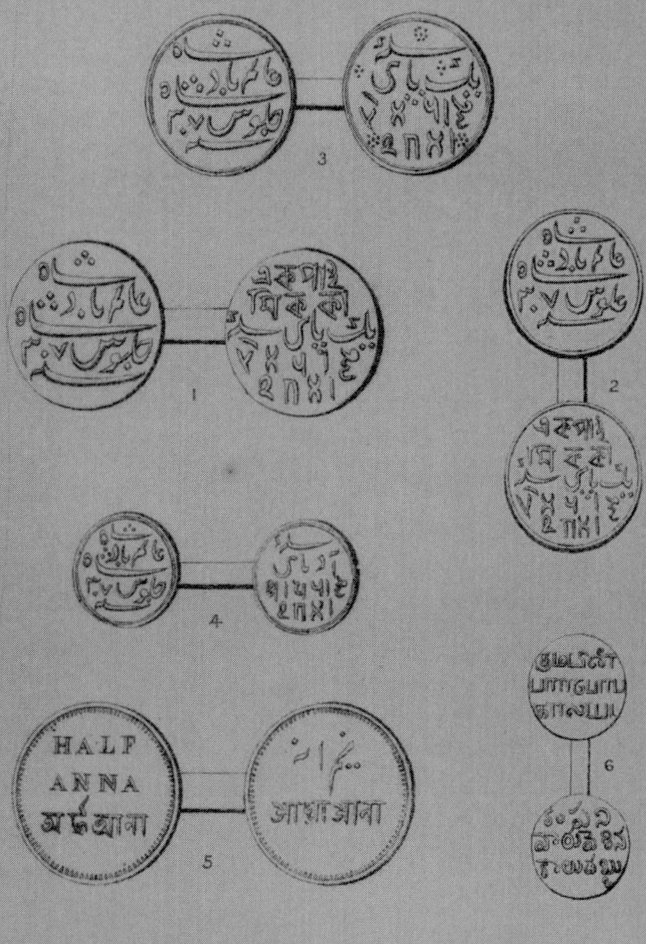

Plate XIV.

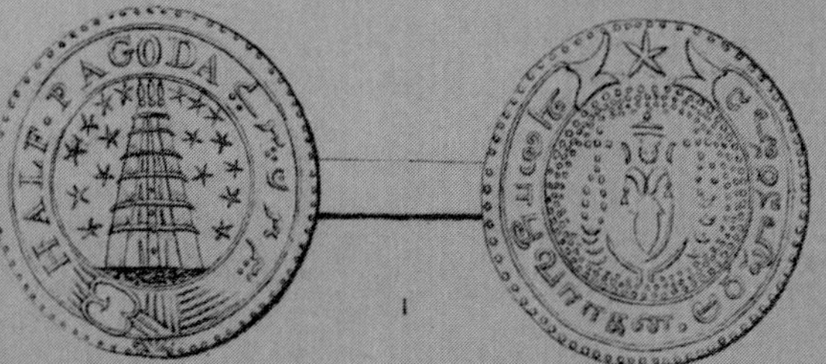

1

2

3

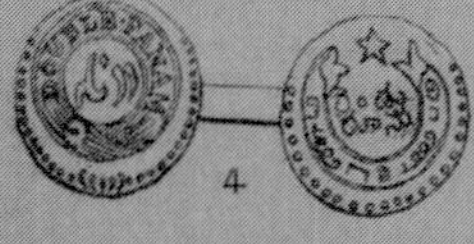

4

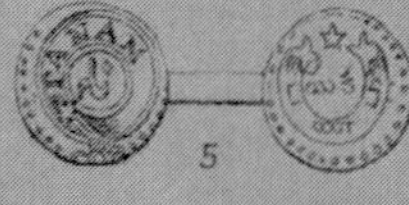

5

6

Plate XV.

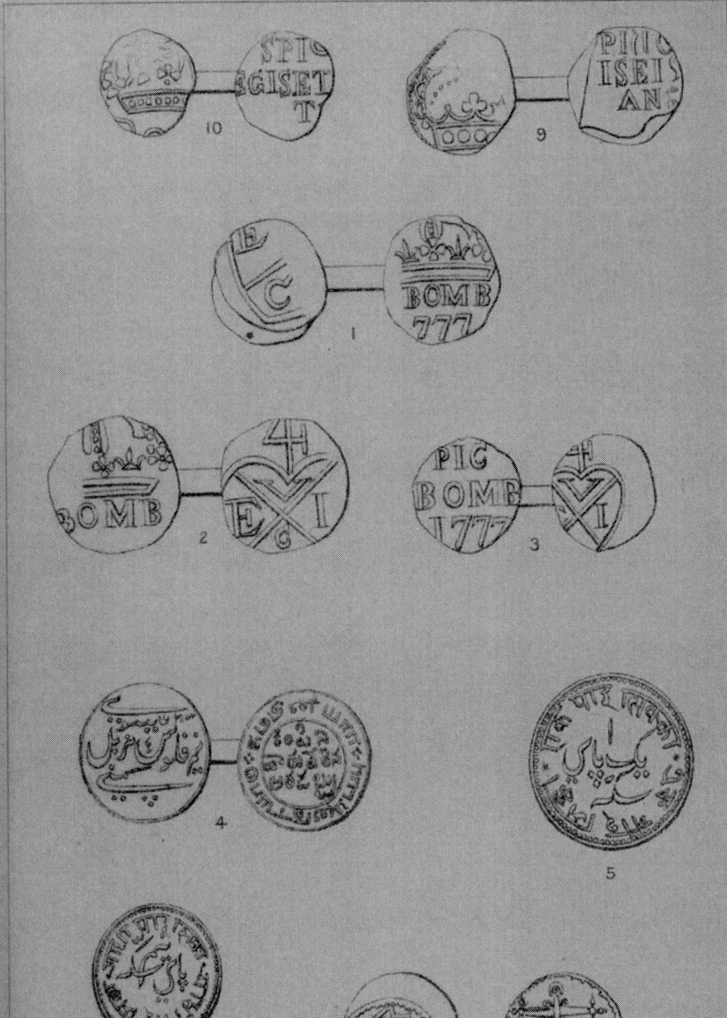

SPI
GISET
T
PIIIC
ISEIS
AN
E
C
BOMB
777
BOMB
E
I
PIG
BOMB
1777
I
10
9
1
2
3
4
5
6
7
8
11

Plate XVI.

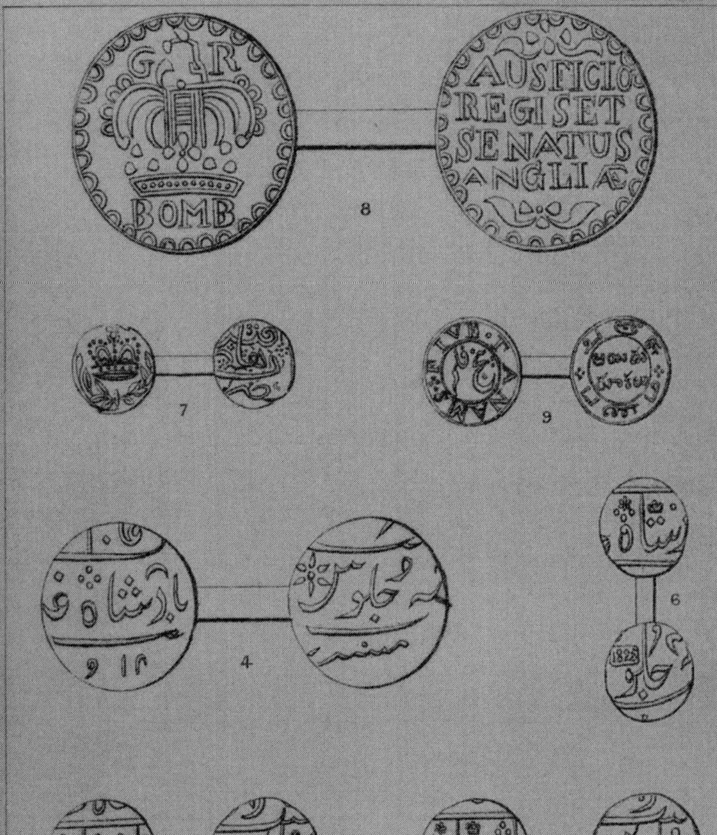

Plate XVII.

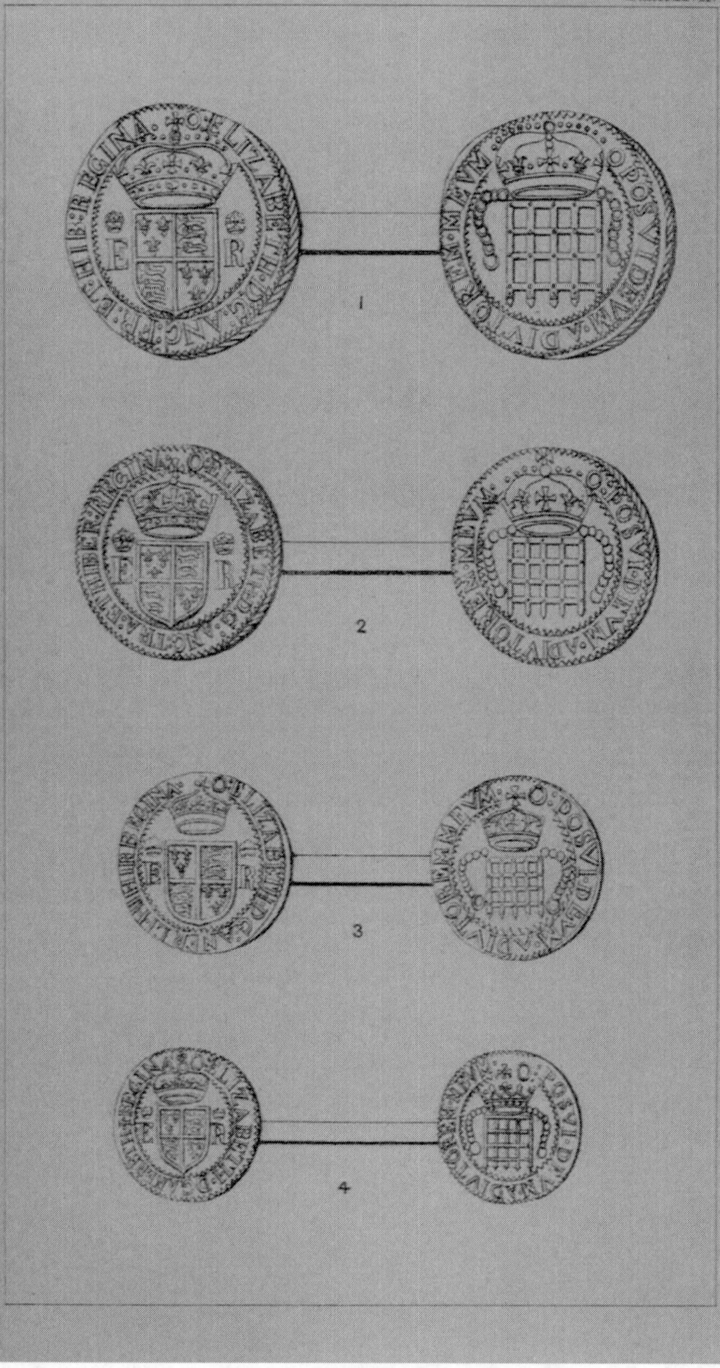

Plate XVIII.

Plate XIX

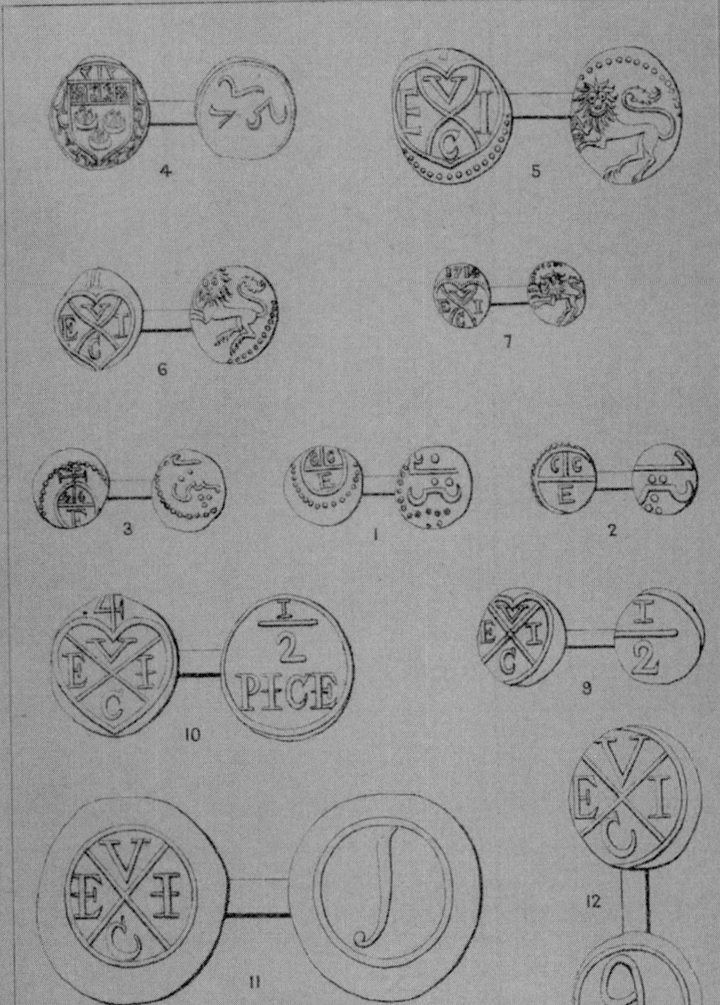

Plate XX

1

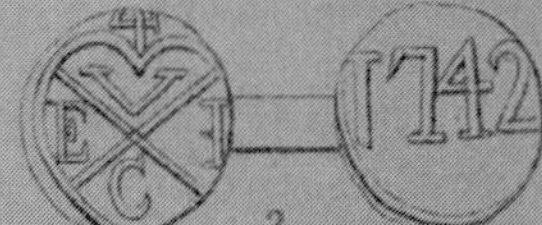

2

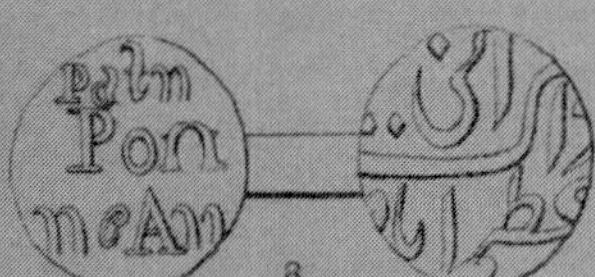

8

4

5

6

3

7

9